Ann Miller

Ann Miller

Her Life and Career

PETER SHELLEY

McFarland & Company, Inc., Publishers

Jefferson, North Carolina

ISBN (print) 978-1-4766-7925-9
ISBN (ebook) 978-1-4766-4092-1

LIBRARY OF CONGRESS AND BRITISH LIBRARY
CATALOGUING DATA ARE AVAILABLE

Library of Congress Control Number 2020041278

Front cover image of Ann Miller, circa 1940s (Photofest)

Printed in the United States of America

*McFarland & Company, Inc., Publishers
Box 611, Jefferson, North Carolina 28640
www.mcfarlandpub.com*

Table of Contents

Preface

$\mathcal{I}$ think I first saw Ann Miller in *Easter Parade*. Playing the other woman in the romance between Fred Astaire and Judy Garland, she was a study in contrast with Garand's persona and style, which was also a plot point in the film. And although the star was playing a vain and selfish character, Miller still made her likeable because she was funny. She was funny in all her films, which gave the glamour-girl image some depth. Miller was beautiful yet also retained a girl-next-door quality which made her more than a clotheshorse or a vamp. She was sexy without being erotically disturbing and there was something touching about her eagerness to perform. And what a performer she was!

Miller was best known as a tap dancer, though she did other kinds of dance, and some of her solo routines are as good as any recorded in film musical history. The *That's Entertainment* series repeatedly celebrated her M-G-M period which saw "Shakin' the Blues Away" in *Easter Parade*, "Prehistoric Man" from *On the Town*, "I Gotta Hear That Beat" from *Small Town Girl*, and "Too Darn Hot" from *Kiss Me Kate*. But her earlier work is just as memorable even if the films themselves are not considered classics, with particular favorites being the star's dance debut in *New Faces of 1937*, "I'm Taking a Shine to You" in *Radio City Revels*, and "Man Is Brother to a Mule" in *The Thrill of Brazil*. She could also sing, and while it wasn't a voice as unique as Garland's, it was more than serviceable. In fact the Columbia musical *Eve Knew Her Apples* had Miller only sing and not dance at all. Perhaps the most fascinating thing about her career is that it had so many chapters. She began as a child, had contracts with three Hollywood studios, retired twice for marriage, had two Broadway comebacks with *Mame* and *Sugar Babies*, and a return to movies in a small role in *Mulholland Drive* (2001).

Some film historians claim that Miller never made it as a star, with choreographer and friend Hermes Pan saying films never captured, exploited or understood the full potential of her many talents. It is true

1

that her leading roles were few and all in "B" movies at Columbia—*Reveille with Beverly* (1943). *What's Buzzin', Cousin?* (1943), *Jam Session* (1944), and *Eadie Was a Lady* (1945)—but that doesn't diminish some of the great work she did in musical comedies. Miller complained that she never had the chance to do straight roles, though the star played non-musical roles in the RKO comedies *Having Wonderful Time* (1938), *You Can't Take It with You* (1938) and *Room Service* (1938) and the M-G-M comedies *Watch the Birdie* (1950), *The Opposite Sex* (1956), and *The Great American Pastime* (1956). She was always convincing when required to express emotions, unlike some other musical comedy stars who were stiffs when they had to act. Miller also played comedy on stage but since the glamourous image was important to her, it's hard to imagine that she would have dropped it in an effort to show her range. We didn't see her do a Marilyn at the Actors Studio bit because she didn't need to. The star had plenty of life experience to draw upon for the feelings her characters had, even in the gossamer show business contexts that most of her movie narratives had. As an actress she had no discernible mannerisms, and the only time Miller moved away from her established persona was to go blonde in Paramount's *Priorities on Parade* (1942) but for no reported reason. She used stage wigs as a late career signature, though they had practical uses, but never sported the glasses the star wore in life on screen.

Miller's forays into theater occurred when film roles were not on offer, first with the *George White Scandals* on Broadway in 1939 and then when her Golden Age of Hollywood film career was effectively over. She also used television for guest appearances in variety shows as a way to keep her in the audience spotlight as a musical performer, and then later made appearances in situation comedies. But it was *Sugar Babies* that Miller said made her the star she had wanted to be, the star that she felt her films had not, despite the fact of sharing the leading role with Mickey Rooney. Miller participated in vaudeville skits but essentially played herself in the stage musical comedy and we were happy to see the star still singing and dancing at an age when her contemporaries were either dead or retired. When she appeared in a regional production of *Follies* in 1998 at the age of 75, Miller sang Stephen Sondheim's "I'm Still Here," the anthem to show business survival, and it fit her like a glove.

The song's line that she had become camp also seemed appropriate for the star with the pristine lacquered appearance which made her a subject of parody in the *Forbidden Broadway* series. Miller was represented as brassy, robust, but dim-witted cheerleader in a sequined leotard with a toothpaste smile and a bouffant wig. But this reductive look at her ignored the star's good nature, a woman whose sense of gratitude for a career that led her to be appointed an international spokesperson for M-G-M in the ailing years of the studio. This became the education that the girl had never received when she started out in show business as a child and, despite her reputation as a kook who believed she was psychic and had lived former lives, helped to cement her legend with the public around the world.

This is the first book to span the star's full career to date. The only existing book, Jim Connor's authorized pictorial biography *Ann Miller Taps*, was released in 1981, though there have been chapters on her in various titles on film history and dance. This study has been enhanced by the star's two memoirs, *Miller's High Life*, co-written with Norma Lee Browning and published in 1972, and *Tapping Into the Force: Ann Miller's Psychic World*, written with Dr. Maxine Asher and released in 1990. However both of these books lack a comprehensive and consistent coverage of her career. No book so far can be considered the definitive study since some of the television work is not available for viewing, with perhaps the biggest regret being not able to see the year 2000 episode of the television show *Biography* entitled "Ann Miller: I'm Still Here."

As much information as possible has been provided herein. Accessing the afore-mentioned sources and any associated biographies and books on co-workers allowed me to consider differing views of some of the events in the life and career and to highlight any apparent inaccuracies. My research had me review the available interviews that she gave for DVD special features and newspapers and magazines, accessing the archives of *The New York Times*, and ebay.com collectibles and entertainment memorabilia and the Getty Images website for photographs of Miller at events. YouTube.com was also invaluable in sourcing interviews.

The book is written as a biography, with the star's career presented in the context of her life. I have not made new chapters for each film, television appearances or stage show. Rather they are mixed into the biography, with work listed in the chronology they were made as opposed to when they opened or were released or broadcast, with that information also given. I have provided an analysis of the work when possible, positioning Miller's place in the project, commenting on her look and performance, and quoting any comments I have found by the star as well as those about her by director and co-stars. I have also given the critical reaction that the work received and information about any awards it earned. To complement the text, I have supplied stills from some of the films. Additionally the book comes with an appendix of her appearances in theatre, film, television, shorts and videos, and a bibliography of reference sources, including her two coauthored books.

· · · · · · · · · · · · · · · · ·

CHAPTER 1

Beginning

$\mathcal{B}$orn Johnnie Lucille Collier at St. Joseph's Hospital in Houston, Texas, on April 12, 1923, she was named Johnnie because her father wanted a boy and she detested the name, saying that in Texas it was known as tacky. Her mother, Clara, had named the girl Lucille after her Texan great-grandmother who was a Cherokee Indian, a medium and a natural clairvoyant. She was of Cherokee, French and Irish descent. Astrologically, the girl was an Aries, with a Taurus rising and her moon in Pisces meaning she had a mystical love of beauty, music and dancing. Always optimistic with lots of energy and ambition, Aries people were also usually psychic and the girl believed in Ouija boards. She would always think of herself as a race horse—nervous, high strung and temperamental—the way a thoroughbred was.

Her father was John Alfred Collier, a red-haired Irish playboy and egotist, who loved to dance, and became a barber. Clara was born in the small Texan town of Brooklyn and had long legs, a great body, and dark rich mahogany-colored hair. After the couple married they moved to a small upstairs apartment in Houston and John began to study law at night. He seemed to have little time for Lucille, she thinking perhaps things might have been different if she was a boy. Her father took her on weekend fishing trips but the girl didn't enjoy it.

When she was eight John took her to the Gulf of Mexico to teach his daughter how to swim. Out beyond the breakers he held his hand under her stomach telling her to paddle with her feet and hands. John promised not to let go but suddenly did and ordered the girl to swim but she sank and blacked out. When Lucille awoke she was on land surrounded by lifeguards trying to pump water out of her by artificial respiration. The girl promised not to tell her mother of the incident but from that day, she no longer trusted the man. Miller would never learn to swim and retained her fear of water. While she could only paddle like a ruptured duck, the star would later sail in Hawaii in an outrigger canoe sitting behind a big strong Hawaiian.

When Lucille was three, playing in her room, she heard someone say her name over and over again though there was no one there. The voice continued, imploring her to listen, and the girl learned to tune into the psychic and spiritual world whenever she needed help. Lucille sensed from an early age her parents did not have a happy marriage since they argued and her mother cried a lot.

One day when the girl was four her father came home from work late and said he had been at his office but she knew he was lying. Lucille had had a psychic flash of him with a lady in a boat in the park, and she told him about it. Apparently the girl's flash was accurate and her father told Lucille not to tell her mother and she agreed. The girl now believed something awful would happen between her parents. On most weekends she and Clara would ride the bus to her grandmother's house Chireno in East Texas, but John always gave work as an excuse not to go. He succeeded in becoming a criminal lawyer and would represent the notorious "Baby Face" Nelson, Pretty Boy Floyd, and Bonnie Parker and Clyde Barrow. The family moved to a red brick house in Houston.

Lucille had become withdrawn and lonely. Hating to go home after school she went off to the forest behind Sutton Elementary School and cried and prayed for her parents to stay together. Sometimes deer and squirrels and frogs would come out and stare at her, and the girl would talk to them, since she had no friends at school. Lucille was nick-named Little Orphan Annie, though she was taller than average. The girl was knock-kneed with rickets so Clara gave her ballet lessons to straighten her legs. They had an encounter with a gypsy fortune teller in the bus depot on the way to the grandparents. After being given a half-dollar coin, the woman held the girl's hand for a long time and then pronounced that she saw a Star of Destiny. Seeing music and lights and dancing and money the gypsy advised Clara to take her to the West. But Lucille hated practicing her ballet steps, finding the music slow and the discipline boring, and would often have to be jolted out of a daydream with a slap on the legs. She just wanted to play with her dolls, blow bub-ble gum and play hopscotch—to be a normal little girl and not a great ballerina.

Clara also had her try piano lessons and violin. When the violin teacher Miss Morrow teased the hungry girl by eating peanut butter fudge right in front of her, Lucille got so angry that she hit her on the head with the violin and ran away. Her mother spanked her for doing so but never again did the girl have to play the violin. It was the great Negro tap dancer Bill "Bojangles" Robinson who gave Lucille her first tap lesson and this changed the course of her life. He was in Houston for a show at the Majestic Theatre and Clara took the girl backstage afterwards to let him see her dance ballet. Robinson watched, then sang "Bye, Bye Blues," clapping out the rhythm with his hands, and asked Lucille to join him in the tap. Having a natural rhythm, the girl took to tap like a duck to water and Robinson told her to buy some tap shoes with wooden soles instead of steel taps, as he used. Now she knew her mother was right about her someday being a dancer, of tap and not ballet. This feeling was confirmed when her ballet teacher brought in a drummer to play with the piano and Lucille discovered her affinity for drums. Maybe it was her Indian blood but the girl just took off and started tapping, even dancing to the drumbeat without any music.

At the age of six she was to participate in a recital at the Houston dancing school at the Majestic Theatre. The girl donned a ballet skirt and tap shoes but succumbed to stage fright and she refused to perform. The experience stopped her from dancing for almost three years, which was fine with Clara's conservative Southern family who had dissuaded their daughter from her own stage ambitions. Clara was wise enough to wait with nothing more said about dancing and classes ceasing. Lucille was just another schoolgirl but soon she begged to be allowed to dance again.

At seven her mother enrolled her in a dancing school and her teacher Halli Preachard put her in a kiddie show for the Big Brothers Club in Houston (another source states this happened when she was 12). She sang "The Boulevard of Broken Dreams" in an apache outfit standing up against a lamppost, and "Egyptian-Nella" in a costume of breastplates, a waistband beading with a gold fringe that hung to the floor, a gold headdress with a cobra and beaded bracelets and cymbals on her fingers. For the second number the girl was meant to stand still as she sang and rattle her finger cymbals as the chorus posed but when the drums started, Lucille automatically went into a belly dance. When it ended, her father almost fainted and the teacher was furious, saying she had not taught the girl the dance, but the performance won Lucille the personality contest at the Club. She believed the dance had come to her because the girl was a reincarnated Egyptian dancer. One of her favorite pastimes was drawing, and she always drew camels and pyramids and palm trees, of which there were none in Houston.

At the age of 10 she saw Bill Robinson again when he came through the city, and it was now determined that Lucille was to be a professional entertainer. With her mother, she visited backstage at vaudeville houses, making friends with the dancers and learning their routines. In the summer of 1934 on school vacation, Clara took her to Hollywood, where they stayed at a small hotel on Hollywood Boulevard. The girl was enrolled in Fanchon and Marco's Dancing Studio, which was the best one in town. Lucille met Marguerite Carmen Cansino, whose father Eduardo Cansino taught there, Jane Withers and Frances Gumm. Clara became a confidant of Frances' mother, Ethel who played the piano for the children's programs, and learned that Ethel fed her daughter pills because she was high strung. These helped her to sleep but made her groggy the next morning so Frances was given pep pills to get her going again.

Lucille did a revue called All Aboard, getting into the show saying she was 15. It featured a number of dramatic scenes which got her offers from two talent scouts for screen tests, one at Warner Bros. and the other at M-G-M. However both studios told her she was too young for them. The Colliers happened to meet their first movie star on the street in Hollywood—Jean Harlow—and asked for her autograph. Harlow liked the look of Lucille and encouraged Clara to try again to get her into films. She registered with Central Casting who put the girl up for two parts as an extra. She had two quickie screen tests which led to her film debut.

The RKO black and white family comedy *Anne of Green Gables* (1934) was shot from August 7 to September 14. It had a screenplay by Sam Mintz and L.M. Montgomery based on the novel by Montgomery, which had been previously made as a silent film in 1919. The new director was George Nicholls, Jr. The story centered on Anne (Anne Shirley), a romantic 17 year old adopted by a pair of elderly siblings in turn-of-the-century Canada. An uncredited Lucille played a schoolgirl though she cannot be positively identified in the many scenes of Anne and her schoolmates. The film was released on November 23 with the taglines "A PICTURE MADE FOR THE MILLIONS WHO LOVED 'LITTLE WOMEN,'" and "FICTION'S MOST BELOVED HEROINE REALLY LIVES!" It was praised by *Variety*, and Andre Sennwald in *The New York Times*. The film was a box office success, with a sequel *Anne of Windy Poplars* (1940) and remade for television as the 1985 mini-series and 2019 TV movie.

She also made the black and white Universal romantic comedy Ferenc Molnar's *The Good Fairy* (1935) which was shot from September 13 to December 17. The screenplay by Preston Sturges was based on Jane Hinton's translation and adaption of the play by Molnar, which had been originally produced on Broadway at Henry Miller's Theatre from November 24, 1931, to April 1932. The film's director was William Wyler. The story set in Budapest centered on Luisa (Margaret Sullavan), a naive girl just out of the Municipal Orphanage for Girls who finds that being a "good fairy" to strangers makes life awfully complicated. An uncredited Lucille played a schoolgirl in the orphanage and again she cannot be positively identified in the many scenes of the girls at the orphanage. The film was released either on January 31 or February 12, 1935, and was a box office hit. It received a mixed reaction from *Variety*, Andre Sennwald in *The New York Times*, and Clive Hirschhorn in "The Universal Story." It was remade as the Universal musical romance *I'll Be Yours* (1947), a 1956 TV Movie, and the Austrian/West German/ Swiss 1969 TV Movie *Die Fee*.

The Colliers went back to Houston and the girl went back to school. Although the clairvoyant Dr. Mary Young predicted she would return to Hollywood and have a career that would last for years, for the moment there were no new prospects. For a while things seemed to be working between her parents, but this was merely the calm before the storm. One weekend Lucille and her mother went to Chireno to see the grandparents but when Clara fell ill, they came home early to find John in bed with another woman. Lucille told her mother that they had to leave, promising to take care of her. They packed their clothes and spent the night at a friend's house then headed back to California. The girl said her life had changed within an hour and she had suddenly grown up from a child of 11 into a woman. They found a one-room kitchenette apartment in Hollywood with a sofa that had two pullout beds so narrow that Lucille used to roll off hers all the time. Clara had some money saved from the housekeeping funds John had given her, but it did not last long. He took advantage of the Texan law that made no provision for alimony, so with no income, he probably thought this would force them to return. Ironically John needed the window dressing of a wife and child in Texas, for appearances as a successful attorney, but they were determined to make it on their own. Clara was unable to hold a job, being nearly deaf in both ears at a time when no operation was available to help her, so she concentrated her efforts into making her daughter a success.

Lucille would be the provider in the jungle that was Hollywood, but she refused to succumb to the casting couch that might have made her a bigger star. The girl would use her talent for dance and the fact that she had a good-looking pair of legs and a stage-struck mother, whom she called Mama-Kat because Clara reminded her of a large Persian cat. It wouldn't be easy and Lucille would work long hours and feel the pangs of hunger.

Their first Christmas was dismal, with no tree or presents, and only crackers to eat. Their landlady gave them a chocolate cake covered with white icing and a bright red "Merry Christmas" she had baked as a Christmas gift, which they had for Christmas dinner. Being broke and homesick Clara was ready to call her husband and tell him to come and get them but something Lucille found in the trash behind the apartment gave them renewed hope. The *Science of Mind* book had a passage from the Bible underlined in ink, saying if you had faith He was with you always.

On New Year's Eve they had no money for the rent and the landlady evicted them. The pair spent the night shivering in their car, which Clara knew she would soon have to sell. Clara went back to the landlady to tell of their desperate circumstances and she sent them to William Morgan's Shop on Sunset Boulevard—which she described separately as a dance shoe and a Capezio shoe store. After seeing Lucille tap, he lent them money and said the girl could rehearse on a special tap board which he would set up in his showroom. Morgan also made special tap shoes for her, which she named Joe and Moe, which Lucille believed would bring her luck.

Clara could no longer afford to send her daughter to the Fanchon and Marco's Dancing Studio but enrolled her in LeConte Junior High where she met the child star Bonita Granville. Lucille was made Captain of the Commissary, having to patrol the lunchroom and keep out those who brought their lunch from home since there were a limited number of tables. Bonita was one of the lunch-bringers who refused to use the outside tables, and would sneak in to be with her friends. After catching the girl three times, Lucille slapped her and the girls got into a terrible cat fight. Teachers broke them up and they were both reprimanded and sent home. The principal said Lucille was right in trying to keep Bonita out of the commissary but that she should not have slapped her.

Every day after school the girl raced down to William Morgan's shop and danced. She had watched the movie musicals of Fred Astaire and Ginger Rogers and now developed her own steps, including the quick machine-gun style tap the star would later be known for. Clara always accompanied Lucille to Morgan's. One day he said that if they could put a little routine together he could supply a piano player and she could audition for luncheon jobs entertaining at the Elks, Rotary and Lions and American Legion clubs. The player was Harry Fields but he believed that an underage dancer named Johnnie Lucille Collier was not going to make it, suggesting she change it to something simpler and easy to remember like Jane Smith or Anne Miller. The girl liked Anne Miller though Fields' numerologist said the e had to be taken off Anne to make it luckier. Clara also changed her surname to Miller to avoid any confusion. In addition Fields said the girl was so tall that she could easily pass for older if they were willing to lie about her age, being unaware that Miller had lied about her age before to get work. The plan worked. The pay was small—from $5 to $10 per performance but the money kept the Millers going.

She now attended Mrs. Lawlor's Hollywood Professional School. This is where children that worked went who didn't have time to go to regular schools, allowing Ann Miller to take grades over again when she needed to. Frances Gumm was also a student and the girl went to an afternoon benefit which Louis B. Mayer attended. When Frances performed, Miller heard how she had a powerful woman's voice in a little girl's body which made everybody jerk to attention, and the singer was signed to an M-G-M contract.

A Sunday night amateur contest at a café-bar on Vermont Street was a humiliating experience. She won, but when the bar customers threw money at her, the girl got down on her hands and knees to scoop it up like a greedy little monkey. A man lent her his hat to put the takings in which amounted to nearly $6 which was a bonanza on top of the $5 she was paid for being in the contest. Miller won another amateur contest at the Orpheum Theatre where she was paid $5 to enter and a two week engagement at $50 a week. The manager, Sherrill Cohen, bought her two costumes and paid for special musical arrangements, and the girl became a regular on the Keith vaudeville bill as a tap dancer with a new style.

This was her first professional break as a dancer. Agent Arthur Silber saw Miller at the Orpheum and booked her into the Casanova Club, a famous nightspot on the Sunset Strip. It was illegal for a minor to be working in a nightclub but she got away with it, perhaps because nobody asked to see her birth certificate. The girl danced there for a year.

She scored another film role in the Grand National black and white "B" musical comedy *The Devil on Horseback* (1936) shot from late June to July on location in Hemet, California, and at the studios of RKO-Pathé and Republic in Hollywood. The film was released in color but the screened copy is black and white. The screenplay was by Crane Wilbur based on his original story, with music and lyrics by Jack Stern and Harry Tobias, and Wilbur was also the director. The story centered on movie star Diane Corday (Lili Damita), who visits the small Latin republic of Alturas while on a publicity tour. Miller is uncredited as a chorus girl in the Fiesta dance sequence, though she cannot be positively identified. Costumes were by Adrienne and the dance director was Arthur Dreifus. The film's release dates are reported as September 30 or October 11, 1936, but it is not known whether it was a financial success. A Spanish version was simultaneously shot by Wilbur with a new cast, though it is possible that Miller also appears in it. *El carnaval del diablo* (1937) was first released in Mexico in December 1936 and then in October 1937 in the United States.

When the Millers saw Eleanor Powell in the M-G-M musical

Broadway Melody of 1936 (1935) her mother believed that someday Ann would be a big star like Powell, who was being paid $150,000 to $200,000 to dance in films at M-G-M. But although they had stormed the gates of the Hollywood studios for a year, it was without success, so they moved to San Francisco for another job. This was at a theater restaurant called the Bal Tabarin Club, also known as the Beau Tamerin. She was hired for three weeks at $100 a week but stayed 16.

The owners, Frank Martinelli and Tom Gerun, felt they had a new star on their hands since no one else could do those Eleanor Powell machine-gun taps. The girl had two big numbers and two changes of costumes, with Clara there waiting to wrap her daughter in a big robe when she came offstage. The show was changed every four weeks so Miller had to keep creating new dance routines, for which she would be given new arrangements and new costumes.

The Millers lived in a hotel which the girl found depressing, since their suite lacked a kitchen, as a place that had one cost more. They had to eat out and lived mostly on hamburgers and hot dogs. In the daytime she did her school lessons via post with the Lawlor School, and sometimes went to a movie in the afternoon, for a ride on a cable car, or down to Fisherman's Wharf for a little snack. Then Miller took a nap before going to do her shows, after which the couple sometimes would have another hamburger at a small restaurant before going back to the hotel. Clara never left her daughter's side the whole time they were in the city.

During the Bal Tabarin engagement she was seen by Lucille Ball, then an RKO starlet, and Benny Rubin, an RKO studio talent scout. Ball was in San Francisco for the premiere of the RKO comedy *Don't Tell the Wife* (1937) and Miller recognized her from the movies. Ball thought the girl was a marvelous dancer and told Rubin he ought to get her a screen test, believing Miller could give Eleanor Powell a run for her money. After the show Rubin went backstage and took the Millers over to Ball's table, and when he asked old she was, they gave the prepared answer. Frank Martinelli and Tom Gerun knew Miller was underage but their hunch paid off as she proved to be popular. They had warned Clara that, if asked she was to say the girl was 18. Rubin and Ball didn't believe that so the screen test was offered with the proviso that a birth certificate be provided. But while Miller could look older on stage and could pass for 18, she looked much younger off stage and it was feared the camera would expose the lie.

RKO had no interest in anyone under 18 because it cost too much money. They required a teacher on the set and couldn't work a full eight-hour day. Miller felt she was sunk since her birth certificate definitely said she was born in 1923 which made her only 13 at the time of the meeting. But Clara said they would bring her daughter's birth certificate when they came for the screen test. Rubin and Ball still had raised eyebrows but smiled sweetly at the girl as they said goodbye and advised they would be in touch. The solution was to get a fake certificate and the only person they knew who could help was John, since a criminal lawyer would know where to obtain one. Plus he was only likely to break the law in this way for his daughter. They composed a frantic telegram to him in Houston appealing as if the girl's life depended on it, and he agreed.

The document was sent special delivery. It stated she was born in Chireno, Texas, on April 11, 1919, as Lucy Ann Collier, a name dreamed up as a combination of Lucille and Ann Miller. She would say that getting the certificate was the only kind thing her father ever did for her. Ironically the night after Ball and Rubin saw her, Joe Rifkin from Columbia came and offered her a screen test too. But the girl felt since the RKO team saw her first they should test her first.

In early 1937 with the engagement at Bal Tabarin ended, the Millers went to back to Hollywood and RKO. To aid the ruse, the girl wore grown-up clothes, high heels, lipstick, and bust pads and was told to say as little as possible. Clara had the fake birth certificate in her handbag in case it was asked for. The test was made by William "Billy" Grady, the RKO casting director, who was testing dozens of girls at the time. When it was her turn, Miller did one of the numbers from her show, and Grady seemed impressed. He asked the girl to walk back and forth across the stage a couple of times then interviewed her with a few questions, and she made her answers as brief as possible. Grady didn't ask Miller's age. She and Clara went to a screening room to watch the test, where several producers were present. Afterwards one of them asked if the girl would like to be in his new film called *New Faces of 1937* where she would do her tap number. Miller said yes and was offered a seven-year contract for $150 a week. This was to be her first steady income, the most she had ever made, and a rather phenomenal contract salary for a starlet in those days.

The girl assumed RKO was interested in her because Eleanor Powell was so big at the time. Miller could do the same machine-gun taps, and she was 14 years younger, though the girl never imagined she was a real threat to the woman she idolized. Miller felt forever indebted to Lucille Ball whom she found to be the most down-to-earth person of all the people she had met in Hollywood, with a good heart. Ball would come to Miller's defense when it was learned that she *was* only 13 and somebody threatened to turn her mother and RKO into the child labor union. Ball stated she was present when the girl's contract was signed and believed she was 18, and the issue was dropped for the time being.

The Millers moved into residences RKO found for them, the St. Francis Apartments in Vine Street and later into the Hermoyne Apartments on Rossmore, with a doorman and a big indoor swimming pool. But she lived under the constant fear that her real age would be discovered and they would lose everything, and worse, Miller and her mother might be put in jail.

The black and white musical comedy *New Faces of 1937* had the working title of "Young People" (1937) and was shot from late March to mid–May. It had a screenplay by Nat Perrin, Philip G. Epstein and Irv S. Brecher, adapted by Harold Kusell, Harry Clork and Howard J. Green from the George Bradshaw story "Shoestring," with the David Freedman sketch "A Day at the Brokers," and uncredited dialogue contributions by Mark Kelly and Philip Rapp. The director was Leigh Jason.

The story centered on Robert Hunt (Jerome Cowan), a Broadway stage producer who tries to cheat his backers by producing a flop and disappearing with the money. Miller is billed 18th as herself and appears as part of two numbers. She dances to the song "New Faces" by Charles Henderson in the Atlantic City tryouts. The girl is introduced by Wallington Wedge (Milton Berle) as being a new dancing discovery found in a San Francisco nightclub that is more like "an upholstered manhole," which may be a dig at the Bal Tabarin.

She is first seen in silhouette and enters wearing silver and solid-beaded pajamas. The routine scores a laugh when Miller looks at her nails at one point as she dances, and director Jason uses two medium shots that detract from us seeing her feet, with the final one having the girl move toward the camera. Her second appearance is in the number "Peckin'": by Ben Pollack and Harry James, with additional lyrics by Edward Cherkose. Miller one of the bridesmaids of Patricia (Harriet Hillard) doing the chicken head move of the title. The film's gowns are credited to Edward Stevenson and dances are staged by Sammy Lee.

The girl's main number was rehearsed in the morning and shot in the afternoon, taking two hours with three cameras on her. She seemed to know instinctively how to pose and to angle her tap dancing so her body would look right from certain angles. RKO head of production Sam Briskin came onto the set to watch her, as did Lucille Ball and Benny Rubin, and of course, Clara. She was not the type of stage mother that harassed producers or directors but wanted to protect her daughter from the Hollywood wolves. So Clara drove the girl to the studio every morning and picked her up at night. If anyone was a bother they were reported.

The film was released on July 2 with the taglines "LAUGH at the looney guys! LOOK at the lovely girls LISTEN to those tantalizing tunes," and "A new show idea sweeps the screen!" *Variety* noted that Miller doing good tap drew a salvo at the screening, but the film was lambasted by Frank S. Nugent in *The New York Times* and Richard B. Jewell and Vernon Harbin in *The RKO Story*. It was not a box office success so that a series of musical revues designed to introduce new RKO talent did not eventuate.

She was immediately cast in two more films. The black and white musical comedy *The Life of the Party* (1937) had the working title of "Three on a Latchkey" and was shot from May 20 to mid–June. The screenplay was by Berk Kalmar, Harry Ruby and Viola Brothers Shore based on a story by Joseph Santley with uncredited dialogue contributions by George Jeske and Jack Mintz. The director was William A. Seiter. The story centered on Mitzi (Harriet Hilliard) a singer who finds Barry (Gene Raymond) to marry to avoid Penner (Joe Penner) as the one her mother found. Miller is billed eighth before the film's title and plays the supporting role of Betty who is a dancer for the band of Dr. Molnac (Billy Gilbert).

She gets one line as advice to Susan (Betty Jane Rhodes), a singer in the band, "You know he wants you to get hot. Go to town!" This is for the "Chirp a Little Ditty" number, a song with music by Allie Wrubel and lyrics by Herbert Magidson, which also has the girl doing a tap routine. She throws off her dark hat and knee-length skirt to display her legs in dark shorts, and dances in between the outstretched legs of the seated band instrument players, though director Seiter cuts away from her for the number's end. She dances for a second time for "Yankee Doodle Band," another song by Wrubel and Magidson, in the cabaret at the California hotel where the band performs. For her part in the number, the girl dances solo, with two male dancers and with the chorus, where she twirls between their raised canes, but Seiter cuts to medium shots of her, one of her dancing feet. The film's dances were staged by Sammy Lee and the gowns by Edward Stevenson.

The film was released on September 3 with the tagline "The greatest comedy cast ever assembled for one picture!" It received a mixed reaction from *Variety*, Frank S. Nugent in *The New York Times*, and Richard B. Jewell and Vernon Harbin in *The RKO Story*. *Variety* commented that Miller had been allowed to follow the Eleanor Powell style too closely, with the costume she wore for "Yankee Doodle Band" a too close approximation of Powell's in the "Broadway Rhythm" finale of *Broadway Melody of 1936*. A comparison of the two costumes does show a similarity between the creations of M-G-M's Adrian and Stevenson, though the former has a top hat and a longer jacket tail. The RKO film was a modest box office success.

Helen Broderick and Miller in *The Life of the Party* (1937).

Her next was the black and white comedy *Stage Door* (1937), shot from June 7 to July 31 at the RKO Studios in Hollywood. The screenplay was by Morrie Ryskind and Anthony Veiller from the play by Edna Ferber and George S. Kaufman which had run on Broadway at the Music Box Theatre from October 22, 1936, to March 1937. In addition there were uncredited contributions by S.K. Lauren, William Slavens McNutt, and George Seaton. The director was Gregory LaCava.

The story chronicled the ambitions, dreams, and disappointments of aspiring actresses who all live in the theatrical boarding house Footlights Club in New York. Miller is not billed in the opening credits, and is 17th in the end credits as Annie. She is also known as String Bean, plays a supporting role with dialogue, and is shown with a tear in reaction to the curtain speech of Terry Randall (Katharine Hepburn). She dances in a chorus and twice with Ginger Rogers who plays Jean Maitland. Annie chews gum in several scenes, including perhaps her best when she speaks to the Broadway producer Tony Powell (Adolphe Menjou) as she rehearses the dance she will do as part of the Club Grotto floor show. Her Texan twang is apparent and the girl's nervousness is funny and appealing. Otherwise Annie gets the action of holding the cat that Eve (Eve Arden) usually holds. Miller and Rogers' part of the dance sequence at the Club Grotto is brief and LaCava conceals the dancing with medium shots, cutaways, and obscuring objects in the foreground. This is a pity since the outfits by Muriel King are dark shimmery jackets and pants with bare midriffs, dark gloves, canes, and top hats. It is interesting to compare Miller's dancing in the two scenes with Rogers, where one's eye goes to Miller and her work is more detailed.

The film was released on October 6 with the taglines "Cast and Story," "GREAT STARS! GREAT STORY! GREAT PICTURE!," and "The gaiety … glamour … foolishness and fun of showbusiness … played on the Great White Way." It was praised by *Variety*, Frank S. Nugent in *The New York Times*, Pauline Kael in *5001 Nights at the Movies*, and Richard B. Jewell and Vernon Harbin in *The RKO Story*. The film was a box office success and received Academy Award nominations for Best Picture, Best Actress in a Supporting Role for Andrea Leeds who played Kay Hamilton, Best Director, and Best Screenplay. It was remade as the Producers Releasing Corporation musical *Career Girl* (1944), and as a 60 minute adaptation for the April 6, 1955, episode of the live television series *Best of Broadway.*

The screenplay was considerably altered from the hit stage play, with LaCava said to have cut all the dialogue but keeping story, structure and scenes of the play. He had his cast improvise as if they were actually rooming together, two weeks prior to filming, and had a script girl take down all their interchanges. It was also reported that writers listened to the actresses talking and joking off set during the rehearsals and incorporated this into the screenplay, and studio stenographers were sent to casting offices throughout Hollywood to take down the conversations among the women waiting for their break.

It is not known whether Miller provided any ad-libs but she stated the film was her first real acting role. However Kathleen Brady in her biography of Lucille Ball, *Lucille*, reports on the girl's response to the news of the death of Jean Harlow on the day production began. She tapped her feet in a time step and smacked gum, murmuring "Oh my gawd, poor Jean Harlow" to the click of her dance shoes.

Miller said her part was written especially for her but for a while it was touch and go as to whether she would actually get to do it. The problem was height, being too tall for Ginger Rogers, whose pal she played. Rogers' initial veto of the girl was particularly painful since the star was one of her childhood idols. To Miller, Rogers was the epitome of glamour and sophistication as a musical performer. The girl had even plucked out her eyebrows trying to look like her, and they never did grow in again. Rogers' decision was changed by Lucille Ball, who was also in the film as Judith Canfield and Roger's best friend, who put in a good word for her. To solve the height disparity Miller offered to wear lower heels and a shorter top hat.

The girl would later give credit to Rogers for also giving her what she called her first speaking part in a film. The dance number, "Put Your Heart into Your Feet and Dance," was additionally important because it introduced the girl to the dance director Hermes Pan, uncredited in the film. He would remain a good friend and was one of the few dance directors in Hollywood who actually could dance. The number was difficult since it interspersed dialogue, which La Cava wrote on the set, with the dance. She initially had trouble dancing and speaking simultaneously but quickly mastered the concept under Pan's patient dance direction.

Planned to be shot in two months filming actually took three and Miller reported there was great tension between Rogers and Katharine Hepburn. Rogers was especially annoyed by her co-star contractual clause to have tea served with cookies on the set every afternoon at 4 p.m. for 30 minutes. In contrast the girl found the activity to be rather wonderful because it gave you renewed energy at a time of the day when you started to wilt, and she would subsequently repeat the practice herself. A lot of people were scared to death of Hepburn, but Miller said the

Miller, Ginger Rogers and Lucille Ball in *Stage Door* (1937).

star was sweet to her. The girl said Lucille Ball and Eve Arden helped relieve a lot of the strain on the set because they were always joking around. But her greatest fear was realized when the truth about Miller's age was revealed.

She had blurted it out after weeks of teasing by the wardrobe ladies about how the girl needed bust pads. One source claims that she confided in Hepburn about this, and the star supposedly told her not to tell anyone else, but the information got back to Rogers and producer Pandro Berman. The film was already in trouble, being over-budget with delays caused by La Cava's form of dramaturgy. When Berman confronted Miller she tried to deny the divulgence, repeating she had the birth certificate proving her age was 18. But while neither Berman nor Rogers believed her, they decided not to report the girl. Rogers was sympathetic to the situation since she was only 14 when she started in the business, and also was as close to her own mother as Miller was. The casting director asked for her birth certificate and Clara provided the fake one, and the girl was relieved when the film was finished.

After it was done she had Ginger Rogers as another new friend, whose house Miller would visit and loved since it had a soda fountain. Rogers would make ice cream sodas and malted milks for her guests, and thereafter the girl wanted her own soda fountain but never got one. Rogers also gave roller skating parties at a rink on Sunset Boulevard which she rented especially for her friends.

Miller worked eight-hour days, beginning at 5 a.m. When she arrived, her hair was washed then rolled out, and an hour was spent doing makeup where she would sit with Ginger Rogers and Katharine Hepburn and Rosalind Russell who were all down to earth and nice which made the experience like a family. Then the hair was combed out, body makeup applied, and the girl was dressed in costume. She got on set at 9 a.m., already worn out, when the shooting day began. Clara came at 6 p.m. to take her home, with the drive taking an hour. Miller had dinner and a bath, then read her script and learned lines for the next day with her feet soaking in hot water because she had danced so hard. The girl also had to do her schoolwork and didn't get to bed until 1 a.m.

It was a tough schedule but they managed to have a holiday in the first year with the studio, horseback riding in Palm Springs. When she was not working on a film Miller practiced dancing from four to eight hours a day, with portrait drawing as a diversion and hobby. Clara also studied dance and coached her daughter. She was also guided by RKO to always look nice when out in public. People didn't want to see stars with their hair in rollers wearing sloppy old pants, but like an 8 × 10 glossy. Even if the girl was only going to the market she was told to comb her hair out beforehand. Miller was a child of Hollywood who grew up there and this was part of the training.

Stockings became an issue. She had a short body and very long legs, which was anatomically quite unusual. The legs came completely together—with no space between the thighs from the crotch down to the flat and dimpled knees—which made her look good in short costumes. At first the wardrobe ladies had to sew the girl's stockings into the elastic of her panties as she stood spraddled and straight so that the seams would be right. If there was a run or one of the stockings popped during filming, which often happened, they were cut off and a new pair put on in the same fashion. This held up production and Miller was often pricked by the needles, when she was already hot from the lights and panting from exhaustion. Willy de Monde, the famed designer for stars, celebrities and socialites from Hollywood, Broadway and Paris, was consulted. The girl asked him to make silk stockings like thick colored ballerina tights, since she was too tall and long-legged for standard ballerina tights. De Monde designed the first pantyhose—seamless semi-free opera hose knitted to her measurements—and also a pair that were elaborately sequined and embroidered.

Miller was reportedly considered for the part of Lady Alyce Marshmorton in the RKO musical comedy *A Damsel in Distress* (1937) but Joan Fontaine was cast instead. The star said she watched them shoot the dance Fontaine did with Fred Astaire for the song "Things Are Looking Up" with the film in production from July 22 to October 16. Fontaine confided that she had never danced before in her life but Miller said to trust her dance partner and the dance director Hermes Pan. Astaire in particularly was such a great dancer that he would lead her and not step on the neophyte's feet. For the number the man lifted her over a fence in a field and made Fontaine dance as if she was a ragdoll that he could make do whatever Astaire wanted. The neophyte was still scared to death and it was hard for her, but she was thrilled at the outcome.

Her next film was the black and white romantic comedy *Having Wonderful Time* (1938), shot from September 24 to November 29 on location at the Big Bear Lake in the San Bernardino National Forest in California and at the RKO Studios in Hollywood. The screenplay was by Arthur Kober, based on his play which ran at the Lyceum Theatre from February 20, 1937, to January 8, 1938. The film's director was Alfred Santell though an uncredited George Stevens did some re-shoots. The story centers on Teddy (Ginger Rogers), a New York office girl who goes on vacation to Camp Kare-Free in the Catskill Mountains and finds waiter Chick (Douglas Fairbanks Jr.). An uncredited Miller plays another camp guest and is seen in two crowd scenes, but it is reported that her speaking part was cut. In the first she laughs in reaction to Teddy's haughty reaction to the social director Itchy (Richard [Red] Skelton), and in the second she is mostly seen with her back to the camera, laughing at Itchy's routine of how guests walk up and down stairs.

The film was released on July 1, 1938. It was praised by Pauline Kael in *5001 Nights at the Movies*, received a mixed reaction from Frank S. Nugent in *The New York Times* and was panned by *Variety* and Richard B. Jewell and Vernon Harvin in *The RKO Story*. It was not a box office success. Interestingly Miller makes no mention of this film in her memoir, *Miller's High Life*.

Her next film was the black and white musical comedy *Radio City Revels* (1938), shot from mid–November to late December at the RKO Studios in Hollywood. The screenplay was by Eddie Davis, Matt Brooks, Anthony Veiller and Mortimer Offner based on a story by Brooks, and the director was Ben Stoloff. Songs had music by Allie Wrubel and lyrics by Herb Magidson. The musical production numbers were directed by Joseph Santley, the dances staged by Hermes Pan, and gowns by Edward Stevenson. The story centered on Harry (Jack Oakie) and Teddy (Milton Berle), a struggling song writing team in New York who take the songs Lester (Bob Burns) sleep-writes and passes them off as their own.

Miller is billed fourth above the film's title and played the supporting part of Billie Shaw, Harry's secretary. She performs in three musical numbers, and we also see her feet tapping under a piano Billie plays, though the key fingering is not shown. Kenny Baker who plays Kenny sings "I'm Taking a Shine to You" on the Radio City radio show and the girl tap dances when she hears it in the corridor. The skirt of the knee-length dark-colored dress moves to complement her twirls, and this number is perhaps Miller's best in the film though Santley or Stoloff cut away to the radio audience watching her. With Harry she sings "Take a Tip from a Tulip" that is played on the piano by Teddy, and dances to "Speak Your Heart" in the Radio City stage show, with her taps heard before she is seen rising on an elevator platform through a trap in the stage floor. The film also features Miller's first screen kiss by Kenny, and she delivers a girlishly gentle rejection of Harry's proposal of marriage.

It was released on February 11, 1938, with the taglines "LOOK WHO'S IN IT!," "More stars of screen and radio than you've ever seen in one mad melodious burst of exciting entertainment!—plus gay romance and rippling rhythm to keep you happy as you laugh till it hurts!," "IT'S SLUG-NUTTY! The Biggest Fun Bargain in Years," "The Lid is OFF! Here comes the BIG show with stars of screen and radio!," "The Roaring Show from Rhythm Row!," "HERE COMES THE BIG SHOW! NOW FOR THE TIME OF YOUR LIFE!," "HOLLYWOOD SHOOTS THE WORKS!

THE CREAM OF SCREEN AND RADIO STAR IN A ROARING MUSI-
CAL SHOW!," and "SEVEN STARS! SEVEN SONGS! SEVEN HUNDRED
LAUGHS AND A MILLION THRILLS!" The film received a mixed reaction
from *Variety*, who wrote that Miller was most definitely on the way up,
carried the romance interest well, was a cute charming personality, and
was a right smart tapster on the Eleanor Powell order. Frank S. Nugent
in *The New York Times* also had a mixed reaction, saying the nimble and
beauteous little dancer was one of the good things. It was panned by
Richard B. Jewell and Vernon Harbin in *The RKO Story*. The film was
reported to not be a box office success, remaindered to the bottom half
of a double bill with the Universal crime mystery *The Jury's Secret* (1938).

However the star, Miller, claims it was a big hit. At a preview studio officials noted the press reviews praising her, so hasty revisions were
made to give her star billing on the screen credits and in the advertising. Miller's salary was raised to $250 a week. A studio publicist drove
her and Clara to the RKO Theatre in Los Angeles for some promotional
shots where "Ann Miller" was in white shining electric lights on the marquee, for the first time in the girl's career. They stood looking at it, holding each other and crying.

Filming of the film's finale saw a near-miss accident for her. Shot
over five days, by the last day at 5 p.m. she was tired and wanted to go to
her on-stage dressing room and rest. The director was anxious to get the
final shot before 6 p.m. since going after 6 would have meant overtime
pay for the large cast. However Miller was insistent and left the set when
suddenly one of the big arc lights on the catwalk fell in the spot where
she had been standing.

The girl said the film's screen kiss was also her first romantic kiss in
life. The day they were to shoot it she was petrified, also because Miller
had a crush on Kenny Baker and again foolishly confided in a wardrobe lady who spread the word. For the rehearsal of the scene the director stopped before the kiss, and for the take, she closed her eyes and
was kissed. But there was no call for cut. When the girl became out of
breath, she opened her eyes to see that only Baker was there and all the
lights were off. They had played a joke on her and he ran off the set. She
was not amused.

After finishing the film Miller and Clara were at the cinema when
she had another psychic experience. The film was only half over when
she had the feeling they had to go home, seeing a box of flowers dying on
her doorstep. Sure enough, when they got back the flowers were there.

The girl was written up for the first time by Louella Parsons in her
column of February 15, 1938. Parsons reported she had won the role of
the dance-daffy ballet-minded daughter in *You Can't Take It with You*. It

would be funny to see Miller, who was such a good dancer, play someone who could hardly get her feet out of her own way. The splendid opportunity was one of the best comic ones in the play, and the deal for Columbia to borrow her from RKO had occurred that day.

Her friendship with Hermes Pan saw the girl give him the nickname of "Bear" and he dubbed her "Annie Crow." Clara adored him for his great sense of humor and because he was a Southerner. She agreed to let Pan take her daughter to the 10th Academy Awards on March 10, 1938, without a chaperone. This was Miller's first Hollywood date, though he was unaware she was only 14. The couple were accompanied by Mr. and Mrs. Walt Disney, and the girl wore her first long evening dress, a yellow taffeta gown with long pearl earrings and three strands of pearls.

Wanting to look 18 and glamourous, she had designed her hair and makeup to resemble Hedy Lamarr. But when Pan arrived he reacted in horror—Miller's thick pancake makeup, blue eye shadow, coal black lashes, and dark lipstick made her look more like Theda Bara as Cleopatra. He washed her face and re-did the girl's makeup with very little lipstick and eyebrow color, and she cried all the way to the ceremony held at the Biltmore Hotel. But her spirits were raised when both Pan and Disney won Academy Awards—Pan for Best Dance Direction for *A Damsel in Distress*, and Disney for the animated comedy short *The Old Mill* (1937) as Best Cartoon Short Subject.

Movie magazine articles appeared about Miller and she became known as the world's fastest tap dancer according to Ripley's Believe It or Not, who attached a speedometer to her dancing feet noting 500 taps per minute.

The girl started work on the black and white comedy romance Frank Capra's *You Can't Take It with You* (1938), which was shot from 25 April 25 to June 29 on location at the Columbia Ranch in California, at the Sunset Gower Studios in Hollywood. The screenplay by Robert Riskin was based on the Pulitzer Prize–winning play by George S. Kaufman and Moss Hart that ran on Broadway from December 14, 1936, to December 3, 1938. The film's director was Frank Capra. The story centered on Tony Kirby (James Stewart), vice-president of a powerful company and from a family of rich snobs, who becomes engaged to stenographer Alice Sycamore (Jean Arthur) from a decidedly eccentric family. Miller is billed sixth after the title and plays the supporting role of Essie Carmichael, Alice's sister, who is the wife of Ed Carmichael (Dub Taylor). Essie is seen dancing badly and cooking Love Dream candy, and she also chews gum. The girl gets a laugh when Essie jumps into the arms of Ed who falls to the floor and her best scene is perhaps when she dances to Brahms' Hungarian Dance music, dressed in her "dancing clothes." The outfit by an uncredited designer is a light-colored puffy-sleeved tutu with a full skirt, and a hair ribbon. Regrettably director Capra photographs the dance with medium shots, obscures the foreground, and uses cutaways to interrupt the number.

The film was released on September 1 with the taglines "You'll love them all for giving you the swellest time you've ever had!," "Only the Magic of Frank Capra ... could transform this beautiful play into the finest picture of all time!," "The Great Pulitzer Prize Play Now the Screen's Outstanding Picture!," and "From the Master Picture Maker...." It was praised by Roy Chartier in *Variety*, Frank S. Nugent in *The New York Times*, and Clive Hirschhorn in "The Columbia Story." A box office "success," it was said not to have recouped its production costs and won the Academy Award for Best Picture and Best Director, and was nominated for Best Actress in a Supporting Role for Spring Byington; Best Screenplay; Best Cinematography; Best Sound, Recording, and Best Film Editing. The film was remade as a 1945 made-for-TV movie, a 1947 British made-for-TV movie, the December 1, 1955, episode of *The Ford Television Theater* anthology series called "The Fabulous Sycamores," the August 25, 1978, episode of the French comedy television series *Au théâtre ce soir*, a 1979 made-for-TV movie, the November 22, 1984, episode of the musical television series *Great Performances*, and a 1987 comedy television series.

Miller said the experience was magical and a great opportunity to work with people of such magnitude. However she pulled a faux pas with Capra on her first day on the set, mistaking him for an office boy, though the good-natured director forgave her. The girl was lucky to have been cast, since although she had taken ballet lessons, Miller lied about being able to do toe work. She received instruction from dance teacher Ada Broadbent, having to reverse from the lithe, lyrically-limbed professional into a clumsy and awkward amateur. The girl took daily footbaths in straight cider-vinegar to toughen

Miller in Frank Capra's *You Can't Take It with You* (1938).

her feet and ankles since, unlike a tap dancer who needed supple feet and ankles, a ballet aspirant's feet had to be firm and fixed.

She was in pain, because Miller did not know to wrap lamb's wool around the toes and stuff them into the shoes for protection, as ballerinas did. Her toenails pushed up into her feet and they were a bloody mess, but it helped the performance. Every night her feet were soaked and bandages applied, and her toenails would be so badly injured that that forever after Miller had two which wouldn't grow out correctly. Naturally she told no one on the film about all this but once Jimmy Stewart caught her crying and he gave her a candy bar to cheer her up. Stewart loved candy but while he remained painfully thin when he ate it, the girl ballooned from 115 to 139 pounds. Despite this, she kept her crush on him.

Frank Capra wrote in his autobiography *The Name Above the Title* that Miller played her part with the legs of Marlene, the innocence of Pippa, and the brain of a butterfly that flitted on its toes. She admired his all-seeing eye and found him to be a real gentleman, although being Sicilian, he could have temper tantrums. Capra never told actors what to do, and if they did something wrong, he would whisper his direction.

After the film had a sneak preview in August of 1938, Columbia sent the girl out a personal appearance tour, accompanied by Clara on the train. She was the only member of the cast to do so and given star billing in the stage show that played in conjunction with the film. Her William Morris Agency agent, Abe Lastfogel, booked Miller into a lot of theaters and she played at least eight shows a day, which was a real grind. However the tour included her first trip to New York where the girl danced on the stage of the Paramount Theatre, and she also got to work with Betty Hutton, Frank Sinatra, and Red Skelton. Skelton played a joke on Miller after she confided to him her terror of being in a plane, which was suddenly required for a trip to Chicago. He gave her a package, advising not to open it until she was on board. Following his instructions, the girl found inside a scrapbook filled with newspaper clippings of airplane crashes with gory pictures that he had gone to the trouble of creating. Naturally this did not help the Millers cope with the flight, but despite the gag she remained friends with Skelton.

Returning from the tour RKO considered her a hot property and Miller was immediately put into the Marx Brothers' black and white comedy *Room Service* (1938). Rehearsals took place in June and the film was shot from June 27 to August 3. It had a screenplay by Morrie Ryskind from the play by John Murray and Allan Boretz which had run on Broadway at the Cort Theatre from May 19, 1937, to July 6, 1938, and with uncredited contributions from Philip Loeb and Glenn Tryon. The director was William A. Seiter. The story centered on Gordon Miller (Groucho Marx), a penniless theatrical producer who must outwit Gregory Wagner (Donald MacBride), the efficiency expert for the White Way Hotel in New York trying to evict him from his room, while securing a backer for his new play. Miller is billed second after the title and played the supporting part of Hilda, the secretary to the hotel's manager. With gowns by Renie she has little to do except be the thankless love interest for Leo Davis (Frank Albertson).

The film was released on September 21 with the tagline "Better.... Battier.... Funnier Than Ever !" It was praised by *Variety*, who said Miller's part was a virtual walk-through, and Frank S. Nugent in *The New York Times*, but lambasted by Richard B. Jewell and Vernon Harbin in *The RKO Story*. The film was not a box office success but was remade as the RKO musical comedy *Step Lively* (1944).

On her first day on the set Miller was introduced to the Marx Brothers. Harpo, in his typical zany fashion, started chasing her, wearing only a high silk top hat and pair of funny shorts which he soon dropped. She was scared to death and ran into her dressing room, bolted the door, and refused to come out until his pants were on. Every day throughout filming he would come up with some new antic, making a face and blowing his horn at her when the girl least expected it. Miller tried to laugh off his jokes but she was relieved when the shoot was done. The girl had a better relationship with Groucho Marx whom she thought was a super guy and they became good friends.

The International News Service on March 7, 1938, reported Miller had proved herself to be a very sensible girl and not one to waste her salary. She and Clara planned to own a house, be covered by insurance and have a large bank account, and had no intention of increasing expenses. The girl had seen too many players zoom to the top ranks one minute and slide back to the bottom to next to take any chances.

Her next film was the black and white "B" *Tarnished Angel* (1938) which had the working titles of "Sing, Sister" and "Miracle Racket," which was shot from August 25 to September 16. The screenplay was by Saul Elkins and Jo Pagano based on a story by Elkins. The director was Leslie Goodwins. The story centered on Carol Vinson (Sally Eilers), Broadway showgirl who becomes the companion of a jewel thief and forms a vaudeville act as Sister Connie. Miller is billed second after the title, playing the supporting part of Violet "Vi" McMaster, Carol's friend and assistant to Sister Connie. She presumably replaced Mitzi Green whom *The Hollywood Reporter* had announced in July to be Eilers' co-star.

The film opens with Miller singing and dancing to the song "It's the

Doctor's Orders" with music by Lew Brown and lyrics by Samuel Fain, though Miller does no tap and director Goodwins uses some medium shots and a cutaway for the number. She dances twice more in the film, when Vi auditions for another club in a reprise of "It's the Doctor's Orders," and when Vi spontaneously moves in Sister Connie's dressing room. The former number is perhaps her best, since she wears a short skirt to show off her legs as she taps, though again Goodwins employs some medium shots and cutaways.

Otherwise the narrative provides the girl with perhaps her most sizable screen role to date, and she gets two funny lines. When her cheek is pinched by Dan "Dandy" Bennett (Vinton Hayworth), Vi says, "I hope you try that on a rattlesnake, one of these days," and she comments to Mrs. Harry Stockton (Alma Kruger) on her home accommodations being better than the hotel where she previously lived with: "It doesn't seem natural not to smell gasoline." One of her gowns by Renie has an odd design, with two white triangular epaulettes on the chest of the dark-colored knee-length short-sleeved dress. In addition Goodwins films several two-shot dialogue scenes between Carol and Vi where only the back of Miller's head is seen.

The film was released on October 28 with the tagline "Sensational Expose of 'Miracle Racket'"! It received a mixed reaction from *Variety* who wrote that Miller was passably fair, and was panned by Thomas M. Pryor in *The New York Times*, and Richard B. Jewell and Vernon Harbin in *The RKO Story*. It is not known whether the film made a profit, though it presumably did not.

Miller described it as a dud and reported that for one of Eilers' scenes preaching to a flock of people, which Ann was in, a camel on the stage caused a problem. First the restless animal's stomping hoofs made the dialogue inaudible, then it relieved itself splashing everyone within reach, with Eilers' gown and shoes ruined. Men scurried in with mops and pails, and the star flounced off the set in a fury, with the incident ending the day's shooting. The scene in the film is brief, perhaps shortened from the shot footage before the camel accident occurred.

She appeared in the December edition of the magazine *Movie Life*, displaying Max Factor's Color Harmony Make-up Set.

In 1939 Miller went to 20th Century–Fox for a screen test for a role in a Sonja Henie film, presumably the musical comedy *Second Fiddle* (1939), which was shot from mid–March to May. For the girl Henie typified the era of glamour because she was a star who loved things that glittered. Her dresses were always beaded and sparkled, and her fingers and arms and neck and ears covered with big diamonds. Attempting to play a sophisticated woman, Miller smeared her face with heavy makeup—only to find Hermes Pan on the sound stage. To her embarrassment in front of everyone he ordered the girl to wash her face before she would be permitted to test. Miller didn't get the role because it was said she looked too young, and she blamed Pan.

She attended the Academy Awards of February 23 at the Biltmore Theatre to see Frank Capra received the Oscar for Best Director and Best Picture for *You Can't Take It with You*. But despite the success of that film her movie career seemed to be at a standstill. Miller had asked for a pay raise and RKO hesitated, but after her agent secured her a spot in the new *George White Scandals* on Broadway they asked for a release from the contract. She had to be convinced this was the right move by Clara, since the girl liked making movies and didn't want to move to New York. But apparently there were other forces at play. M-G-M was not happy about the build-up she was getting at RKO, spending a fortune for their own big musical productions, with Miller regarded as a threat to Eleanor Powell. Both Powell and she had the same agent, though the M-G-M star brought more money to them, and they told the girl that RKO had no more musicals planned for her and she would be better off getting a release. George White's shows had fallen out of favor, and Miller wondered if her agent was deliberately setting her up to fail, so that they could offload her. But she still left for New York.

CHAPTER 2

Broadway

*T*he Millers moved into the Gorham hotel and rehearsals began in the summer, with Clara buying a white fox fur for her daughter's 16th birthday to wear to the opening. The show was the 13th *Scandals* for George White, though he had not done one for three years. His productions were fast revues featuring showgirls wearing provocative costumes and burlesque comediennes doing risqué skits. White did the staging, though the dialogue by Matt Brooks, Eddie Davis and White was directed by William K. Wells. The songs had music by Sammy Fain with lyrics by Jack Yellin and additional lyrics by Herb Magidson. He gave Miller two solo numbers, and although White was the show's choreographer, he allowed her to create her own dance, hoping she would invent one that would become as popular as "The Black Bottom" which he had introduced. Her songs were "The Mexiconga" and "Are You Having Any Fun?" and she would also dance in a medley of all the songs in the show. In addition, White cast her in some of the skits.

The premiere took place at the Garden Pier Theatre in Atlantic City on August 8, 1939, and the week's run saw standing ovations and rave reviews. They moved on to Boston for two weeks, with the critics alarmed at the blue material, though the city was known for its puritanical atmosphere. Miller claims that Clara was so alarmed by the vulgarity of the skits she demanded her daughter be removed from them, though another source says the girl was cut to shorten their running time. Feeling disappointed, she begged to quit the show but White refused.

The Broadway opening night was August 28 at the Alvin Theatre, and Miller was so frightened that she screwed on her earrings tight so that pain forced her to forget the fear. Her mood changed when "The Mexiconga" began halfway through the first act. The show's leading lady, Ella Logan sang the song and then Ann was in a spotlight, supported by the Kim Loo Sisters pounding out the rhythm on conga drums. Her waist-length hair was dyed blue-black, and she wore heavy Moorish eye makeup and a Mexican costume by Madame Berthe of New York comprised of a colored short bodice overlaid with shimmering layers of silver bugle beads, a ruffled red frontless rhumba skirt, big jeweled cuffs and a bugle bead Mexican sombrero.

Miller danced faster and faster and, when the chorus appeared, the number worked up into an exotic, sensuous whirling dervish finale. It stopped the show and she got a standing ovation. Not knowing how to react, the girl danced into the wings and into the arms of White who told her to do the number again, which the company did. "Are You Having Any Fun?" in the second act gave her a spectacular Madame Berthe Folies Bergère showgirl costume: a white beaded and rhinestone leotard with a train of ostrich feathers, long rhinestone gloves, and a hat with a long doodad of ostrich feathers. Miller danced alone in a spotlight, whirling and turning with the crash of the tympani. This too brought down the house and at the end of the show when the cast took their bows, she stood there crying.

It was praised by *Variety* who wrote that Miller was the finest tap dancer seen on Broadway boards in many seasons and easily the show's individual hit, and Brooks Atkinson in *The New York Times* said she tap danced with virtuosity.

The season ran at the Alvin Theatre to November 5 and then transferred to the Hollywood Theatre for a run from November 6 to December 9. George White attributed to Miller the show's success, and paid her the ultimate compliment by asking Ann to be his date after the opening night instead of Ella Logan. This allowed her to wear the coat Clara had purchased and at the Stork Club the columnist Walter Winchell invited them to his table. He wrote marvelous things about the girl in the *New York Daily News*, nicknaming her Ann "Legs" Miller, a name that stuck throughout her career and something she felt had always brought her luck. Back at the hotel Clara told her daughter to go straight to bed because of the lateness of the hour instead of schoolwork which she was still doing via post with Mrs. Lawlor.

Miller was the toast of Broadway and also obtained a better billing in the show, almost equal with Ella Logan, which the star wasn't happy about. She was the cover girl for all the important newspaper Sunday supplements and magazines, and she made the rotogravure section of *The New York Times* in her Mexican costume. *Vogue* used a full-page cover picture of her in color with the Kim Loo Sisters and their drums, and *Life* did a photo series of her dance. Kyle Chricton wrote a lengthy story for *Collier's*, uncovering the genuine birth certificate that revealed she was just 16. He wrote that while on stage the girl had sex appeal radiating from all directions, at home she was a long-legged tomboy who had never had a date with a boy alone, didn't smoke or drink and always said her prayers before going to bed.

Those who pursued Woman Incarnate would have been better sending her dolls. And she was pursued—all the rich playboys in New York who habited the late-hour night spots always had an eye for Broadway's pretty showgirls. Miller went out with some of them, with Clara as chaperone, to the Stork Club and 21 and El Morocco. At El Morocco at the wolves' table they made bets on who would be the first to take her out alone but they all lost. She was also pursed by older men, courted with champagne and caviar and white orchids and many expensive gifts which Clara made her send back. One went to the show every night, always sitting in the front row, and sent flowers and a diamond bracelet. But her mother said it wasn't right to accept such gifts unless you were in love and expected to marry the man.

The girl became friends with Mary Martin who lived in the penthouse above, whose little boy used to drive them crazy running all over the place night and day, and grew up to be Larry Hagman. She also befriended Carmen Miranda who was appearing at the Sert Room at the Waldorf-Astoria Hotel. She wrote in *Miller's High Life* that at this time she went to the Metropolitan Museum to see the Egyptian collection, and was mesmerized by her facial similarity to that of the lioness sphinx Queen Hatshepsut of Egypt. However in her 1990 Sally Jessy Raphael interview the star would say this occurred when she was doing *Mame* on Broadway. Later four psychics would tell her that she was the Queen in another lifetime, though Miller says that Tina Turner also believed she was the Queen and the star believed they should have let the two women in a room to let them fight it out.

She felt her success was like too much too soon for 16 years old and the show helped to get more money when Hollywood wanted the girl back. Now she received four offers from producers when six months before nobody had anything for her. But Miller could not be tempted, and stayed with the show for the national tour, with seasons at the Forrest Theatre in Philadelphia for two weeks from December 11, and the Erlanger Theatre in Chicago from December 25. In 1940 it continued on to Detroit although the dates and location are unknown, and Los Angeles at the Biltmore Theatre for two weeks from March 24, 1940.

The opening night in the Curran Theatre in San Francisco on April 15 proved an embarrassing moment. The girl's number in the second act followed The Three Stooges in a pie throwing skit, where a rubber mat was usually on the floor to catch the pies, but on this night the stage manager had forgotten it. So after entering she stated tapping and slid across the floor, with her ostrich feathers preventing her from landing in the orchestra pit, but kicked one pie all over the conductor's white shirt and another down the tuba. Miller got up and danced into the wings, with the audience finding the accident hysterical and clapping, but her costume was ruined. It was announced there would be a short intermission and the lights were blacked out and prop men came with mops and buckets to clean up the mess.

The highest dollar film offer came, ironically, from RKO for $3,000 a week to star in the film version of *Too Many Girls* (1940) which had run on Broadway from October 18, 1939, to May 18, 1940. In New York she had met George Abbott, who had produced and directed the Broadway show, and dated him with Clara as chaperone. He was signed to direct the film version and urged her to stay in New York to pursue a career on Broadway and then she could return to Hollywood as a big star. But although both Millers liked the man and the girl respected his opinion, she decided to accept the film, being homesick for California.

The black and white sports musical comedy *Too Many Girls* (1940) was shot from June 22 to September. It had a screenplay by John Twist based on the musical play by George Marion, Jr., with music by Richard Rogers and lyrics by Lorenz Hart. The story centered on Connie Casey (Lucille Ball) an heiress who goes to Pottawatomie College where her father (Harry Shannon) has arranged for her to have four football players as her bodyguards. The actors are billed after the film's title and Miller is billed third after the title, playing the supporting role of Pepe, a student at the college, who had been played by Diosa Costello in the stage show. Pepe has a few lines, even some in Spanish, but mostly sings and dances, and her hair is worn in a shoulder-length style and off her forehead. She sings and dances in the chorus for "'Cause We Got Cake" and "Spic 'n' Spanish," sings in "Look Out!" and the reprise of "You're Nearer," and dances in the "Conga" finale. The dances are staged by LeRoy Prinz and Ann's best number is perhaps when she dances with Desi Arnaz, who plays Manuelito. She wears a light-colored long-sleeved and belted gown by Edward Stevenson with a matching cap that has a full skirt which complements her twirling. Her dancing is the "Conga" finale is also noteworthy for its wildness in response to Manuelito's drumming, which matches the general hysteria level of the number.

The film was released on October 8 with the tagline "It's knee-deep in gorgeous gals and gaiety!" It was praised by *Variety*, who wrote that Miller displayed a fresh and youthful personality with plenty of showmanship behind it, received a mixed reaction from Bosley Crowther in *The New York Times* who said she sang and danced with pleasing exuberance, but was panned by Richard B. Jewell and Vernon Harbin in *The RKO Story*. It is not known whether the film was a box office success.

Miller with Hal LeRoy in *Too Many Girls* (1940).

Miller thought her salary, billing, and star dressing room was odd considering the small part. However she was grateful to RKO and had high hopes for their future plans for her. The girl's friendship with Lucille Ball continued on the film, and she claimed to have introduced Ball to Desi Arnaz, when Miller and Arnaz were rehearsing and Ball walked in. Miller saw it was love at first sight and it was not a surprise that Lucille's eyes lit up when she the man, since Arnaz was the cutest thing around with a great personality. The girl herself had dated him. No one could play the drums like Arnaz, who was a Don Juan that all the girls were mad for, and now she had the psychic sense that he and Ball would marry. Miller joined them on double-dates, with George Abbott as her beau, going to the Cuban nightclub El Zarape on Sunset Boulevard. Both men were marvelous dancers and she learned to do a mean rhumba, which was a big craze at the time.

The clairvoyant Mary Young moved to Los Angeles, and the Millers introduced her to many stars and friends to make predictions for them. The predictions included how the girl would marry but not be happy and that her greatest stardom would occur later in life.

She was loaned out to Republic for two films. The first was the black and white musical comedy *Hit Parade of 1941* aka *Romance and Rhythm* (1940). The latter title was a re-edited re-issue of the film running at 52 minutes, which cut 30 minutes from the original, and the only one available for viewing. The film was shot from early August to September 6 at the Republic Studios in Hollywood. This was a sequel to the Republic musical *The Hit Parade* (1937). The new screenplay was by Bradford Ropes, F. Hugh Herbert and Maurice Leo, with additional comedy sequences by Sid Kuller and Ray Golden, and unconfirmed contributions from Vera Caspary, Gordon Rigby, Rian James and Manny Seff. The director was John H. Auer.

The story centered on the radio station WPX Brooklyn which is saved from bankruptcy by a backer, Emily Potter (Mary Boland), on the condition that her daughter Annabelle (Miller) sings on television. She is billed fourth after the title, playing a supporting role. It is not known whether it is her voice that is used to display Annabelle's bad operatic singing, but otherwise the girl sings with the off-stage voice of Pat Abbott (Frances Langford) on "Who Am I" and "In the Cool of the Evening" both with music by Jule Styne and lyrics by Walter Bullock. Director Auer uses cutaways for these numbers which is acceptable given that it is not Annabelle really singing, and he uses medium shot coverage of her brief dancing after the operatic singing.

However Auer also uses cutaways for Miller's dancing part of the "Swing Low, Sweet Rhythm" number, also by Styne and Bullock. Her taps are heard before she is seen on the top of a piano though Miller's best dance number is the "South American Ballet" aka Pan American Conga with uncredited music by Styne and Walter Scharf. Here Auer keeps her in long shots and uses no cutaways, and she wears a diaphanous floor-length long-sleeved costume with silver turban by Adele Palmer, one of many flattering Palmer outfits. The girl makes Annabelle's ambition and flirting with David Farraday (Kenny Baker) funny, and equally funny is a line Emily's assistant Carter (Franklin Pangborn) has about Annabelle—"Nature has endowed [her] with a superb pair of limbs but since she is not a grasshopper and can make no sound by rubbing them together her value as a vocalist is nil."

The film was released on October 15 with the tagline "Romance.... Rhythm.... Revelry combined to give you a musical extravaganza of matchless beauty and entertainment" It was panned by Bosley Crowther in *The New York Times* but he wrote that Miller made the most of her conventional assignment and managed to get in a few lively tap dances. It was a box office success and was nominated for the Best Music Score and "Who Am I?" for the Best Original Song Academy Awards. There were three Republic sequels—the musical romance *Hit Parade of 1943* (1943), the musical comedy *Hit Parade of 1947* (1947), and the musical *Hit Parade of 1951* (1950)—but none of them featured Miller.

The credited dance director Danny Dare was reportedly moved up to co-director in the middle of shooting and he asked Hermes Pan to complete the dances. The exact nature of Pan's contribution is unknown but in his book, *Hermes Pan: The Man Who Danced with Fred Astaire*, John Franceschina suggests that he contributed to Miller's routines for "Swing Low, Sweet Rhythm" and "South American Ballet."

She appeared on the radio broadcast "Of Stars and the States" on August 5. The second film for Republic was the black and white musical western "*Melody Ranch*" which was shot from September 16 to October 5 on locations in California and at the Republic Studios in Hollywood. The screenplay was by Jack Moffitt, F. Hugh Herbert, Bradford Ropes and Betty Burbridge based on an uncredited story by Herbert and Moffitt, with special comedy sequences by Sid Kuller and Ray Golden. The director was Joseph Santley. The story centered on Gene Autry (playing himself) who is invited to his Arizona hometown of Torpedo to be the honorary sheriff of the Frontier Day Celebration. Miller is billed second after the title, playing the supporting role of Julie Shelton, an actress and singer on the radio show that Autry is on. With him, she sings the title song with music and lyrics by Jule Styne and Eddie Cherkose, and "We Never Dream the Same Dream Twice" with music and lyrics by Autry and Fred Rose.

Alone she sings and dances to "My Gal Sal" with music and lyrics by Paul Dresser though there is no credited dance director. As the only time Miller dances in the film, it is perhaps her best musical scene, and she is dressed in an Adele Palmer shimmery knee-length dress with feather collar and matching shimmery and feathered hat. However director Santley limits our view of her with foreground obscuring, a cutaway, medium shots, and bad framing of long shots where the feet are cut off. The Palmer wardrobe also features Julie in different hair ribbons. Otherwise in the film Ann gets to ride a horse, though a stunt-double is presumably used when she falls off and has to avoid an oncoming horse-drawn carriage. She is funny in the early scenes, being uppity and condescending to Autry's cowboy ways, but soft and appealing when she falls in love with him, where Santley provides her with some good close-ups.

The film was released on November 15 with the tagline "Join the fun with Public Cowboy No. 1 in the gayest, most melodious fun-festival he ever made." It received a mixed reaction from Bosley Crowther in *The New York Times*. The film was not a box office success.

This was the first musical Gene Autry had done and he especially asked for Miller to be his leading lady. Autry told her she was the first girl he had ever kissed on screen, though he wrote in his autobiography, *Back in the Saddle Again*, that it was with Ann Rutherford in the Republic musical adventure *Comin' Round the Mountain* (1936). There was a lot of advance publicity about the new kiss and Republic was flooded with letters from the kids saying "Don't let Gene Autry kiss Ann Miller in the picture—that's sissy!" So to please the fans the kiss was cut. In the film, you see the couple move to kiss and then part from the kiss, so the actual contact is not shown.

Miller now had new agents, Frank and Orsatti, who had bought out her Morris office contract and signed her for a one-picture deal with Columbia. She was cast in the black and white musical *Time Out for Rhythm* (1941), shot from February 24 to March 24, 1941. The film had the working titles of "Show Business" and "Time Out for Music." The screenplay was by Edmund L. Hartman and Bert Lawrence based on a story by Bert Granet and a play by Alex Ruben. The director was Sidney Salkow.

The story centered on New York theatrical agents Daniel "Danny" Collins (Rudy Vallee) and Mike Armstrong (Richard Lane) putting together a television show. They discover Kitty Brown (Miller), the maid of nightclub star Frances Lewis (Rosemary Lane). Miller is top-billed but after the title, although Vallee has the leading role. She doesn't appear until 24 minutes into the narrative and is heard singing before her legs are seen through a window before all of her is revealed. The hair is now shorter but still shoulder-length and costume designer Saltern gives Kitty hair ribbons. She sings and dances three songs by Sammy Cahn and Saul Chaplin: "A-Twiddlin' My Thumbs," "Obviously the Gentleman Prefers to Dance" twice, and as part of the title song.

Director Salkow employs cutaways, medium shots and foreground obscuring but "A-Twiddlin' My Thumbs" has a dance with her mirrored reflection, and the second version of "Obviously the Gentleman Prefers to Dance" shows Miller's funny disapproval of the dancing of her

"TIME OUT FOR RHYTHM"
Rudy VALLEE, Ann MILLER, Rosemary LANE, Allen JENKINS, Joan MERRILL, BRENDA and COBINA, The THREE STOOGIES, Printed in
Richard LANE, SIX HITS and a MISS and Glen GRAY and his CASA LOMA BAND · A COLUMBIA PICTURE

Miller in the title song number in *Time Out for Rhythm* (1941).

partner Off-Beat Davis (Allen Jenkins). The star's best showcase is perhaps her part of the finale of the title song, where she dances wearing a Saltern shimmery outfit with a low-cut black and silver top with torso holes, sheer split skirt, winged shoulders, long gloves, and a large feathered headdress. The film's musical numbers are staged by LeRoy Prinz.

Miller also gets dramatic scenes, with the best being her underplayed choice to give up her theatrical career to help Danny.

The film was released on June 5 with the tagline "A Stage Show and a Love Story Too Big for any Stage … Only the Screen Could Bring You." It was panned by *Variety* who wrote that only the tap dance numbers of Miller momentarily lifted the onlooker out of slumping seats. Bosley Crowther of *The New York Times* said she was lovely and lively, simply wouldn't be suppressed and danced charmingly and with ease. The film was a huge box office hit.

Miller reported in her memoir that while making this film she was visited on set by a very famous and much older star lady. Later she identified the lady as Marlene Dietrich who was said to have been simultaneously making a film at Columbia. However the production dates don't match up. It is more probable that Miller was visited on the set of her next film.

During shooting Columbia did a publicity stunt of insuring her hands and lightning feet for $25,000. She described the film as a nervous "A," not quite big enough to rate as first-class but having more production values than the ones designated as the second feature slot on theater double bills. It saw the beginning of her professional relationship with composer Saul Chaplin, whose name appeared in the credits of Miller's films more than any other person. He and Sammy Cahn were hired by the studio to make a series of quickie musicals for her.

She had not met Harry Cohn while making the film, but he asked to meet her after its success, offering her a new contract with Columbia. She says it was for seven years but other sources say it was six. Cohn was an awesome sight to behold, sitting behind a big desk looking like a huge grizzly bear. When he shook hands with her the star thought the man was going to break her arms. Cohn had a temper and cursed, roaring like a bear and kept a riding crop on his desk which was cracked at anyone who got out of line. He ran the studio with an iron hand and was known as one of the most hated men in Hollywood but Miller felt his bark was worse than his bite. Cohn's kind and decent side was expressed to her, always being polite and kind, and if anyone cursed when she was in his office he called them down. The man was like a Mother Hen, always polite and kind to the star and Clara, respecting her mother for bringing up her daughter strictly and teaching her to work hard. Although probably having all kinds of girls, Cohn was never a wolf with Miller.

She now became "The Queen of the Bees," since her films were made quickly and cheaply but resulted in millions at the box office. Her childhood friend Marguerite Carmen Cansino was now known as Rita

Hayworth and the studio's big star. Compared to her, Miller was a little star, as Hayworth got the big budget Technicolor films. But the money the little star was earning was good and she enjoyed making the films, hoping one day that Cohn would think Miller was good enough to do an "A" film. At Columbia she also felt the same sense of family as her days at RKO, with Hayworth in makeup at the same time in the morning and people drinking coffee and having donuts. The women retained their friendship, visiting their sets to watch each other dance, and Miller learned how Marguerite had been transformed into Rita, her black hair lightened and painful electrolysis used to remove an inch from on her forehead.

Cohn would use the little star as a threat to Hayworth, as when she went off and married Orson Welles in 1943 and left her career temporarily. The studio head Cohn would say she would be replaced by Miller unless the star came back on a certain date, and this strategy worked for a time. This was similar to what 20th Century–Fox studio boss Darryl F. Zanuck did to Miller's friend Linda Darnell to keep Loretta Young in line. Miller and Darnell had met on Catalina Island where their respective studios had sent them for a benefit and the two Texans hit it off immediately. But the two Columbia ladies were very different and choreographer Jack Cole said Hayworth's instinctive, marvelous erotica was something her supposed rival didn't have. To Miller the threat was silly because she could not compare in terms of glamour with the sex goddess. Miller was also a witness to the hard time Cohn gave her friend, since he had a yen for her and Hayworth was always trying to get away from him.

This era was a new beginning for the girl who was now 18, a legal adult, and had finally finished her schoolwork. She repeated the RKO work hours of getting up at dawn to be at the studio and in makeup by 6 a.m. Again Clara always drove her there and back. Many times Miller, after a full day of work, was in the rehearsal hall until 11 p.m. preparing the numbers for the next day's shooting. When making a film she wore a leotard and tennis shoes and never went out in the evening, but in her time off the star loved to dress up in something pretty and go out. Although Miller had been on the Hollywood scene a long time it was almost like she was tasting for the first time what the girl had dreamed about.

There was dinner at LaRue's or Romanoff's or Victor Hugo's or Chez Roland at the Beach and then dancing at the Mocambo and Ciro's. The places were glamourous, glistening and gay. The Mocambo had a cage full of exotic parrots that hung above the dance floor, and gave a prize every night to the lady with the best hat and Miller and Linda

Darnell often won. She also tied with Ginger Rogers in the winning of a champagne bucket at the Charleston contest the club held. At Ciro's one night the star saw Marlene Dietrich in a beaded gown and a floor length white fox coat get her foot got caught in the hem of her dress and fall flat on her face. This was very funny to Miller. She was also there the night a very popular and beautiful dark-haired Big Star made love to a well-known director behind the bar. The young star thought if Clara knew about it she would never let her go again.

Miller's second film for Columbia was the black and white "B" western *Go West, Young Lady* (1941), shot from July 16 to August 14. It had the working titles of "Cowboy Joe" and "Lady Buckaroo." The screenplay was by Richard Flournoy and Karen DeWolf and based on a story by DeWolf. The director was Frank R. Strayer. The story was set in the town of Headstone and centered on the romance between new arrival Belinda "Bill" Pendergast (Penny Singleton) fresh from an Eastern ladies' seminary and Tex Miller (Glenn Ford), the new sheriff who must contend with the masked bandit known as Killer Pete. Miller is billed 3rd after the title, playing the supporting role of Lola, the Crystal Palace dance hall entertainer and girlfriend to wealthy rancher Tom Hannegan (Onslow Stevens). She sings and dances in 2 numbers both with music and lyrics by Sammy Cahn and Saul Chaplin: the title song and "I Wish That I Could Be a Singing Cowboy" which the star performs with Allen Jenkins who plays Hank. Although director Strayer uses foreground obscuring, medium shots and cutaways in both numbers, the better showcase for her is the first. Here she wears a Walter Plunkett shimmery dark-colored low-cut corset with a large white flower on the hip and in her hair, with stockings to show off her legs, and when Miller tap dances on top of a bar Strayer keeps to long shots. For the comic ""I Wish That I Could Be a Singing Cowboy" she recites rather than sings the lyrics and wears spurs on her boots. The hair is longer and done in a sculptured period style with ringlets, and Lola dons cowboy drag for the climactic catfight with Bill. This scene is disturbingly vicious and somewhat humiliating for Miller, since she loses, though no apparent body doubles are used. The film also sees her sit on a horse, with a body double perhaps used for the riding scene. The film's dance director is Louis DaPron.

The film was released on November 27 with the taglines "It's jam-packed with melodrama, music and mirth!," "Rip-Roarin' Rhythm," "Gunfire and Gayety" and "SEE and HEAR BOB WILLIS and his Texas Playboys deliver a solid stack of sizzling song hits!" It was praised by Theodore Strauss in *The New York Times* who wrote that Miller tripped rhythmically across the bars of Headstone, and not so rhythmically when she tried to act, but received a mixed reaction from *Variety*, and Clive Hirschhorn in "The Columbia Story." *Variety* said she was unusually attractive although her specialty tapstering was only seen briefly, and deserved a better break than being submerged in this subordinate role.

The star wore special rubber legs guards to protect her shins from the spurs while rehearsing the "I Wish That I Could Be a Singing Cowboy" number, which took two weeks, and also wore the guards when recording the taps. In his book *Glenn Ford: A Life*, Peter Ford wrote that his father romanced her when the film was being made, with the 18 year old being attracted to the older man of 24. Ford doubts the affair was intimate but says it certainly was affectionate and the sweet Miller became a dear and close family friend.

Marlene Dietrich made the romantic comedy *The Lady Is Willing* (1942) at Columbia from August 11 to October 24, so this is thought to be the film she visited Miller on. She writes that the lady watched her do her big production number, observing in a strange way. The next day there was a note saying Dietrich had enjoyed watching the dance, and an invitation to have lunch in the lady's dressing room. Miller was thrilled, sending a note back accepting and received a dozen long-stemmed red roses back. Word about the lunch went back to Harry Cohn, who didn't want it to happen. On the day and each day throughout the shoot she was kept on the set rehearsing during her lunch hours and her meals brought to her. Years later the star learned that Cohn's objection was due to the rumor that Dietrich liked girls better than men and he wasn't about to let his young naïve new player into a situation like that. She also learned from the wardrobe ladies that the lady had a reputation for coming to work in filthy underwear.

Miller appeared in the short *Meet the Stars #8: Stars Past and Present* shot at the Republic Studio, which was released on July 24. Directed by Harriet Parsons it had stars past and present gathered to take part in the ceremonies at Republic's new sound stage, dedicated to the memory of Mabel Normand. The short was the eighth in the *Meet the Stars* series that were all released that year.

A musical short the star appeared in was *Screen Snapshots Series 21, No. 1* made by Columbia and released August 15. Directed by Ralph Staub, it had vaudeville performances and featured the contract players from Columbia, 20th-Century Fox, RKO Radio, and Universal.

On October 3 she appeared in Los Angeles Superior Court to sign a new contract with Columbia which called for $400 weekly, increasing to $1250 a week over a five year period. Miller reportedly had $5,000 in the bank and had bought her first home for Clara and herself, a Frank

Lloyd Wright structure built high in the Hollywood Hills overlooking the lights of the city. The receiving hall was on the second floor and the sunken living room was known as Miller's High Life Room, with the figure of a tall witch doctor with black high top silk hat, grass skirt, bangles, and holding a bottle of beer at the entrance. The room was decorated with jungle scenes on the walls, with a baby grand piano, fake palm trees, ceiling lights that blinked on and off, and a thatched hut bar with a fake skull hanging over it. While Ann didn't drink, the room was a wonderful place for parties.

The house was also furnished with all custom-made pieces and antiques with her bedroom done in all white and deep-pink satin. Miller's friend Linda Darnell visited often and, while the two mammas talked, the girls gossiped about their studios and all the goings-on there. She also met Kathryn Grayson at another benefit and they became a close threesome. Everything looked rosy for the Millers. They were finally eating three regular meals a day and had bought a new car and Clara went to the beauty salon to have her hair set and nails done instead of doing them herself at home.

The star was loaned to Paramount for two films. The first was the black and white musical comedy *True to the Army* (1942), shot from late October to mid–November at the Paramount Hollywood Studios. It had the working titles of "Sergeant Yoo-Hoo" and "Private Yoo Hoo." It was a remake of the Paramount musical comedy *She Loves Me Not* (1934). The new screenplay was by Art Arthur and Bradford Ropes, adapted by Edmund Hartman and Val Burton from the novel by Edward Hope and a play by Howard Lindsay. The play *She Loves Me Not* had run on Broadway at the 46th Street Theatre from November 20, 1933, to September 22, 1934. The director of the film was Albert S. Rogell.

The story centered on carnival tight-rope walker Daisy Hawkins (Judy Canova) who hides from gangsters in the nearby Fort Bray army camp in disguise as a man. Miller is billed third above the title and plays the supporting role of Vicki Marlow, the daughter of camp commander Colonel Marlow (Clarence Kolb). She sings and dances in the Swing in Line camp show number "Jitterbug's Lullaby," with music by Harold Spina and lyrics by Frank Loesser and partnered with an uncredited Conrad Wiedell, and briefly dances the rhumba with Lieutenant Danvers (William Wright) and Private Bill Chandler (Allan Jones).

The star's best number is her dancing to music that accompanies the target range tape routine, choreographed by an uncredited Jack Donohue. Her taps follow the sound of machine-gun fire, and accompany a clock ticking and the sound of a typewriter. She even taps sitting

in a chair, with the dance complemented with the light and dark verti-
cally striped skirt of the dress she wears with a military jacket, though
director Rogell uses cutaways and foreground obscuring. Miller's hair
for the film is shorter and still worn off her forehead and the uncredited costume designer gives her ribbons in it. She gets a funny line after
being suddenly kissed by Private Bill, saying "You've got more nerve
than an aching tooth."

It was released on March 21, 1942, with the taglines "It's All-Out
Fun When Judy Canova Crashes This Man's Army!" and "From 'Taps'
to revelry.... FUN is the order of the day!" It was praised by *Variety* who
wrote that Miller was a standout with her dancing with some of the best
hoofing seen in pictures, and John Douglas Eames in "The Paramount
Story," but panned by Theodore Strauss in *The New York Times* who said
she had a pair of miraculously nimble toes but her acting was woefully
limited. The film would be remade as the Fox comedy *How to Be Very,
Very Popular* (1955).

It was reported that during rehearsals for the target range routine
Miller set a new world record for tap-dance speed—the almost unbe-
lievable speed of 840 taps to the minute. The speed record's authentic-
ity was attested to by Army artillerist Colonel Charles Ide, screen dance
authority Danny Dare, and songwriter Johnny Mercer. The number was
filmed on the stage of the Biltmore Theatre in Los Angeles, with no audience except for the film crew.

She appeared uncredited in the documentary short *Hedda Hopper's
Hollywood No. 2*, released December 5. Directed by Herbert Moulton
it showed Hopper playing hostess at a party for her grown son William DeWolfe, Jr., attending the dedication of the Motion Picture Relief
Fund's country home and the Mocambo where the star was seen, and
the world premiere of *Hedda Hopper's Hollywood No. 1*. (The series continued with numbers 3, 4, 5, and 6 all released in 1942 though Miller was
not in them.)

Although *True to the Army* had been made before the bombing
of Pearl Harbor on December 7, its setting in a stateside army camp
seemed to prefigure America's involvement in World War II. Moviegoers would seek relief from battle news, civil defense, and blackouts
and rationing in the Hollywood escapism shown at local movie palaces.
The star now secured a niche in Hollywood's musical films, becoming
the toast of servicemen and American citizens, though she had her own
form of sacrifice. Silk was in short supply and leg makeup was used on
her instead of stockings, which was a helluva job for the studio makeup
ladies.

In 1941 RKO announced they would remake their 1929 musical

comedy *Hit the Deck*, which had been an adaptation of the Broadway musical that had run at the Belasco Theatre from April 25, 1927, to February 25, 1928. The new version was to star Ray Bolger, with Miller to play Looloo, the owner of a seaside coffee shop, but in the end was not made. However she later appeared in the 1955 M-G-M remake.

Next was the Paramount black and white musical comedy *Priorities on Parade* (1942), shot March 26 to April 21, 1942, at the Paramount Studios in Hollywood. The working title was "Priorities of 1942." The screenplay was by Art Arthur and Frank Loesser and the director was again Albert S. Rogell. The story centered on the members of the swing band Johnny Draper (Johnnie Johnston) and the Six Dixie Pixies who get defense jobs at the Eagle Aircraft plant entertaining the employees. Miller is billed first after the title though she has a supporting part, playing Donna D'Arcy. The star goes blonde for this film and her hair is longer, worn in a shoulder-length sculptured style off her forehead.

She sings but doesn't dance for "Kiss the Boys Goodbye" with Johnston that has music by Victor Schertzinger and lyrics by Frank Loesser, sings and dances to "I'd Love to Know You Better" with music by Jule Styne and lyrics by Herb Magidson, and is part of the "Payday" finale, with music by Styne and lyrics by Frank Loesser. Her best number is perhaps "Cooperate with Your Air Raid Warden" with music by Styne and lyrics Magidson where she only dances, accompanied by the singing of Jerry Coronna who plays Jeep Jackson and Vera Vague who plays Mariposa Ginsbotham. Although director Rogell uses cutaways and medium shots, he has Miller with a flashlight illuminating her shoes dancing in the blacked out room, dancing on spilled sand, and with an unsynchronized shadow. In addition she does the radium dance where only her light-colored shoes, belt, hair ribbon, hands, and necklace are seen. When lit she wears an outfit by the uncredited costume designer of a dark-colored pants suit with shimmery pants side lines and a shimmery brooch on one side of the top. The film's musical numbers were staged by Jack Donohue.

It was released on July 23 with the taglines "The first big swing show of the swing shift!," "First Big Swing Show Hits the Ceiling for Fun!," "It just keeps swinging along!," "Six big hit parade songs!," "The jive charmers who turn out the dive bombers!," and "Meet the boys and girls who are sending for Uncle Sam." Miller appeared in a stage show at New York's Paramount Theater to accompany the release but it is not known what she performed. The film received a mixed reaction from Theodore Strauss in *The New York Times*, who wrote that Miller made dexterous use of a spectacular pair of legs, but even that talent had its limits of

A blonde Miller for *Priorities on Parade* (1942).

enjoyment, and John Douglas Eames in "The Paramount Story." It was a box office success.

She celebrated her 19th birthday during filming but reported that having her hair bleached was an unpleasant experience because it damaged her jet-black hair and took a long time to repair.

The star returned to Columbia for the black and white musical comedy *Reveille with Beverly* (1943) shot from November 19 to December 9. It had a screenplay by Howard J. Green, Jack Henley and Albert Duffy based on a story by all three, though it is said to have been based on the radio program created by Jean Ruth. The director was Charles Barton. The story centered on Beverly Ross (Miller), who moderates a 5:30 a.m. radio show on KFEL with swing music, dedicated to the local servicemen. Miller is billed eighth after the title, though she plays the leading role. Back to being a brunette, her hair is shorter though still shoulder-length and worn off her forehead.

She briefly dances for Elmer (Doodles Weaver) when Beverly visits the record store where Beverly used to work but her big number is singing and dancing for "Thumbs Up and V for Victory" with music by Ted Fio Rito and lyrics by Paul Francis Webster at an army camp broadcast. The star is dressed by an uncredited designer in a white floor-length cape with army jacket with a dark-colored V pattern on the front, epaulettes, a matching white cap and a shimmery silver short skirt. She dances to the sound of a marching solider chorus behind her and the number climaxes in the dance over flames that erupt from the floor in a V for Victory pattern, although director Barton disappointingly uses some medium shots in coverage. The designer also has Miller in two notable wide-brim hats in the narrative. Barton gives her one good close-up and the actress is funny in her role and touching in her tentative wave goodbye to the departing soldiers at the film's end.

The film was released on February 4, 1943, with the taglines "Get 'Hep'! Fall Into Step! Here's A Pep!," "HOT HITS! TWINKLING TOES! RACY ROMANCE!," "The HOTTEST rhythm in pictures!," "Romance on the beam! Rhythm in the groove! Laughs on the loose!," and "Great Big Star-Studded Musical! Full of Rhythm, Rhumba and Romance!" It was praised by *Variety* who wrote that Miller walked through her role until the final production number where she got hot with a spirited hoofing routine. However the film was lambasted by Theodore Strauss in *The New York Times*. It was a box office success.

Ann reported that the dance through the flames singed her costume, hair and eyelashes. The flames were meant to spring up behind her as she twirled up and down a platform. The man who controlled them turned a flame in front of her and the star had to leap out of the way, not leaping quite fast enough, which resulted in the singes. Frank Sinatra appears in the film as one of the musical acts, singing "Night and Day." Miller felt that even then he was great and his voice sent tingles up your spine, but the singer was so skinny that he looked like an upside-down drain pipe. It was said that a besieged garrison at Corregidor ran this film over and over again to keep up morale, though this was the only film they had. Colonel Douglas MacArthur told the star that he must have seen it at least 100 times.

She and Jean Ruth, whose radio shop had inspired Columbia to make the film, attended the graduation dinner dance held at the Beverly Hills Hotel on an unknown date in 1943 for the navigation students of the 90th Squadron at Santa Ana California Air Base. The women were the sweethearts of the party, with Miller chosen as the Squadron's favorite film girl.

Clara finally decided to let her daughter go out alone with men who met her approval. She would have an early dinner-and-dancing date but had to be home by midnight, and if late could not go out with that man again. Every time the star had a date she would buy a new hat and new kind of perfume, as she had started into a collecting phase that also included earrings. One of her most frequent escorts was her agent, Vic Orsatti, though there was no romance between them. It was the custom for Hollywood agents to be seen around town with their clients, and anyway, he was madly in love with Linda Darnell. They often double-dated with Miller's other frequent escort Warren Cowan. Some of the other beaus were department store heirs Al Bloomingdale and Jerry Orbach but her most serious was shoe tycoon Harry Karl. He knew the darkly beautiful Spanish spitfire Lupe Velez and introduced her to the star. On January 30 Miller appeared on the radio broadcast "Command Performance."

The black and white musical comedy *What's Buzzin', Cousin?* (1943) was shot from March 16 to April 16. The screenplay was by Harry Sauber, based on a story by Aben Kandel with additional dialogue by John P. Medbury. The director was Charles Barton. The story centered on Freddy Martin (playing himself) and his band on vacation, who come to the deserted Palace Hotel in Waterhill. Miller is top-billed after the title, having the leading role in terms of number of scenes. She plays Ann Crawford, one of the owners of the hotel and sings and dances in two numbers: "Knocked-Out Nocturne" by Jacques Press and Eddie Cherkose and "Eighteen Seventy-five" ($18.75 War Bond Cost) by Wally Anderson.

Although dance director Nick Castle has her end her part in the latter number by bursting through a giant poster for war bonds, the former number is the better showcase. Barton uses some medium shots and there are a lot of cuts to show the star at different angles, but the foreground obscuring at the end has a narrative context where the camera pulls back to reveal that she has been performing to no audience. Another distraction is Miller's ugly costume by an uncredited designer, a shimmery silver and black long-sleeved jacket with vertical triangles at the shoulders, with black bra, a sheer floor-length skirt that is pulled off-stage to reveal a short black split skirt, black necklace, and a shimmery silver cap with sparkles in the hair. The film has her cry for the first time on screen, and Barton gives the star some close-ups, though she is saddled with some bad lines.

The film was released on July 8 with the tagline "Triple Header for Joy! ROCHESTER and his riotous revels! Freddy MARTIN and his jivin' gentlemen playing sweet and hot! Ann MILLER dancing dynamo of rhythm!" It received a mixed reaction from A.H. Weiler in *The New York Times* who wrote however that Miller's dancing left nothing to be desired.

She had wanted to do a Barefoot Stomp in the film but the idea was scrapped because it was impossible to record barefoot taps. Nick Castle considered her the best all-round female dancer of the last 20 years, topping Eleanor Powell, Vera Zorina, Adele Astaire, Marilyn Miller and Marie Bryant.

On April 12 there was a double birthday party for the star and Jane Withers. Harry Karl sent a watch and small ring as presents, which Clara allowed her daughter to keep because she liked him too. Linda Darnell had also been at the party and now Miller repaid her by being Darnell's maid of honor for her marriage to Pev Marley on Sunday April 18 in Las Vegas. Darnell and Marley had been to the star's house on Friday April 16 and after leaving, he proposed. Darnell wanted her to leave with them for Vegas on the Saturday, but she was working till 4 p.m. The couple picked her up at the studio and the wedding party then drove to Vegas. After the ceremony they all returned to Los Angeles where Miller and her mother gave a reception at their house.

She was photographed at the Mocambo on June 15 with Linda Darnell, Pev Marley and Phil Roffin.

The star had hoped to be cast in the title role in Columbia's "A" musical comedy *Cover Girl* (1944) but it was given to Rita Hayworth. When the film went into production on July 3 Miller was sent by the studio to another benefit, this time in Boston for the Russian War Relief, where she had a glorious time. On July 15 the star appeared on the radio broadcast "Mail Call."

Her next film was the black and white musical *Hey Rookie* (1944), shot from August 30 to October 2. The screenplay was by Henry Myers, Edward Eliscu and Jay Gorney based on a musical play by E.B. (Zeke) Colvan and Doris Colvan that was originally presented by the "Yardbirds of Fort MacArthur." The director was Charles Barton. The story centered on Pendelton "Pudge" Pfeiffer (Joe Besser) who joins the army and helps with the camp show created by Jimmy Lighter (Larry Parks). Miller is top-billed after the title, though she plays the supporting role of Winnie Clark, Jimmy's former leading lady. The star sings and dances in three numbers: "There Goes Taps/Take a Chance" by Sgt. J.C. Lewis, Jr.; "Streamlined Sheik" and part of "You're Good for My Morale" by Henry Myers, Edward Eliscu and Jay Gorney; and she sings in the finale medley of the reprise of "You're Good for My Morale" and "It's a Swelluva Life in the Army/It's Great to Be in Uniform," also by Lewis. The finale has Miller dressed in an army uniform with her hair in a nape roll, and "Streamlined Sheik" has her emerge from a basket in a daring Arabian outfit of an uncredited designer to belly dance. But the star's best number is "There Goes Taps/Take a Chance" despite the obvious cutting and use of a medium shot by director Barton. She wears a long-sleeved floor-length low-cut dress with a sparkly jacket and light-colored skirt to dance an adagio with Bill Shawn. It is unusual for Miller to have a dance partner and also, as she does in "Streamlined Sheik," to use a non-tap style. The film's dance director is Val Raset.

The film was released on April 6, 1944, with the taglines "THE KHAKI-GO-WACKIEST MUSICAL SHOW OF 'EM ALL!," "HI, LO, JACK AND THE DAME—Singing team of the FRED ALLEN RADIO SHOW!," "JUDY CLARK AND THE SOLID SENDERS—The Hottest Swing!," "JEEPS! Look what's coming," "THE KHAKI-GO-WAACY MUSICAL!," and "Smiles and Miles of Entertainment!" It received a mixed reaction from Clive Hirschhorn in "The Columbia Story."

During filming Miller acted as mascot for the Yardbird Club's football team. A set statistician attached a pedometer to her leg during her dance rehearsals and clocked 48 miles during the 12 days. Ann felt that "Streamlined Sheik," accompanied by the drums of Thurston Knudson, was one of the best numbers she ever did. When the star was in Cairo years later fans begged for her to do it again, which she tried.

Her next film was the black and white musical comedy *Jam Session* (1944), shot from November 29 to December 22, 1943, at the Columbia Hollywood Studios. The screenplay was by Manny Self, based on a story by Harlan Ware and Patterson McNutt, and the director was again Charles Barton. The story centered on Terry Baxter (Miller), a never-say-die Hollywood newcomer from Waterfall, Kansas, determined to make it big at the Superba Studio. She is top-billed after the title, playing the leading role. The star only has one song and dance number, "Vict'ry Polka," with uncredited music by Jule Styne and lyrics by Sammy Cahn, divided into three parts. The first has a notable chorus of female factory women using tools and machines and Miller wears a shimmery black pants suit with white long sleeves and black cap by an uncredited designer. This section is regrettably marred by director Barton's use of obscuring foreground and smoke but there is a transition of a turning wheel over the star.

She returns for the third part in a fluffy knee-length white dress with horizontal back stripes and low-cut black jacket with white puffy sleeves and a striped hair ribbon to dance with Bill Shawn. Miller is also seen dancing to show studio director Berkley Bell (George Eldredge) and Lloyd Marley (Eddie Kane), and with George Carter Haven (Jess Barker) as part of the crowd in a dance club. She is funny showing Terry's enthusiasm, and we see her in a slip, and wearing old lady makeup and a gray wig twice for comic scenes, also speaking as the old lady in one.

The film was released on April 13, 1944, with the taglines "ITS A CARNIVAL OF SWING!," "SHE PUTS THE M-M-M-M IN MUSIC!," "IT'S A JIVE HIT!," "IT'S SOLID MUSIC!," "IT'S A SUPER CELEBRATION WITH THE SWING STARS ... OF THE NATION!," "READ 'EM AND LEAP!," "TEDDY POWELL PUTS THE JOY IN JIVE!," and "Leap for joy as this

Miller and Bill Shawn in the "Vict'ry Polka" number for *Jam Session* (1944).

jive-jammed lyrical session of laffs and love!" It received a mixed reaction from *Variety*, who wrote that Miller did well in the finale dance routine and attempted to inject interest in the trivial plot, and Paul P. Kennedy in *The New York Times*, who said she sparked up the show. However the film was panned by Clive Hirschhorn in *The Columbia Story*.

This was the last film she made with Charles Barton whom the star said was her favorite Columbia director.

She made an uncredited appearance as herself in the Columbia black and white comedy *Sailor's Holiday* (1944), shot from November 29 to December 17. The screenplay was by Manny Self and the director was William Berke. The story centered on two merchant marines, "Marble Head" Tomkins (Arthur Lake) and Jerome "Iron Man" Collins (Lewis Wilson) on leave in Hollywood. Miller appeared in one scene where the sailors tour Apex Pictures (played by the Columbia Studio), and is said to be one of the studio's leading stars. The film was released on February 24, 1944.

Her next was the black and white musical comedy *Carolina Blues* (1944), shot from April 6 to May 27. The working title was "Battleship Blues." The screenplay was by Joseph Hoffman and Al Martin based on a story by M.M. Musselman and Kenneth Earl with additional dialogue by Jack Henley. The director was Leigh Jason. The story centered on band Leader Kay Kyser (playing himself) wanting to take a holiday, but scheduled to give shows in New York. Miller is billed second after the title, playing the supporting role of Julie Carver, the daughter of 68-year-old Phineas Carver (Victor Moore), whose family owns the Carver Corporation defense plant where the band performs. Her hair is mostly worn in a nape rolled updo by an uncredited dresser, and gowns by Jean Louis include one light-colored suit that has a notable black and white striped scarf and matching large gloves.

She performs in three numbers: singing and dancing "Thanks a Lot" with music by Jule Styne and lyrics by Sammy Cahn, and singing "Mr. Beebe" by Jule Styne and Sammy Cahn and Dudley Brooks, and among those who sing "Thinkin' About the Wabash" by Styne and Cahn. A source claims the star dances with Harold Nicholas in the "Mr. Beebe" number but this is incorrect, but regrettably the one number that she does dance in, staged by Sammy Lee, is almost sabotaged by director Jason with extended cutaways. Otherwise Miller is funny in her cartoonish flirting with Kyser, and genuine when she apologizes for trying to deceive him, with Jason redeeming himself somewhat by giving Miller close-ups.

The film was released on December 20 with the taglines "SOME-

THING NEW IN DIXIE FUN!," "RIGHT THIS WAY! For the GAY WAY ... to MUSIC ... MIRTH and M-M-MAIDS!," "6 SWELL NEW SONG HITS!," "MUSICAL MAGIC FROM KAY TO Z!," "THE GAYEST OKAYEST MUSICAL EVER TO COME FROM DIXIE!," "Carolina Blues will chase your Blues away!," "Your head will spin to those Kay Kyser Melodies!," "Your sides will split at those Victor Moore insanities!," and "Your feet will tap to those legnificent Ann Miller dances!" It received a mixed reaction from Bosley Crowther in *The New York Times* who wrote that Miller's role had her virtually brushed off.

She was next in the black and white musical comedy *Eve Knew Her Apples* (1945), shot from July 10 to 22, 1944 with the working title of "Once Upon a Mountain." It had a screenplay by E. Edward Moran based on a story by Moran and Rian James. The film was a remake of the Columbia romantic comedy *It Happened One Night* (1934) and, according to the star, done without Harry Cohn's knowledge since he planned to remake the film for Rita Hayworth. The new director was Will Jason. The story centered on Eve Porter (Miller), a Continental Broadcasting Station radio singing star who wants a vacation during her show's summer hiatus. Miller is billed above the film's title but plays a supporting role to William Wright who plays *Los Angeles Bulletin* reporter Ward Williams. In the film she sings four songs, with the writers all uncredited, but surprisingly never dances. The songs are "I'll Remember April" by the uncredited Don Raye and Gene de Paul, "An Hour Never Passes" by Jimmy Kennedy, "I've Waited a Lifetime" by Eddie Brandt, and "Someone to Love" by Robert Warren. Miller also reprises "I've Waited a Lifetime" and "Someone to Love."

The best showcase for her, however, is "I'll Remember April" since this number is not hampered by cutaways like the others. Here she wears a sparkly light-colored floor-length low-cut long-sleeved gown by an uncredited designer and her hair is worn with a nape roll. The star looks fetching in Ward's black and white vertical striped pajamas, and her longer shoulder-length hair is worn loose. She makes Eve funny, is touching when she believes that Ward has only a financial interest in her, and gives a surprising subtle reaction to being forced to drink a glass of soap and water. Jason shoots the latter scene in close-up, and he gives her a lot of other close-ups in the film.

It was released on April 12, 1945, with the taglines "This Eve played hide and seek with ROMANCE! This Adam tried to throw a wrench into their LOVE AFFAIR!," "Meet the Modern Eve! She carries a compact instead of a club! Uses perfume instead of apples!" and "YOU'LL SEE THE MOST TEMPTING COMEDY OF THE YEAR!" It was praised by *Variety*, who wrote that Miller's comedy playing was neatly presented, but panned by Clive Hirschhorn in *The Columbia Story*. The film was a box office success, which Miller said dissipated Cohn's fury, and remade as the Philippine romantic comedy *Niña bonita* (1955) and the Columbia musical comedy *You Can't Run Away from It* (1956).

While making it, the star received a fan letter from an American GI stating that a large pinup photograph of her had been found on a wall in a captured German staff headquarters, presumably taken by the Germans from a captured American soldier.

CHAPTER 3

. . . .

Louis B. Mayer

$\int$ he first met Louis B. Mayer in mid–1944, introduced by her agents, since Frank Orsatti was one of Mayer's close companions. The M-G-M studio head was still married to Margaret Shenberg but the couple had been separated for years, and would not divorce until 1947. Mayer was suffering from a broken romance with Ginny Simms, whom Miller had a resemblance to, since the singer had turned down his proposal and married someone else. His friends were worried about the man's emotional health, though the Czar of Hollywood was known to be a sentimentalist who cried easily. Miller had heard terrible things about him yet the Orsattis said she was just the person to bring Mayer out of his funk, being gay and happy hearted and loving to dance as much as he.

The Czar was eager to meet the star, knowing her from the Columbia films and especially after being told she was a good girl and a real mother's girl, as he loved mothers. Frank Orsatti gave a dinner party in Bel Air to introduce them and Miller was dazzled by the sight of orchids everywhere, her favorite flower. Mayer adored Clara from the moment he met her, which the star thought added to his attraction to the daughter. Listening to him talk, she found the man brilliant and brainy. Mayer told Miller he enjoyed her dancing on the screen and asked if she would go to dinner and dancing with him one night. The star was sure that Clara would not allow this; his age suggested he would better dating her mother. She asked if Clara could accompany them and Mayer agreed. This would be the arrangement for all of Miller's nights with the Czar, although Clara did not join in the dancing.

Ann found him to be a superb dancer. He was not handsome but virile and strong in line with his star sign of Cancer the Bull. Mayer looked and acted like a man half his age and the star was physically attracted to him. To her he was always a perfect gentleman, always immaculately groomed, and never cursed or told an off-color story. Mayer was mostly kind and compassionate, with a soft heart, loving beauty and goodness, and who respected responsibility. However they did argue when he got jealous of Miller wanting to see other men.

The star was having the time of her life and called him L.B. and never Louie. His brother Jerry often joined them at the Mocambo with the Orsattis and Clara. There were also fabulous Sunday-night dinner parties at Mayer's home, a palatial mansion at 910 Benedict Canyon Drive in Beverly Hills, which had once been the dressing room of Marion Davies on the M-G-M lot built for her by William Randolph Hearst. The parties were attended by the Czar's table of stars and their partners, and after the meal the group would all go to the Mocambo. On other nights they went into the house's projection room to see a film that had yet to be released or screen tests of people being considered by M-G-M. Clara and Ann would stay and talk with him long into the night, hearing calls he received from his lady stars offering their charms for a part in a film. Mayer respected Miller for not operating like those women. One time he wanted to borrow her for a musical being planned at his studio, but nothing came of it. Mayer also went to the Millers for dinner, enjoying how their Texas cook made roast beef and soufflés, and bringing his favorite whisky Rock and Rye. He liked the same music as the star and they would listen as they talked for hours, or just listen to the radio together. Other times they took walks up and down the Beverly Hills streets.

Meanwhile her next film was the Columbia black and white musical comedy *Eadie Was a Lady* (1945) shot from 11 September to 7 October with the working title of "Sadie Was a Lady." It had a screenplay by Monte Brice based on his story and the director was Arthur Dreifuss. The story centered on Edithea "Eadie" Alden (Miller), a Boston Glen Moor College student who leads a double life by working at night as a dancer in New York's Foley's Jollities Burlesk. Miller is top-billed after the title, playing the leading role.

She sings and dances in three numbers: "You Came Along" with music by Saul Chaplin and lyrics by Sammy Cahn, "I'm Gonna See My Baby (On Victory Day)" by Phil Moore, and "Eadie's Back Again" by Chaplin and Cahn and "Eadie Was a Lady" with music by Richard A. Whiting and Nacio Herb Brown and lyrics by Buddy G. DeSylva. We also see her dancing in the burlesque chorus, doing stiff classical moves at the rehearsals for the college's annual play, and at the show's performance entitled "The Greeks Never Mentioned It." "Eadie Was a Lady" has Miller bursting through a poster and doing some Mae West–style sashaying and line readings dressed in a Naughty Nineties gown.

Her best showcase is perhaps "I'm Gonna See My Baby (On Victory

Day)," choreographed by the uncredited Jack Cole, despite director Dreifuss' medium shots, foreground obscuring, and cutaways. The star's feet are seen first and she emerges from behind swing doors wearing a slinky, sequined, black, knee-length, long-sleeved low-cut dress with a split almost to the waist, leg garter, a fur piece, high-heeled shoes, and turban. Cole has her strike some jazz poses before the inevitable tap steps and the effect is enhanced by his stylized chorus in darkness as opposed to her spotlight. Eadie also some funny lines. Defending working in burlesque she says, "I tried every high class producer on Broadway and they all looked at me as if I was a side dish they hadn't ordered." After she is hit in the face with a cake doing a Marie Antoinette sketch in a pompadour blonde wig, Tommy Foley (William Wright) asks if Eadie heard them laughing, and she replies, "How could I help it? They were laughing at me!"

The film was released on January 23, 1945, before *Eve Knew Her Apples*. The new film's taglines were "A MUSICAL PEEK INTO THE PRIVATE LIFE OF A PUBLIC FIGURE ... WHAT A FIGURE!," "IT'S BREEZY ... IT'S TEASY ... IT'S EASY ON THE EYES!," "GLITTERING WITH GAGS ... GALS AND GAIETY!," "YES, INDEEDIE, 'EADIE'S' THE MUSICAL SWEETIE YOU GOTTA SEE!," and "IT'S A BREEZY-TEASY MUSICAL COMEDY!" It was praised by *Variety*, who wrote that Miller did a slick job singing and cleaned up with her deft tapstering as usual.

This was the first of two films with Jack Cole whom she nicknamed Pussycat. He reported that once she asked him about a script, which he found to be bad. After Cole told her so, Harry Cohn called Cole and said not to advise the star about scripts since she had refused to do the film. Cohn agreed that the script was bad but said it shouldn't matter to Miller who was just a dumb broad with large things and he was paying her a lot of money. Cole agreed to tell the star to do the film after all.

In the fall Mayer suffered a painful accident at his Perris Valley farm on a weekend when the Millers were staying with him. A horse that had a reputation for being a brute had thrown him and the Czar was taken to Cedars of Lebanon Hospital in Hollywood. His pelvis was fractured and he developed pneumonia, and the star went to him almost every day, helping in Mayer's recovery. He gave her a topaz ring for Christmas, which Clara allowed her daughter to keep. On December 29 Miller appeared on the radio broadcast "G.I. Journal."

However when the Czar presented a diamond and ruby bracelet watch and then proposed marriage all hell broke loose. Miller was shocked, too dumb to realize his romantic fixation on someone who only considered herself his dancing partner. Clara was against it because of Mayer's age, but Vic Orsatti disagreed, telling her to think

Miller after having been hit in the face with a pie and William Wright in *Eadie Was a Lady* **(1945).**

of the advantages and that it was better to be an old man's darling than a young man's slave. Ann theorized that part of her appeal to the Czar was because she was a virgin and he could be like her father. He called her child or Annie, and the star probably had the maturity of a teenager needing a father figure, since she had lost her own. Miller was sure this was why Clara allowed her to go out with him but marriage was another matter. Mayer pleaded with her but she was adamant, even though he was prepared to wait in the hope that one day there would be a change of heart. Another source claims that Miller's belief that Mayer wanted to marry her was a misinterpretation and an exaggeration of the seriousness of his intentions. His friends said he appreciated her on the dance floor and took a professional interest in the star as a possible replacement for Eleanor Powell who had left M-G-M at this time, but that was it.

The fact was that she wasn't in love with the man, though flattered that he liked her enough to want to marry her. Miller admitted she might have gone ahead and done so, against her mother's wishes, until finding out there was a plot against her. The star was being pushed into the marriage by others for the most appalling reasons. There was the Orsattis, and then Harry Cohn, who had refused to sell her Columbia contract to

Mayer. Cohn called Miller into his office and said she was going to star in a lavish musical called *The Petty Girl*, a property he had bought especially for her, to spite Rita Hayworth. It would be Miller's first "A" film and a big career break. The Petty Girls were all the rage at the time, the long-legged beauties drawn by George Petty featured in *Esquire* magazine. Cohn's decision was based on a means to use her as a bargaining tool with the M-G-M chief, since an "A" star would have a higher asking price, like a thoroughbred racehorse. The Orsattis would also get a sizable percentage, which explained their support of the marriage. When she found out about all this, Miller was furious. She was not going to be a lamb going to the slaughterhouse, and as they said in Texas, the star decided to jump the corral.

Naturally she would have loved to have become an M-G-M contract player, but not this way. Everyone in town knew Miller was dating Mayer and if her Columbia contact had been sold to him, no one would believe that she had any talent. They would assume it was because the star was his paramour, which she denied, though another source claims that they had had a threesome with Katharine Hepburn. Miller wanted to become an "A" star on her own, not with a For Sale sign on her legs or on a producer's casting couch. Maybe that was naïve and a mistake but it was how she felt. Miller didn't tell Mayer of Cohn's bargaining plot because she felt the Czar would have been hurt if he knew, but their relationship had changed.

Naturally he *was* hurt by her rejection of the marriage proposal, and told her to go and see other men, with Mayer thinking she would come back to him. He continued to ask the Millers to the Sunday-night dinners and sometimes they went and sometimes also to the races at Santa Anita or Hollywood Park or to his Perris Valley horse ranch for Sunday lunch. One time they were invited to the ranch to witness the birth of a foal where the star saw Mayer weep for the only time. But she didn't change her mind about marriage. He had the habit of asking his favorite stars and friends to name his horses for him and picked a black-maned filly to match Miller's brunette hair and asked her for the name. She chose Eiffel Tower because the star had a yen to go to Paris and the animal became one of Mayer's best race horses and had many children for him.

She looked for romance elsewhere, finding the multimillionaire Reese Milner through friends at the Mocambo. He was 31 years old, blond, blue-eyed, virile, and handsome and a marvelous dancer and Miller started dating him. Clara approved because Milner always brought her home by midnight. She didn't know that much about him, except that there was an attraction between them which the star thought was love. After three months he proposed, and promised she would never have to work again. Miller was simultaneously seeing Harry Karl who now also proposed.

In late December she was to start in *The Petty Girl*, but instead of being thrilled all the star could focus on was Harry Cohn's manipulation of her. She decided to solve the problem by marrying Milner and leaving her career and went to Cohn's office to tell him. His jaw dropped and Cohn asked her to repeat what she had said. He called this a mistake and regaled her with stories of Milner's escapades with women but the star didn't believe them and left the office. No sooner had she got home than her agent called in hysterics, forbidding her to marry this man, which Miller found crazy. But having an uneasy feeling, she decided to tell Milner that night. He denied Cohn's stories and the star was relieved until the man suddenly became a raving maniac accusing "that fat old Jew" Mayer of spreading lies. She was stunned but then even more stunned when Milner stated that if Miller didn't marry him he didn't want to live. The man apologized for the Mayer slur, being insanely jealous of him for having previously dated her, and reiterated his love. So she accepted Milner's marriage proposal and after telling the elated Clara, the three went out to dinner together to celebrate.

Miller also had to tell Harry Karl, who had given her a silver fox coat and a diamond and ruby bracelet as added incentives to matrimony. But although he was kind and patient and extremely generous, she wasn't in love with him. The star called Karl to tell him to collect the gifts and why, and in two minutes flat his chauffeur was at the front door to pick them up. Karl has also given her a beautiful clip and pair of earrings that he didn't want back, and he later sent a ring to match.

She had to give the news to Mayer before he heard it from someone else. The Czar knew Miller was seeing Milner, and Karl, but didn't think she would marry either. Unable to face Mayer, she telephoned him at home. The star was aware that this was not good timing after his doctors feared, but had not confirmed, he had lung cancer, but she had to tell him. Miller tried to be gentle but after breaking the news, there was a long pause and then she heard sobbing. She begged him to stop but it continued until finally, without having said a word to her, Mayer hung up the phone. Later that evening his chauffeur came to her house, asking the star to accompany him as the Czar had tried to kill himself by taking a whole bottle of sleeping pills. Despite his condition, he had kept calling for her.

When they arrived doctors were pumping his stomach and an ambulance was waiting to take him to hospital. She was in hysterics, blaming herself since Miller was the third woman in a row he had dated and proposed to, who rejected him. However she also knew the man was prone to melodramatic acts and wondered if this was something he had done to win her back. The star did not go to see Mayer in the hospital, fearful of the publicity, but telephoned him. She was still going to marry Milner but asked the Czar to forgive her for hurting him. He said they would always be friends but their relationship could never be the same, and warned that her fiancé was not right for her having heard the same stories as Cohn. Determined to go ahead with the marriage, Miller felt that the reaction of the two moguls was like a curse, and she was due for bad karma after all the evil things the star had done to men in previous incarnations, as when she was the lady Pharaoh.

When Miller had been free she had played all the Army camps and Navy and Air Force bases as part of the effort to support the war. The star and Martha Raye once did 30 shows in one day at the Coral Gables Hotel in Florida which had been turned into an emergency hospital. Miller and Linda Darnell each received citations for their work with the war wounded and they were set to go to Bataan and Corregidor but the tour was cancelled due to bombings.

The year of 1946 saw her in Columbia publicity photo entitled "Greetings to 1946," lying on the ground with her legs up against an armless clock, and her fallen dress showing her legs.

The engagement to Milner was on-again off-again since he revealed himself to be as dynamic and melodramatic as Mayer. She had believed his request for her to abandon the career was an appreciation of the struggle the star had endured all those years, but then learned it was because the man had promised his family to never marry an actress. She broke the engagement over this but then they made an agreement. Miller still had a film left to do on her contract and Milner agreed to let her do so before retiring. She writes in *Miller's High Life* that this decision was made while shooting *The Thrill of Brazil* so that he was allowing her to finish the film. However her dates appear to be wrong, since the marriage occurred before that film had started production though it is possible that the production had been scheduled to start earlier but postponed.

The New York Times adds to the date confusion by reporting that the star had announced her wedding for January 20 but it was postponed until her next film had been completed. The film was not to be *The Petty Girl* which Columbia would finally make in 1949 starring Joan Caulfield and release in 1950. Harry Cohn was still against the marriage. He even brought in three women who had dated Milner to tell how he had beaten them up, but seeing this did not change the star's mind, he agreed to give her two weeks off for a honeymoon in Mexico.

She finally got her marriage license on Valentine's Day February 14 and was married two days later at the All-Saints-by-the-Sea Church in Montecito, California. The *Times* reported that the couple planned to set up housekeeping in Beverly Hills. Linda Darnell, Betty Bloomingdale and Marjorie Reynolds were her bridesmaids, and it was Reynolds who had tried to explain the facts of life to Miller when she learned that Clara had not. This information seemed to be useful as within a few weeks she was pregnant. However the marvelous news became soured when the star began to realize there was something wrong with her husband. She was ignorant of his wealth until after they had married. Milner had told her the family was in the scrap-iron business but Miller didn't know what that meant, and she was not even sure he had money enough for them to live on. The man had said he was barely making ends meet while Columbia was paying $100,000 a year, so the star figured they could use her savings to support his meager income.

It was after the wedding ceremony when Milner revealed he was Reese Llewellyn Milner, whose family had made all the Llewellyn elevators. He was from a blueblood Social Register family, rich scion of the Llewellyn Iron Works company and heir to the family fortune. The man had not told her of his wealth, fearful that she would want to marry him for his money which saw him worth at least $7 million. So while Miller was sorry to give up her career, she was also exhilarated that her husband could take care of her mother and herself from now on.

He owned the Rancho La Vista near Ojai, California, but their home was on Delfern Drive in Holmby Hills, a $250,000 mansion. They had hand-carved furnishings and a dinner table that could seat 24, chandeliers and marble floors, four gardeners, a chauffeur, an upstairs maid, cook and butler, and a nursery to decorate for their coming baby. But after two weeks of marriage Miller saw the temper she had been warned about. Milner was like Jekyll and Hyde, with a change of personality occurring when he drank as it reacted against the steel plate he had in his head. The star was horrified and felt trapped. She hadn't told Clara about the pregnancy and now Miller was afraid her life was in in danger. She hoped that the baby would make a difference and help her husband get control of himself.

The black and white musical *The Thrill of Brazil* aka *Dancing Down to Rio* (1946) was shot from April 20 to June 25 with the working titles of "Rendezvous in Rio," and "Rio." In terms of running time this was an "A" film but Miller plays a supporting role. It was a remake of the Columbia romantic comedy *His Girl Friday* (1940) with a screenplay by Allen Rivkin, Harry Clork, and Devery Freeman; the director was S. Sylvan Simon. The new story was centered on Steve Farraugh (Keenan Wynn) a revue producer in Rio de Janeiro who is still in love with his ex-wife Vicki Dean (Evelyn Keyes) but his star Linda Lorens (Miller) is in love with him. Miller is billed third after the title and sings and dances in three numbers by Doris Fisher and Allan Roberts: the Samba tap routine "The Custom House," "Man Is Brother to a Mule," and part of the finale of the Brazilian macumba or voodoo to the title song.

Although both of the first two numbers have medium shots, foreground obscuring and cutaways, the better showcase is perhaps "Man Is Brother to a Mule," where she wears a Jean Louis outfit of white knee-length ruffled skirt and top with a bare midriff, black necklace and arm band and bracelets, and a white flower in her hair. She enters from behind window shutters and ends by going behind a beaded curtain and back behind the shutters. The dances were staged by Eugene Loring and Nick Castle, though an uncredited Jack Cole did "Thrill of Brazil." Miller's hair is styled by Helen Hunt in a new way for her—with period bangs. Miller makes the Linda character initially funny even if her later jealousy of Vicki and bitterness towards Steve reads as nasty.

The film was released in September 6 or 30 with the taglines "Looking for a new THRILL?," "SOUTH AMERICAN FIESTA OF MUSIC AND LAUGHTER!," and "Romantic Rio on a heart-to-heart hook-up with music ... laughter ... love ... is for you!" It was praised by *Variety*, who wrote that Miller's singing and dancing were tops and that she gave an impressive account of herself as star of the revue, but received a mixed reaction from Bosley Crowther in *The New York Times*, and Clive Hirschhorn in *The Columbia Story*.

Jack Cole had hired Nick Castle to supervise her tap dances for the film. She was said to have been terrified of the temperamental Cole who supposedly left the studio for three days after being disgusted with one dancer and came back with his head shaved. She knocked herself out to prevent any similar outbursts, though another source claims that her self-confidence matched that of Cole.

Being pregnant, the star said she found the finale where she had to climb up high on a platform to dance difficult, though Miller's memory may be faulty since we do not see Linda climb to get to the platform. Perhaps she confused the finale with "Man Is Brother to a Mule" where the star moves up and down a ramp in high heels. This action would not have ordinarily bothered her but now she was frightened of getting dizzy and falling. The number had to be reshot many times, even after 6 p.m. when Miller normally left to go home. After getting it right she was about to leave when her husband burst onto the set, grabbing the star by the arm. Dragging her to his car, he shouted all the way home that those Hollywood people were breaking up their marriage. Milner now

Portrait of Miller in the "Man Is Brother to a Mule" number in *The Thrill of Brazil* aka *Dancing Down to Rio* (1946).

forbid his wife to go back to the studio, though she had only two more scenes to do. At home he beat her, the first time this had been done to Miller by anyone. She tried to escape into the bathroom beyond their bedroom but Milner caught her and knocked the star to the floor. It was two weeks before she was able to report to work because her nose was swollen, an eye was cut, and Miller was all black and blue. When she did return to Columbia, the star had to be covered with extra thick makeup to hide all the welts and bruises, and she vomited between takes. Harry Cohn's attitude surprised her. He wasn't angry that Miller had held up production, didn't want to cut her out of the film, and didn't say "I told you." However Cohn did sue Milner for $150,000 for making his wife break her contract and demanded she return to Columbia when the marriage broke up, which he was certain it would.

After completing the film the star was interviewed by Hedda Hopper for the 1947 Look Awards Broadcast.

In July she became involved in the love affair of Linda Darnell and playboy millionaire Howard Hughes, whom Darnell had been dating after a separation from Pev Marley. One source claims Miller had encouraged this new relationship though another says she did not because of the man's reputation for seeing many women simultaneously, using and dumping them. At the time she knew Hughes was also involved with Lana Turner, Gene Tierney and Paulette Goddard who all wanted to marry him. But he refused to marry anyone, including Darnell, and wanted her friend to be the one to tell her.

Hughes contacted Miller by telephone at 2 a.m. and she agreed he could come for her at 9 p.m. and take the star to dinner. She got all dressed up but he did not arrive until 11.45 p.m., wearing his work attire—a dirty old coat with grease spots and patches on the elbow, a beat-up shirt, wrinkled trousers, and old tennis shoes. Miller had expected a millionaire to dress well and she refused to go out with him in that condition. He retrieved another shirt, trousers and tie from his Chevrolet and changed in her powder room. However Hughes still wore the awful coat and the tennis shoes, which he refused to change, though the star later claimed the man wore new shoes as well.

The couple climbed aboard his beat-up and battered car and drove to Perino's, considered one of the most elegant restaurants in town. Leaving Miller at their table, Hughes went to the restaurant's kitchen and re-emerged with a huge bowl of salad that he had made himself, since the man never let anyone touch food he ate. He asked the waiter to bring a toaster and a loaf of bread and when these arrived, Hughes made his own toast. After their meal, he told the star that it was Pev Marley's demand for money before he would agree to let his wife go that put the playboy off her, and he planned to marry Lana Turner instead. Miller agreed to tell Darnell but halfway back their car ran out of gas so she had to wait again while Hughes got a can from the filling station four blocks back.

It was now 2 a.m. But, after filling the tank, the car would not start.

It was Ann who had to push it along the road and then jump in real fast when it got going. They drove back to the filling station to return the gas can, and then on to her home where they made love after which he told Miller she was too flashy for his taste. Naturally this did not go over well, but neither did the news Miller had to convey to Darnell, who apparently became so hysterical that Ann had to stay with her for 10 days fearing her friend might commit suicide. She thought Darnell was more in love with the idea of being Mrs. Howard Hughes than with the actual man, since his peculiarities made him unlovable. Her friend got over it and Miller tried to keep in touch with Hughes but he did not return her phone calls.

She now realized her marriage was a mistake. Milner was hard to live with and rude to her friends, never wanting to let her invite any of them to their dinner parties, which were populated with only *his* friends. He didn't trust his wife, calling at a restaurant where she would go to lunch with a girlfriend or showing up uninvited to see if Miller was really seeing a man. Milner accused her of affairs with Louis B. Mayer and Harry Cohn, and the fighting escalated. She stayed with him only because he was the father of their child, and the star didn't think it was right to have a fatherless child. By October she was nine months pregnant and Milner did allow her a baby shower with Linda Darnell and Marjorie Reynolds among the guests.

But November saw more trouble. The couple spent a few days at his ranch and there was a row which resulted in the star falling down a flight of stairs. Sources differ as to whether she slipped or her husband was drunk and he knocked her down, but either way Miller landed on her back and was screaming in pain. She was put into the back seat of their station wagon and rushed to Good Samaritan Hospital in Los Angeles. The star was sure her back was broken, and then labor pains started. The baby was born with a club foot, ironic for the child of a dancer, but it died three hours later. When she was informed, Miller became so hysterical that she had to be sedated.

The star lapsed into a semi-comatose state, only remembering seeing nurses and doctors but not Milner or her mother. When her husband appeared he went through the same let's-forgive-and-forget routine, and Miller said she loved him, but the loss of the baby made her know it was over. She refused to live with him again; she just wanted to be free and to have a chance to regain her health. Her back was not broken but it had been badly injured, with her doctors saying Miller would never dance again and could have no more babies. From her hospital bed she filed for divorce and never went back to the mansion in Holmby Hills.

The star recuperated at Clara's house, where an osteopath was consulted who had worked with race horses. He suggested natural fusion, and had her sleep harnessed in a hospital traction bed, loaded down with weights of all shapes and sizes, to keep the pinched nerves of the spine apart. This practice would continue for a year and ultimately saved Miller from a back operation. She was determined to dance again and did everything possible to speed up her recovery, sometimes lying all day immobile in the traction bed. Clara was a marvelous nurse, attending to every comfort, pampering the star like a baby, and doing everything possible to keep her spirits up. Christmas was a particularly difficult time because Miller couldn't help but think she was meant to have had a new baby then. Clara gave her a baby doll, since the star loved dolls, but it had the opposite effect and again she had to be sedated.

But Miller was making progress which amazed her doctors. She could walk, though she needed to wear an uncomfortable steel brace, and Willy de Monde presented her with the annual "Golden Calf Award" for the most beautiful legs in the world. Not surprisingly Milner was not in touch, but Harry Cohn sent his attorney, Jerry Geisler. He helped with a suit for $375,000 damages in a civil fraud case against her husband for tricking the star into signing away interest in the Holmby Hills mansion. However Geisler later talked her into dropping the suit, and she suspected this was because Milner had paid him off. Miller testified in court at the divorce hearing that he had committed acts of violence toward her and she feared further harm from him. The star was not required to be too specific and avoided mentioning the fight and her fall down the stairs, but strangely the newspapers said the baby's death was due to a car accident where Milner was driving. She let it go at that because he was known as a reckless driver and had been in quite a few accidents.

The property battle was settled out of court with Miller asking and getting compensation for her medical bills and $20,000 tax free as lost income. She felt this was a minimal request but Milner still told everyone he could that his wife was a gold digger and had taken him for a million dollars. The interlocutory divorce decree was granted on January 22, 1947, less than a year after the star had married.

In early 1947 the star attended the sale of Louis B. Mayer's racing stable, one of the saddest experiences of her life because his horses were like movie stars to him. In the week ending April 12 she was photographed with Philip Reed having dinner at the Chanticlair restaurant. Miller was still in and out of the traction bed and steel brace when she heard in the mid-year about an opportunity at M-G-M replacing Cyd Charisse. The star had known her as a child in Texas as Tula Finklea and had taken dancing lessons from Nico Charisse whom Cyd later married. On the set of the M-G-M musical comedy *On an Island with You* (1948)), which had been in production from June 1, Charisse had fallen and torn a tendon in her leg, having to wear a cast for two months. This meant she was out of what was to be her next film, the musical romance *Easter Parade* (1948) to star Fred Astaire.

Producer Arthur Freed was testing replacements and Miller was ready to try for it. She had not danced a step in months and prayed to God for help. Her Columbia contract had by now lapsed but Harry Cohn still wanted her back. Also Rita Hayworth had stopped making musicals and would soon leave the studio altogether for a marriage to Prince Aly Khan in 1949 for what she thought would be the rest of her life. But Miller had other ideas. M-G-M had lost Eleanor Powell to marriage and retirement and while the studio had Charisse, Vera Ellen and Lucille Bremer under contract as dancers, there was no whirlwind tap dancer. The new opportunity was especially exiting, as to be in a film that starred Fred Astaire was every dancer's dream.

She swallowed her pride and telephoned Mayer. This was not to ask him to get her the role, because the star didn't want it that way. She felt insecure because of the tumultuous recent months, being incapacitated and out of circulation for so long. Vic Orsatti could have gotten her the test without Mayer's help, but Miller wanted the studio head's personal reassurance. He was polite and solicitous, but she could detect a faint aloofness in his voice. The man had warned that he would never feel the same way about her again which was now apparent. The star asked about the test and Mayer said he could arrange it with Freed, but if she didn't do well, the man couldn't help any further. Miller said numerous other dancers tested but she was considered the best choice. A myth arose that it was her prior relationship with Mayer that secured her the part but the star said the opposite was true, since the studio head was so hurt and ego-damaged by her rejection of his marriage proposal. The decision to cast her was made by Freed and Astaire.

She had known Fred Astaire at RKO because of her friendship with Hermes Pan, who also worked on the Astaire/Rogers films. Pan was a fabulous chef and held dinners with Astaire and Rogers and Miller as guests. But Miller had never worked with Astaire, though she reported he would watch her do tap numbers at RKO. He screened her ballroom number from *Hey Rookie* since she was mainly known for tap and thought the star would be fine. The only problem was height since she was taller than he. This was solved by her agreeing to wear ballet shoes in the dancing scenes with him; even in the rushes everyone had to watch closely to see that her feet didn't show in the flats. Miller also had to wear her hair flatter than usual.

Louella Parsons wrote in her July 26 column that Mayer had personally signed the star to a contract and wrote on August 13 she would be in *Easter Parade,* to be followed by *Belle of New York.* In the week ending September 25 Miller was photographed with the Maharaja of Cooch Behar at the Mocambo. On October 2 she was photographed with Cesar Romero at the Ice Follies of 1947 in Hollywood. The star learned that Rita Hayworth had started her own production company at Columbia called the Beckworth Corporation and it was to produce the music adventure film *The Loves of Carmen* (1948). Miller said that Hayworth was a very smart woman who had an inner strength, stood up for herself, and always did what was right for her when it came to her rights.

The powers that be at M-G-M decided that the star needed a nose job to make her more photogenic but unfortunately the surgeon she was ushered off to did a botchy job. He left Miller's nose slightly crooked with an indentation on the tip that required her to wear a prosthesis that was studio property and kept in their safe.

CHAPTER 4

. . . .

Easter Parade

Easter Parade was titled onscreen as *Irving Berlin's Easter Parade* and shot in Technicolor from November 19 to mid–February 1948 with retakes on March 12 at the M-G-M Hollywood studios. The screenplay was by Sidney Sheldon, Frances Goodrich and Charles Hackett, based on an original story by Goodrich and Hackett, with uncredited work by Guy Bolton. Songs were by Irving Berlin, and the director was Charles Walters. The story is set between the Easter Sundays of 1911 and 1912 and centered on nightclub entertainer Don Hewes (Astaire), who hires Hannah Brown (Judy Garland), a naive chorus girl, to become his new ballroom dancing partner.

Miller is billed after the title and plays the supporting role of Nadine Hale, Don's former partner. She sings one song, "Shakin' the Blues Away" where the star also dances, gets a dance duet with Astaire on "It Only Happens When I Dance with You," which is reprised, and dances as part of "The Girl on the Magazine Cover." The latter number is noteworthy for the gorgeous Irene floor-length low-cut white dress with a red ostrich feather skirt that she wears with matching large red ostrich feathered fan. However Miller's best effort is perhaps "Shakin' the Blues Away." Wearing a yellow floor-length dress with black bodice and yellow long gloves, and her hair loose, she pulls the skirt to the side to expose her legs to dance on a theater stage in front of flowing gray curtains.

The film's musical numbers were staged and directed by Robert Alton, though the star said he was assisted by the uncredited Nick Castle and Hermes Pan. While Alton uses some medium shots, he doesn't have cutaways and foreground obscuring as in the other numbers. The Technicolor shows some odd choices: Jack Dawn's makeup seems to overdo the rouge on her and the shorter shoulder-length hair by Sydney Guilaroff is two-toned with the front worn off her forehead brown but the back black. She makes Nadine's narcissism and manipulative nature funny and looks glamourous in a green suit with a spit skirt worn with a fur jacket and muff and a green wide-brimmed hat.

The film was released on June 30, 1948, with the taglines "The Happiest Musical Ever Made is Irving Berlin's Easter Parade" and "Full of melody! Full of young love!" Miller attended the New York premiere. It was praised by *Variety* who wrote that she made an especially bright contribution and shined in "Shakin' the Blues Away," by Thomas M. Pryor in *The New York Times* who said the star did an especially graceful ballroom dance with Astaire and somehow paired better with him than Garland, and by John Douglas Eames in *The MGM Story* who said she displayed a vivid dancing personality. It received a mixed reaction from Pauline Kael in *5001 Nights at the Movies*. The film was a box office success and won the Academy Award for Best Music Scoring of a Musical Picture.

Miller reported that in the rehearsal room preparing the production numbers she was scared stiff to be dancing with the master but Astaire was as charming off the screen as he was on and put her at ease right away. The star found the man to be a blithe spirit, always in a good mood and only ill-tempered at himself. He was a perfectionist but so was Ann, which is why they got along so well. After exhausting hours of rehearsal when they all thought it was just right, Astaire would say, "C'mon Annie. Let's do it one more time." He had such a way with women that it was as though Miller had always danced with him. The man tried to do the steps that made her look good which was very unusual in a male dancer, and which she appreciated. He also acknowledged the hard work that was tap-dancing, saying it was next to ditch-digging.

The hard work was added to by the fact that Miller was in excruciating pain with her back. She couldn't dance in a steel brace so had to be taped up each day, from just under her bust to a little below the navel, and each evening went through holy hell pulling that tape off. By the end of the shoot her skin was almost raw. The star also had to take Darvon pain pills and she hated taking pills of any kind. Each night her mother strapped her back into the harness and the traction bed, but it was all worth it to be in a film with Astaire and her old friend Frances Gumm now known as Judy Garland.

Miller said that "Shakin' the Blues Away" was one of the best tap numbers she ever did, all the more remarkable because of the courage it took for her to do it in the physical condition she was in. She was thrilled to work with Robert Alton whom she considered a great choreographer. Arthur Freed was M-G-M's pet and very avant-garde and the star also liked Charles Walters, saying he was one of the cutest people she had met on the lot. Miller and Garland gave him a hard time,

Miller performing the "Shakin' the Blues Away" number in Irving Berlin's *Easter Parade* **(1948).**

carrying on and laughing, but Walters said that he found the star to be a kookie darling.

Fred Astaire wrote in his memoir *Steps in Time*, that she was a terrific performer, and in later years the pair would have dinner with Hermes Pan every now and again. Miller said Astaire and Garland got along

just great because they were both great pros and fantastic entertain-
ers so it was a happy union because they liked to work and work hard.
The star became friends with Astaire's daughter Ava Astaire McKenzie
and her husband Richard who had many anecdotes about the woman
they described as "inadvertent." At a Chinese restaurant sitting next to a
table of obvious hookers and some gentlemen, Miller said of the hookers "Those girls could hear a dollar bill hit the floor." At the end of a party
one night when standing on the curb waiting for their cars Miller asked
if they wanted to go out "honky-tonkin." And visiting the McKenzies
once in Pennsylvania when on tour in *Sugar Babies* Miller apologized
for looking like Mush Mush of the North, dressed demurely in a fur coat
and her hair pulled back in a ponytail held by a barrette.

Garland could be late on the set, but if so, came in with a marvelous joke and got everybody laughing, though producer Freed was not
pleased. She knew what to do, not needing to have to go over and over
it again, but getting her on the stage in her body makeup and her costume with her hair done took time and being late went against her. If a
star delayed production that made the budget go up though Garland was
worth it and the studio was wise enough to know that for the time being.
If she was on time, preparation would be done with the other M-G-M
ladies and her great sense of humor meant that they would walk out on
the set giggling and laughing. The star felt that Garland went down in
history as one of the greatest performers there had ever been, and was
so down to earth that she didn't know what the phrase Queen of the Lot
meant.

Garland was sophisticated way beyond her years, an old lady men-
tally at a very young age, and a great clown. Her loving to laugh made
Miller think it was compensation for not having enough laughter in
her life. But while admitting she was a fantastic genius the star also
saw there was a waste of talent, since her inner torments and frequent
absences made her an increasingly hazardous risk to any production.
Another problem arose if Garland brought her baby daughter Liza with
her to work, as this caused a distraction to cast and crew. Miller now saw
firsthand Garland's drug addiction and felt she was mixed up in a clique
of strange people that certainly didn't help her very much.

There was an intricate spider web of yes people and people who
were supposed to be Garland's friends but really weren't because they
worked to destroy her. One was a "Dr. Feelgood" on the lot who was
always there to give Garland a pill when she wanted one, anything to get
her out on that set and working. Miller said this was a business decision
but she felt like she could have taken a pot and hit him in the head. Her
friend was a victim so she didn't blame her but Miller imagined the long

working hours and the small amount of private time must have been a living hell for someone on drugs. There was a time when Garland had Vincente Minnelli to help her as her husband, who was one of the most charming men you could possibly meet, and greatly talented. They had a lot in common, both being in show business and having mutual friends, and they could talk about scripts when they went home at night. But when the couple separated she didn't have anybody to really cling to or guide her, and Miller thought Garland was a person who had to be guided. By the time of her end at the studio, she became almost paralyzed, not being able to get on stage on time or remember lines, and having fights with people around her.

Irving Berlin, whose songs were used in the film, was an initial stumbling block over Miller's casting, but became so pleased with her work that he toyed with the idea of writing a Broadway show especially for the star.

She next made a contribution to the Technicolor musical comedy western *The Kissing Bandit* (1948), after a preview screening where the studio thought the film was a dud and needed salvaging. Miller claimed to have been at the preview and said the film was the worst ever made. New scenes were shot in mid–March after the film had been in production from mid-May to early August 1947. The screenplay was by Isobel Lennart and Briard Harding, and the director was Laslo Benedek. The story was set in 1830 California and centered on Ricardo (Frank Sinatra), the milquetoast son of a Mexican bandit who is forced by his family to follow in his father's footsteps and become "The Kissing Bandit." Miller is billed ninth below the title, and played the supporting role of an unnamed specialty dancer in the Fiesta. She appears in one dialogue scene having two lines. Her one musical number, created by Robert Alton, is known as the "Dance of Fury" with music by Nacio Herb Brown.

Miller's Jack Dawn makeup has a less jarring rouge here and she presumably wears what is a long shoulder-length brown wig by Sydney Guilaroff. Her Walter Plunkett ankle-length red and yellow dress has gold short sleeves, a full skirt with a green undelay, yellow bandana and gold hairpiece, and red shoes. She emerges from the behind the black cape of Ricardo Montalban and fights with the now recovered Cyd Charisse in the dance for his attention, sometimes using a black fan. One's eye goes more to her than Charisse, and Alton makes uses of their swirling skirts, though occasionally uses medium shots.

The film was released on November 18 with the taglines "HILARIOUS! EXCITING! ROMANTIC!," "MGM's big, bold, different Technicolor musical!," "THE SINGING STARS OF 'ANCHORS AWAY' TOGETHER

Cyd Charisse, Ricardo Montalban and Miller performing the "Dance of Fury" in *The Kissing Bandit* **(1948).**

AGAIN!," "The hilarious misadventures of a timid outlaw and the gorgeous gal whose kisses almost kill him!," "Ricardo Montalban and Cyd Charisse in the fiery 'Dance of Fury,'" "Ann Miller will thrill you!," "Sono Osato is the screen's new sensation!" and "The Boldest Spectacle Ever Told in Song, Spectacle and Technicolor!" It received a mixed reaction from *Variety*, Bosley Crowther in *The New York Times*, and John Douglas Eames in *The MGM Story*. The film was still a notorious box office failure.

In his book *The Frank Sinatra Film Guide*, Daniel O'Brien reports that Laslo Benedek was replaced by George Sidney early in the shoot, and for the "Dance of Fury." Even after M-G-M had done the re-shoots, the studio still delayed the film's release.

This was Miller's first film with producer Joe Pasternak, one of the three musical comedy producers at M-G-M. She said that he was very European, loved the singers, and was great in his own way but didn't have the cabinet of talent that Arthur Freed had around him. She had never done anything like the "Dance of Fury" before and thought it was the best thing about the film. In the past the star had created her own tap steps but since the "Spanish dancing" to be used was not her forte, she was happy to follow the moves that Robert Alton devised. When Montalban had to lift and swing her and Charisse it was like lifting two bags of potatoes because of the heavy costumes. Doing so injured his leg, though he was too proud to complain at the time, and it was never the same again.

On June 30 Miller was one of the guest stars from New York on *The Tex and Jinx Show* NBC radio show. The program was a salute to Irving Berlin and the New York premiere of *Easter Parade* that night.

She loved working at M-G-M., sometimes having to pinch herself to see that it was all true. When you got to there it was like the Ziegfeld Follies—you had arrived at the top. The other studios like 20th Century–Fox tried but they were never comparable. The studio catered to all needs, with Miller kept in expensive custom-made and extra-long Willy de Monde silk dancing stockings. All the stars were pampered like French poodles. Each had a beautifully decorated dressing room, personal makeup man, personal body makeup lady, personal hairdresser, and personal wardrobe woman at their disposal. You were almost carried around on a satin pillow with a bowl of cream.

Miller arrived at the studio at 6 a.m. and gave different accounts of the M-G-M process for her. One was that she went into an individual cubicle with her own makeup person before being sent to the big open room with a long table for hairdressing, though as a brunette the star's hair needed less attention than the blondes. Twenty dressers often dealt with 20 stars simultaneously, all being supervised by Sydney Guilaroff, who gave personal attention only to Elizabeth Taylor and Lana Turner. Miller's second recollection had her treated at her dressing room on the set, where body makeup, costume, hair and face makeup were done by different people before she was ready to go to work.

If she was in the hairdressing open room Miller reportedly talked a mile a minute, chatting and gossiping about the seamy side of Hollywood hushed up by the publicity men who were also paid to keep some stars out of the papers. The studio had its own lesbian scandal when two of the biggest ladies were caught in bed together in Palm Springs, but another was caught three sheets to wind in an elegant Madrid hotel piddling in the front lobby. But while Hollywood had its vices and its dens of iniquity, she felt it also had class, a quality, and an elegant sheen that would soon become nonexistent.

M-G-M treated her like a piece of merchandise. Louis B. Mayer only wanted the best and he told the press department that Miller was to be given star treatment. She was seen by the staff photographer once a month for all-day sessions, posing for 100 magazine covers with clothing changes supplied by the wardrobe department, some with a seasonal theme like a scanty Santa Claus for Christmas. There were also location layouts at home, on bicycles, and romping in the surf. The star loved going to these sessions as she otherwise dressed in ballet tights and old sweaters and slacks for rehearsal. If Miller had to attend a premiere, the publicity department would provide a new dress and hat and fur from wardrobe and a limo and escort if necessary. He would be a young handsome contract player, always a gentleman and usually gay. The star felt like Cinderella, and while it was fun, the studio kept careful tabs on her so it all looked good in print.

She ate lunch in the same commissary as Clark Gable and Spencer Tracy and saw Greta Garbo there once, when Garbo went to visit George Cukor. Strangely Miller rarely saw Mayer on the lot, only in the commissary where he nodded at her. She learned of the M-G-M diet also known as the noontime footraces and the backlot scramble to lunch which the star needed track shoes to get through in time. It took 15 minutes to get out of her costume, into her own clothes, and 10 to sprint to the commissary which was half a mile from the soundstages. Once there, there was no class division—you lined up with the electricians, carpenters, and Cowboys—to order your food. When it arrived you had another 10 minutes to eat and then race back to the set with a soggy ham on rye minus the pickle. Your body makeup had to be reapplied, your costume put back on, your face makeup retouched and your hair re-combed, so by the time you were back on the set you were worn out. Most people never knew how hard they worked or how much they all loved it.

The star also took ballet classes with Janet Bennett, along with Cyd Charisse, Vera-Ellen, Leslie Caron, Debbie Reynolds, and Zsa Zsa Gabor. Reynolds said Miller was unique because she could kick her leg right up to her ear, which no one else was able to. Sometimes the star would socialize with her co-stars or other M-G-M friends after the day's work. They might go out for dinner or just stay in the dressing rooms and have champagne, laughing and scratching and telling funny stories until the guard told them to leave because the studio was closing.

On September 4 she was photographed with Greer Garson riding elephants at a circus for charity in Los Angeles. On September 20 Miller was a guest at the wedding of her childhood friend Jane Withers to William "Bill" Moss, an oil man from Texas. The star found him charming and noticed how much he looked like Reese Milner.

Mayer's wife finally divorced him and he remarried in December to Lorena Danker. Miller often saw the couple around at parties and out dancing at the Mocambo or Ciro's and found Danker to be very warm and friendly. Now in her personal golden years, Ann was looking for a real Prince Charming after the disaster of her marriage. As M-G-M's new dancing queen her name was up in lights all over the place and she was in constant demand for public appearances and social functions.

Miller went everywhere she was asked, meeting shahs and maharajas and Spanish bullfighters and international playboys. Serious beaus were Ernie Byfield, Jr., Jack Seabrook, Gilbert Swanson, Jim Kimberely, Randolph Churchill, and Charles Isaacs. But her greatest beau was William "Bill" V. O'Connor (spelled O'Conner by Miller in *Tapping Into the Force*), a man the star had fallen madly in love with but who was not free to marry. She met him through her good friend Margaret Pereira, wife of the famous architect, William "Bill" Pereira. O'Connor was an attorney, who eventually became Chief Deputy State Attorney General of California and Governor Edmund "Pat" Brown's right arm. His prominence in politics was why the relationship had to be discreet, and they did manage to stay out of the gossip columns for a while, but being a Catholic meant there was little chance his wife Adele would ever divorce him. Nevertheless Miller continued to hope for nearly 12 years.

O'Connor was her "Big Rabbit" because he was politicking like a rabbit, always hopping around a room and shaking someone's hand. She felt they had a psychic rapport from the very beginning, with the star falling in love with his photograph in the *Los Angeles Times* before meeting him. Without telling Margaret Pereira about the photograph, she called and asked her to visit her to work the Ouija board. Miller and Clara often used it together and were amazed at how fast the planchette on the board went through the alphabet to spell out words like a typewriter. Biblical messages and philosophies came through, like "Take the up elevator and not the down elevator," which became her life credo. But mother and daughter soon learned that what seemed like fun could be something to be reckoned with.

The star realized she was a wide-open channel for both positive and negative forces and strange things began to happen in the house. One night she felt fingers touching her face, then later heard loud raps and noises in her room for weeks. Miller became unable to sleep and after praying, they had a minister of the Spiritualist Church come to exorcise and bless the house. He said to stop using the board since she didn't know how to protect herself from the earthbound spirits. The star took his advice and would only observe others using it at parties where there were psychics or sensitives present, warning about the use of the spirit world as entertainment.

Margaret Pereira worked the board at her house, where one time Edgar Bergen was in attendance. When he laughed, the planchette went into a fast spin, flew off and landed in his lap. When the man asked the board a serious question he turned white at the answer and stopped laughing. At the home of the hostess Dolly Green, it said she would never marry her long time beau because he would die, which became true. When a psychologist friend asked if the LSD he had been experimenting with on patients like Cary Grant was harmful, he was told it was, so the man stopped using it. Later it was proven that LSD was a dangerous drug.

The board had said Miller would meet a tall, dark and handsome man that was an attorney in a private home. She showed O'Connor's photograph to her friend, hoping this was the man and Pereira laughed since she knew him well. O'Connor and Adele were legally separated and Pereira said she would have a dinner party and invited him and Ann. On the night she was all a-flutter with anticipation so it was a let-down when O'Connor arrived with his wife. Miller learned the couple had on-again off-again periods, sometimes sharing their Bel Air home and sometimes his taking the apartment in Beverly Hills. The next time the Pereiras gave a dinner party and invited her, O'Connor came alone. They were seated together and it was Kismet.

In spite of their religion, the O'Connors had agreed on a divorce that was not yet final, but as a devout Catholic he could not remarry unless Adele died or signed the papers permitting it. Doing otherwise would risk excommunication from the Church. And there was his political aspiration to consider, which any scandal might hamper. O'Connor did not promise to marry Ann but she kept up hope, even taking catechism classes studying to be a Catholic as an added persuasion. Miller knew he loved her and that he gave her true happiness. Agreeing not to appear in public together they went to the same parties but she would be with someone else like Freddie de Cordova, Gilbert Kahn, Greg Bautzer, the Maharajah of Cooch Behar, or Ernie Byfield, Jr. The columnists were always marrying her off, with the four most mentioned bridegrooms-to-be being Byfield, Conrad Hilton, Eddie Lasker, and Bob Rhodenberg.

It was good copy even when the star denied the rumors, but the real story broke in 1949 so O'Connor could now escort Miller to many of the important social-political-film industry functions. Clara told her daughter that it was wrong to be so devoted to him because the man would never marry her, and insisted she have other beaus. The star did see other men, but what was disturbing was that O'Connor saw other women, such as Joan Crawford and Rhonda Fleming. This broke Miller's heart but she knew better than to try to hold too tight a rein on him.

On February 12, 1949, the star was photographed with Elizabeth Taylor at a dinner party in Hollywood. Seated next to each other, Miller turned her head so that Taylor could get a better view of her new diamond earrings, though the star wouldn't say whether they were from an admirer. In February all the 58 M-G-M stars under contract were gathered together on the biggest soundstage with executives and exhibitors for a gigantic luncheon for the studio's 25th anniversary silver jubilee. Black and white film was taken of the stars, as was a group photograph known as a "family" picture. Both the film and official photographs were arranged alphabetically, and the film saw the group eating lunch. The surviving footage is incomplete and shows Miller entering the sound stage behind Agnes Moorehead but not being introduced by the MC, George Murphy. She wears a dark fur coat over a light-colored patterned knee-length dress with fur-lined sleeves and a hat with a large flower on top. When the stars are shown seated we see her in between Moorehead and Jules Munshin, chatting with him.

Miller's next film was the Technicolor musical comedy *On the Town* (1949), which went into rehearsals from February 29 and filmed from March 28 to mid–July on locations in New York and at the M-G-M Hollywood Studios. The screenplay was by Adolph Green and Betty Comden, based upon the musical play whose book was by Green and Comden from an idea by Jerome Robbins. The Broadway show had run from December 28, 1944, to February 2, 1946. The film's directors were Gene Kelly and Stanley Donen, with Kelly reportedly the uncredited choreographer. The story centered on three sailors—Gabey (Kelly), Chip (Frank Sinatra) and Ozzie (Jules Munshin)—on a day of shore leave in New York City looking for fun and romance before their twenty-four hours are up.

Miller is billed fourth above the film's title and plays the supporting part of Claire Huddesen, a student at the Museum of Anthropological History, the role that Betty Comden herself had played on stage as

Claire DeLoone. She sings and dances in three numbers, all with music by Roger Edens and lyrics by Green and Comden: "Prehistoric Man," "On the Town," and "Count on Me." Miller is part of the chorus of Kelly, Sinatra, Munshin, Betty Garrett (who plays Brunhilde Esterhazy) and Vera-Ellen (who plays Ivy Smith) for "On the Town," and Kelly, Sinatra, Munshin, Garrett and Alice Pearce (who plays Lucy Shmeeler) for "Count on Me," getting one verse.

For "Prehistoric Man" she sings with Kelly, Sinatra, Munshin, and Garrett dancing as her chorus, wearing a Helen Rose green knee-length dress with a black and white checkered collar and sleeves and a split skirt. The number is her best showcase and has the startling moment where Munshin as the prehistoric man drags her across the floor by the hair, although directors Kelly and Donen uses cutaways and medium shots which detract from the star. Otherwise Rose gives her a notable off-the-shoulder watermelon-colored ankle-length dress, and a Coney Island multicolored coochie dancer outfit. Miller's shoulder-length black hair by Sydney Guilaroff is shorter than it was in *The Kissing Bandit* and her makeup by Jack Dawn is back to be over rouged as it was in *Easter Parade*. She makes Claire funny and gets to deliver a deliberately hammy speech to the Professor (George Meader) about the sailor's appreciation of the museum dinosaur that has collapsed, accompanied by Brunhilde on piano.

The film was released on December 8 with the taglines "Come On, Everybody, Let's the Town!," "M-G-M's Big Technicolor Musical !," "They're painting the town red, white and blue!," "Twice as gay as 'Anchors Aweigh'!," "Championship Musical of Them All!," and "They Paint the Joy!" It was praised by *Variety*, Bosley Crowther in *The New York Times*, John Douglas Eames in "The MGM Story," and Charles Higham and Joel Greenberg in "Hollywood in the Forties," but had a mixed reaction from Pauline Kael in *5001 Nights at the Movies*. The film was a box office success and won the Academy Award for Best Music Scoring of a Musical Picture. It was remade as the 1966 Finnish TV Movie *Loistokaupunki* and the December 22, 1993, episode of the television series *Great Performances* entitled "On the Town in Concert," PBS.

This was the first musical to be shot partly on location and Miller took credit for persuading Louis B. Mayer to do it in New York claiming she had never been there, seemingly forgetting her time on Broadway in the *George White Scandals*. However other sources say that the idea came from Gene Kelly. In her book, *Betty Garrett and Other Songs: A Life on Stage and Screen*, Garrett writes that the star was unhappy when she learned that only Kelly, Sinatra and Munshin would be going on location. Miller went to producer Arthur Freed and cried crocodile

Gene Kelly, Frank Sinatra, an obscured Jules Munshin, and Betty Garrett at right performing as the chorus behind Miller in the "Prehistoric Man" number in *On the Town* (1949).

tears so he relented and the female stars went too. They stayed at the Waldorf Hotel for a week and while the men were shooting, they went shopping, to Broadway shows and saw friends. There are two shots in the film where it seems the star is on location, unless they are convincing studio lot approximations, and Garrett reported that the one where the women wave goodbye to the sailors at the Brooklyn Navy Yard had to be later re-shot with doubles because there was a hair in the camera aperture.

She was paid less than Kelly and Munshin and more than Stanley Donen, but felt Donen was a genius. During camera rehearsal for the "Prehistoric Man" number her dress flared out and hit the reconstructed dinosaur that was behind them on the set, collapsing to the floor. The cast were told to go to lunch while the crew reassembled it, and came back late in the afternoon to shoot the number. Miller reported that the very thin Sinatra had to wear prosthetic padding to fill out the seat of his sailor's uniform, something he was extremely sensitive about and unappreciative of movie set horseplay involving his lower half. She did not get to know Vera-Ellen very well during the shooting, not socializing after work. Yet Vera-Ellen told friends that the star called her Vera-Girl and how much she admired Miller for the extraordinary extra taps she could generate, sometimes wondering where all that sound came from.

After finishing the film Miller had a great restlessness come over her, something she assumed was the gypsy soul that gave the star the great urge to keep dancing and be on the go, though she had to wait until a beau called for a date to do so. She believed it was dancing that had brought her to the present place in films but she didn't want it to be the boundary of her career. Miller could be a comedienne and wanted to do the type of parts that Ginger Roger played, but without giving up dancing. She was happy to have kept the financial promise made to her mother, with whom she lived in Beverly Hills, and there was no wolf outside their door anymore. Ann and Clara remained close and if she had no date, they would go out driving together the radio playing music to urge them on, since Miller loved to drive next best to dancing. She wondered if her slippers had the tinge of red that made them kin to the red shoes that danced poor Moira Shearer to her death in the British musical romance *The Red Shoes* (1948), which the star found unforgettable and had seen many times. But Miller's thoughts were not always so serious since that could enmesh the dancer's feet and bind them to the earth, and then what would be the use of her cry, "Let's Dance"?

She was touted by M-G-M as the star of their forthcoming film *Singin' in the Rain* in mid–1949, to play Kathy Selden.

Miller gave a birthday party for Bill O'Connor on June 12 and her good friend Cobina Wright speculated in her society column whether the next cake the couple will cut would be their wedding cake. But the star felt any hope of marriage plans was slowly disintegrating, although she was still deeply involved with the man.

She appeared in the M-G-M color documentary short *Mighty Manhattan, New York's Wonder City*, directed by James H. Smith. This was shot on locations in New York and was released on July 30. Miller is seen entering the Starlight Roof restaurant of the Waldorf Astoria, escorted by the president and chairman of the board of directors of American Airlines C.R. Smith, president of the hotel Frank A. Reddy, and its resident manager Henry B. Williams. She is also seen at a table talking with Smith. The star wears a black evening gown with spaghetti straps, and her hair is brown and worn off her forehead and in a neck roll.

Arthur Freed had reportedly considered casting her in the musical romance *Pagan Love Song* (1950) as the half-Caucasian, half-Tahitian Mimi Bennett, but chose Esther Williams instead. In early 1950 Ann attended a party at the home of Conrad Hilton. The black-tie affair had an orchestra that played fast-paced rhythmic Latin songs and the crowd moved to the sidelines to make room for the host and his star companion. When Hilton danced across the floor with her everyone clapped merrily in time with the music.

Miller's next film was the black and white "B" crime and romantic comedy *Watch the Birdie* (1950), shot from May 1 to mid–June on location in California and at the M-G-M Hollywood Studios with the working title of "The Cameraman." This was a remake of the M-G-M silent family romantic comedy *The Cameraman* (1928). The new screenplay was by Ivan Tors, Devery Freeman and Harry Ruskin, with uncredited work by Buster Keaton who had starred in the original film; it was based on a story by Marshall Neilan, Jr. The director was Jack Donohue. The story centered on Rusty Cameron (Red Skelton), a cameraman who helps Lucia Corlane (Arlene Dahl), an heiress, to get rid of her financial adviser who wants to get her money. Miller is billed third above the title and plays the supporting role of Miss Lucky Vista, a beauty prize winner whose real name is not given. Her hair by Sydney Guilaroff is shorter and she wears notable clothes by the uncredited designer that includes a dark-colored one-piece bathing suit, a silver floor-length strapless low-cut silver dress, and a fur stole. This is a non–musical comedy role for the star though she has a hard time in the narrative being chased by turkeys, pushed by Mrs. Shanway (Pam Britton) and slapped by Lucia. Her best scene is when Miller attempts to seduce Rusty for the purpose of getting incriminating film he has taken for Grantland D. Farns (Leon Ames), where she is funny.

The film was released on December 11 with the tagline "Clicks with the Chicks." It was praised by *Variety* who found Miller to be fun and said her gams registered, but lambasted by Bosley Crowther in *The New York Times* who wrote that she bore up rather bravely in a small and humiliating role. It was a box office success. Miller did not want to do the film though she adored working with Skelton, whom the star taught a new rhumba step between takes. She also became friends with Arlene Dahl, who shared her interest in the spirit world.

Miller went to the wedding of Elizabeth Taylor and Nicky Hilton on May 6 and the reception they gave at the Bel Air Country Club as a friend of the groom's father, Conrad Hilton. They had all been on a double-date when Nicky broke the news about the marriage, also telling the star that she would make a glamourous stepmother. The wedding reception was almost unbearably beautiful which made it unbearably painful to see how the marriage so quickly disintegrated.

By the time the musical comedy *Singin' in the Rain* (1952) went into production she was not in the cast, reportedly considered too old at 28 for the part of Kathy, and 19-year-old Debbie Reynolds was cast instead.

When Judy Garland cut her throat on June 19 after being suspended by M-G-M, Miller said she was always an emotional girl and by that time was like somebody drowning with no one to help. So it was a relief when Garland was released from her contract on September 29.

Around this time Maurice Woodruff, one of England's most famous psychics, came to the star's home, saying amazing things about her past and present life and predicting that Clara would have a lingering illness. He also saw that Miller would have later success in a stage play on Broadway.

She learned that her friend Rita Hayworth was to return to films after the marriage to Prince Aly Khan had failed and she had returned to the Unites States. The star commented that while Hayworth was really a passionate Spanish gypsy in her heart she was also a very soft-spoken easy-going, down-to-earth person who loved to put on old clothes and just chew the fat. Khan was a playboy who lived for parties and beautiful women and gambling and drinking, and not prepared to give his wife the time at home she wanted. It was strange how life worked out since the very thing her friend had run away from was the very thing that saved her, going back to her career out of the financial necessity of being a single mother.

Miller was lent to RKO for her next film, the Technicolor musical *Two Tickets to Broadway* (1951), shot from November 4 to mid–January 1951 on the Paramount backlot and the RKO Hollywood studios. The screenplay was by Sid Silvers and Hal Kanter based on a story by Sammy Cahn and the director was James V. Kern. It centered on Nancy Peterson (Janet Leigh) from Pelican Falls, Vermont, who goes to New York to be a Broadway star. Miller is listed fifth after the title, playing the supporting part of chorus girl Joyce Campbell. She sings and dances in two numbers—"The Worry Bird" and "Big Chief Hole-in-the-Ground" both by Jule Styne and Leo Robin, and dances in a rehearsal montage.

The star's showcase is in the former, where she is the main dancer of the chorus of Leigh and Barbara Lawrence who plays S.F. Rogers, for the singing by Gloria De Haven who plays Hannah Holbrook. Miller is dressed in a Michael Woulfe green and white horizontal striped top with white sleeves and collar, ankle-length green skirt and green gloves, and her hair is by Larry Germain. The coverage uses some medium shots and foreground obscuring, with the film's musical numbers created and directed by Busby Berkeley. Other notable Woulfe costumes for her are an American Indian outfit with a long black plaited wig and tropical makeup by Mel Berns for ""Big Chief Hole-in-the-Ground" and a blue bathing suit for a rehearsal. Director Kern actually opens the film with a shot of the star's legs, and has another close-up of them later at a rehearsal. Otherwise she gets a comic bit with an out-of-control exercise bike in a scene at the gym.

The film was released on November 1, 1951, with the tagline "Get set for a Racy Romp up and down the Big Street!" It was praised by *Variety*, who wrote that Miller did some flashing footwork, and Bosley Crowther in *The New York Times*, who said she personified one of the film's major attractions. But it received a mixed reaction from Richard B. Jewell and Vernon Harbin in *The RKO Story*. The film was not a box office success but received an Academy Award nomination for Best Sound Recording.

The star was to have had a big solo number for the Styne and Robin song "It Began in Yucatan," choreographed by Nick Castle and set on top of a two-storey high Peruvian pyramid. However she got dizzy with vertigo when dancing and tripped and fell, rolling all the way down the pyramid side. Miller sprained a leg and ankle and hurt her back and was hospitalized for a now-unknown period of time. The number was cancelled though it appears that a snippet of it, with her tapping solo, is seen in the rehearsal montage. She was sure her injury cost the studio a lot of money and this led to her hearing again from producer Howard Hughes, whom the star thought had borrowed her from M-G-M as a thank you for the favor she had once done for him. Miller writes in *Miller's High Life* that he telephoned, though in her 1997 *Private Screenings* interview she says he came to the studio to talk to her. Hughes was sorry that the star had been hurt and her number had to be cut. In the interview she stated he came to say *why* the number was cut, which was because they could not afford to wait for her to heal, though this version of the story contradicts the legend that Hughes never set foot on the RKO lot when he owned the studio.

Janet Leigh wrote in her memoir *There Really Was a Hollywood* that Miller was wacky, kooky, and spirited. No one knew what would pop out of her mouth, she least of all, and the woman had absolutely no idea how funny she really was.

In 1950 the star named a pair of beloved tap shoes "Moe and Joe" and she would keep them for the next 40 years. In the *Photoplay* of January 1951 for an article by Vicky Riley entitled "Glad Hands" she was photographed giving her nails their weekly manicure, because everybody in Movietown said she had the prettiest hands. Miller reported she gave herself three or four polish changes a week.

Her next film was the Technicolor musical comedy *Texas Carnival* (1951), shot from February 2 to late March with the working title of "The Carnival Story" on location in California and at the M-G-M Hollywood Studios. The screenplay was by Dorothy Kingsley, based on a story by George Wells and Kingsley. The director was Charles Walters. The story centered on the Bellrows Western Carnival Show team of Debbie Telford (Esther Williams) and Cornelius "Cornie" Quinell (Red Skelton) who are mistaken for a cattle baron and his sister at a swank hotel. Miller is billed fourth above the title and plays the supporting role of Sunshine Jackson, oil millionairess and daughter of the local sheriff.

She sings and dances in two numbers: "It's Dynamite," with music by Harry Warren and lyrics by Dorothy Fields, and "Deep in the Heart of Texas," with music by Don Swander and lyrics by June Hershey. Though the latter gives the star a solo dance as part of the number where she leaps over male dancers and does a series of fouette turns, the former is the better showcase for her, despite the use of some medium shots. Miller fires six-shooters, kicks a bass drum, dances on the vibraphone keys of a player and on tables as the chorus boys remove the tablecloth under her one by one, plays bongo drums, and finishes dancing on the lid of a grand piano. The star's costume is a Helen Rose black long-sleeved knee-length dress with white fringes and red kerchief with a removable skirt. The dance numbers were choreographed by Hermes Pan. Otherwise in the film, her Texan accent is more pronounced, though she gets little else of consequence to do.

The film was released on October 5 with the taglines "M-G-M's High, Wide and Handsome TECHNICOLOR Musical!" and "FOR THE MILLIONS WHO LOVED 'THE GREAT CARUSO' AND 'SHOW BOAT' ANOTHER BIG MGM MUSICAL!" It was praised by *Variety* but received a mixed reaction from Bosley Crowther in *The New York Times*, who said that Miller's dancing in the one fast number she had was highly stimulating. The film was a box office success.

This was her first film for producer Jack Cummings, who ran the third musical comedy unit at M-G-M. He was Louis B. Mayer's sophisticated nephew and had great taste. Cummings didn't do as many musicals as the other producers, and like Joe Pasternak didn't have the cabinet around him that Arthur Freed had, but knew how to do them. The star had a ball on the film and loved working with Esther Williams, who had a marvelous sense of humor, was always smiling and laughing, and never moody. Producers were always chasing Williams around because she was considered one of the sexiest actresses on the lot—but when the swimmer's eyes half-closed the sexy look came from her being nearsighted. This is why Miller called her Esther Hazy. Williams wrote in her autobiography *The Million Dollar Mermaid* that they became friends on the film, not resenting the screen time the star received. This was because she had given birth the previous October to a child that was difficult at home and was glad someone was sharing some of the work.

Arlene Dahl wrote about Miller's makeup secrets in the *Tribune* of February 23. For sheer winsome sweetness there was no one else whose face looked like a valentine with a personality to match.

On June 6 she attended the Hollywood premiere of the M-G-M musical biography *The Great Caruso* (1951) with Charles Isaacs, who was reported to be her beau for some time. It was also said that the star had recently injured her back which had delayed her next appearance in movies.

The musical comedy *The Belle of New York* (1952) was in production from mid–June to October but Miller was not in the cast, with the leading role taken by Vera-Ellen. Dore Schary took over control of production at M-G-M either in June or July, with sources differing on the date. Louis B. Mayer was said to have either resigned his position on June 22 or been fired on June 23 after 23 years as head of the studio. Schary had been made vice president in charge of production on July 1, 1948, after 1947 had seen the studio experience their first-ever end-of-year financial loss. M-G-M faced a hard time adapting to the postwar filmmaking environment, and Mayer's splashy, wholesome entertainments were seen to be old-fashioned in comparison with the more realistic message pictures that Schary preferred.

The industry in general also faced the issues of rising labor costs and unrest, political turmoil, the threat of television and the Paramount decree that had forced the studios to sell the theaters which had previously guaranteed the exhibition of their films. Schary and Mayer had co-existed and some of Schary's personal productions helped the studio make a profit but their philosophical differences came to a head with the 1950 production of the war drama *The Red Badge of Courage* (1951). Mayer was vehemently opposed to making it because it had no marquee names or female roles and he predicted the film would flop. He was right and in 1951 Mayer presented an ultimatum to Nick Schenck, head of the New York parents company Loews. He wanted Schary fired but Schenck supported his rival, so Mayer decided to leave or was let go.

Miller attended the July 27 Hollywood premiere of the M-G-M family musical *Show Boat* (1951) with Dan Dailey, with the couple described as Hollywood's newest surprise twosome; they were photographed holding hands. In the week ending September 28 she was photographed at a Los Angeles Orphanage Guild event with the French-born actress and West Coast socialite Jetta Goudal, now known as Mrs. Harold Grieve.

Miller's next film was another Technicolor musical comedy for producer Jack Cummings, *Lovely to Look At* (1952), shot from late September to mid–November at the M-G-M Hollywood studios. It was a remake of the RKO musical comedy *Roberta* (1935). A potential new version had been publicized in the *Los Angeles Times* on November 19, 1948, with Betty Garrett for the part the star played. The new screenplay was by George Wells and Harry Ruby, with additional dialogue by

Andrew Solt, based on the musical play "Roberta" from the novel by Alice Duer Miller. The play had run on Broadway at the New Amsterdam Theatre from November 18, 1933, to July 21, 1934. The film's director was Mervyn LeRoy though Vincente Minnelli directed the fashion show finale after LeRoy had to leave the production prematurely.

The story centered on Al Marsh (Red Skelton), Tony Naylor (Howard Keel) and Jerry Ralby (Gower Champion), Broadway producers struggling to get backing for their show who inherit a half interest in a Parisian fashion house. Miller is billed sixth above the title and plays the supporting role "Bubbles" Cassidy, a showgirl at New York's Club Sirocco. She has only one solo number, "I'll Be Hard to Handle" with music by Jerome Kern and lyrics by Bernard Dougall, though is seen dancing with Al in the cast crowd at the fashion show finale with the reprise of the film's title song by Kern and additional and revised lyrics by Dorothy Fields. For her number, Miller sings and dances with a male chorus wearing wolf masks and ends up riding on two of their backs. Her leg emerges from behind a curtain and she appears in an Adrian designed pink, glittery, low-cut sleeveless short dress with a floor-length back skirt that has a large bow, long gloves, a headpiece with a large feather and fishnet face mask, and with a long cigarette holder. Choreography is by Hermes Pan and there are some medium shots and foreground obscuring. Adrian also gives Miller a notable sparkling, silver-patterned, low-cut, knee-length sleeveless dress with matching jacket that has fur cuffs. The star makes "Bubbles" funny and is given a tart reply to Stephanie (Kathryn Jackson) about how she is, saying "I'll pull through." Miller also gets to deliver a silent reaction to the romantic overtures of a drunken Al and a believable dramatic confession to Stephanie that she never loved Tony.

The film was released on May 29, 1952, with the taglines "One of the Grandest Romantic Musicals in Years!" and "M-G-M's Technicolor spectacle! Jerome Kern's music!" It was praised by *Variety*, who wrote that the star displayed talented feet and shapely gams, and John Douglas Eames in "The MGM Story" but received a mixed reaction from A.H. Weiler in *The New York Times*, who did say she exhibited both her beautiful legs and staccato tapping. The film was not a box office success but it was remade as a TV movie entitled *Roberta* broadcast on September 19, 1958, and November 6, 1969.

Miller became good friends with Zsa Zsa Gabor who plays "Zsa Zsa" while making the film. She said Gabor had a flair and a flounce and electricity about her whether it was in a film or on a talk show. Her mother Jolie had groomed all her daughters to be a wife for a wonderful man and whoever got one of these girls got themselves a thoroughbred.

Gabor was initially piqued that Miller was seeing Conrad Hilton, since he was her ex-husband, but there was no romance between them because of Miller's continued love for Bill O'Connor. O'Connor had introduced her to Hilton so she was sure his friend knew the situation—he could take the star out when O'Connor could not. She and Hilton always had a great time together because he was a terrific dancer and she was his favorite partner. Together they danced all over the world at the Hilton Hotel openings which were as glamourous as Hollywood premieres in those days.

Miller went to the openings in Havana, Hong Kong, Tokyo, Mexico City, in the Caribbean, Cairo, Madrid and Istanbul. Hilton always held rehearsals with his orchestra and the star so they could be the first ones on the floor when their theme song "Varsovienna" was played, which he considered his lucky tune. Hilton was also one of the few who could keep up with Miller for the rhumba, that she was considered one of the best practitioners of in Hollywood. The star felt the secret to the man's youthful energy and looks was that he always liked to be in the company of younger people, and Hilton was also always invited to her annual Christmas Eve parties. They loved going out on the town together and often double-dated, but he was only ever a friend.

On December 28 *The New York Times* reported that the star had been assigned one of the two female leads in *Lili* which had been first announced under the title "The Seven Souls of Clement O'Reilly." She did not end up appearing in the film, which was shot from early March to late April 1952 and starred Leslie Caron. It was released in 1953 and Zsa Zsa presumably played the part of Rosalie, a magician's assistant, that Miller might have played.

She again worked for Joe Pasternak on the Technicolor musical romance *Small Town Girl* (1953) which was shot from mid–June to mid–July at the M-G-M Hollywood Studios. The screenplay was by Dorothy Cooper and Dorothy Kingsley, based on a story by Kingsley, and the director was Leslie Kardos. It centered on Cindy Kimbell (Jane Powell), a Duck Creek salesgirl and daughter of the town's judge, who meets New York millionaire playboy Rick "Ricky" Belrow Livingston (Farley Granger).

Miller is billed third after the film's title, and plays the supporting role of Broadway star Lisa Bellmount who is also Ricky's fiancée. She has two musical numbers, singing and dancing in "I've Gotta Hear that Beat," with music by Nicholas Brodszky and lyrics by Leo Robin, and dancing in "My Gaucho," also by Brodszky and Robin. "My Gaucho" is notable for being a flamenco dance without taps but, despite some medium shots, the former is the better showcase for her. Dressed in a Helen Rose sparkly low-cut black leotard with a fringed skirt, long black gloves, and a veiled sparkly black hat, the star is revealed after an open curtain and two large tom-tom drums on either side of the screen. She taps on a sloped stage from which 100 musical instruments and the hands of the disembodied musicians play protruding Dalí-esque from the floor and against a back wall, and moves up and down a staircase. The number ends after an aerial shot of Miller in a spotlight moves in to reveal her alone on the stage, a trick presumably accomplished by the blackout around the spotlight allowing for a cut. The film's musical numbers were staged by Busby Berkeley. Otherwise she is funny as Lisa, particularly when rejecting Ludwig Schlemmer (Bobby Van)'s romantic advances and career aspirations; the star is also seen in footage from *On the Town* in a nightclubbing montage. Helen Rose's wardrobe for Lisa includes a white knee-length suit with jarring long red gloves and a red and white vertical striped scarf.

The film was released on April 10, 1953, with the tagline "THE NEW HIPPITY-HOP MUSICAL!" It was praised by *Variety* who wrote that Miller exposed her 3-D gams in two production numbers but received a mixed reaction from Howard Thompson in *The New York Times*, who said she was perfectly cast as a peppery Rialto gold-digger who turned one tap routine into a personal rhapsody, and John Douglas Eames in *The MGM Story*. The film was not a box office success but received an Academy Award nomination for Best Music, Original Song for "My Flaming Heart."

This was one of the star's favorite films because of "I've Gotta Hear that Beat," which became the scene it was best remembered for. She felt the film did not receive the publicity it deserved. Her choreography in the number was aided by William "Willie" Covan who had worked with Eleanor Powell, and she said it came off as surreal, spectacular and typical of Busby Berkeley's genius. But Berkeley was also a devil, because he had no sympathy for the performers. He just wanted to get his shot, make it great, and go home.

Doing takes for the number gave her a painful and bloody blister on one of her heels and Miller wanted to stop to get a bandaid but the director refused. That would take time while she removed her stockings to apply it. Berkeley said he didn't care about Miller or her blister. The man had promised the studio he would have the number done that night and the genius said if she didn't like it that was too bad. The star just had to think about something else and do it, and Berkeley had a way of hypnotizing her. When she got up on the platform that was a high as a three-storey building Miller also got dizzy with vertigo and more than once she slipped and almost fell. But the star did it.

Miller performing "I've Gotta Hear that Beat" in *Small Town Girl* (1953).

Another complication was the temperature of the set. Those holding the instruments under the platform became heated and wore jockey shorts for relief, with one of them fainting from the ordeal. Miller said the warmth was caused by the fans they normally ran being turned off, since the studio was not air conditioned. However this claim is disputed in other sources since certain stars like Joan Crawford and Betty Hutton demanded air conditioned sets, and they could be refrigerated for films that had Arctic locales.

After making the film, Ann and Jane Powell became good friends, calling each other Mutt and Jeff. Powell reported that Miller was unique. She was the first to admit to not being practical—the star couldn't boil and didn't want to learn. Miller gave her profession on her income tax forms as "star." She and Jane Powell would later travel together for a Brazilian film festival in Rio de Janeiro, and on the plane she was found sitting on the closed toilet seat with her arms flung over her chest. Miller had lost "Moe and Joe," the flop chickies (also known as flap chickies), what the star named her bust pads though she also used these names for her beloved tap shoes. The pads were eventually found in Miller's bunk.

Farley Granger wrote in his memoir *Include Me Out: My Life from Goldwyn to Broadway* that he and the star got along like kindred souls. She would always tell him not to make her laugh because that would make her fake nose flip. At around 5 p.m. when the ravages of a long day began to show on everyone's makeup, Miller would touch her loosening nose and say it was Shangri-La time.

She was considered for a role in the musical comedy *Give a Girl a Break* (1953), though it is not known whom she would have played.

The star appeared in the Woman's Home Companion magazine advertising luster-cream shampoo to keep her hair always alluring, since its care was vital to her glamour-career.

CHAPTER 5

Kiss Me Kate

*A*nn Miller's next film was the Technicolor musical comedy *Kiss Me Kate* (1953) for producer Jack Cummings, shot from early May to July 4, 1953, at the M-G-M Hollywood Studios. The screenplay was by Dorothy Kingsley based upon the play by Samuel Spewack and Bella Spewack and after the uncredited play *The Taming of the Shrew* by William Shakespeare. The original Broadway musical ran from December 30, 1948, to July 28, 1951, and won the 1949 Tony Awards for the Best Musical, Best Book and Best Musical Score. The film's director was George Sidney.

The plot centered on Lilli Vanessi (Kathryn Grayson) and Fred Graham (Howard Keel), an ex-husband and wife team who star in a musical version of *The Taming of the Shrew.* Miller is billed 3rd after the title, playing the supporting role of singer and dancer Lois Lane that had been originated by Lisa Kirk on stage. She sings and dances in six numbers, all by Cole Porter, and is seen dancing with Bill Calhoun (Tommy Rall), "Gremio" (Bobby Van) and "Hortensio" (Bob Fosse) in a segue. The Porter numbers are "Too Darn Hot," the duets "Why Can't You Behave" and "Always True to You in My Fashion" with Rall, "We Open in Venice" with Grayson and Keel and Rall, "Tom, Dick or Harry" with Rall and Van and Fosse, and "From This Moment On" with Rall and Van and Fosse and specialty dancers Carol Haney and Jeanne Coyne.

Despite director Sidney's use of medium shots and foreground obscuring and cutaways, the star's best effort is "Too Darn Hot," which she performs in a Walter Plunket–designed, watermelon-colored, beaded, low-cut leotard with matching long gloves and neck ribbon, and a black fan. Miller dances on tables and in front of a mirror that shows two reflections, and throws her gloves and scarf and jewelry at the screen as a 3-D effect which is repeated when in "Why Can't You Behave" she throws dice at the screen. The film's choreography is by Hermes Pan, though Bob Fosse contributed his own dance to part of

Miller in the "Too Darn Hot" number for *Kiss Me Kate* (1953).

"From This Moment On." In the play "Lois" wears a waist-length black wig by Sydney Guilaroff and plays the harp.

The film was given a test screening for the cast and crew, wearing 3-D glasses. It was released on November 5 with the taglines "THE FAMED STAGE HIT ... NOW A BIG COLORFUL MUSICAL!," "IN 3D !!!," "A Great Big M-G-M Musical in COLOR!," "Hollywood's First Important Big MUSICAL in Perfected 3-D," "On the Vast Panoramic Stereophonic Sound.... Color Too!," "Broadway's Long-Run Musical Smash Hit—Now on the Screen.... All the Spicy Splendor!," "MGM presents Hollywood's first important BIG MUSICAL in 3-D on our Panoramic Screen with MIRACULOUS STEREOPHONIC SOUND! COLOR, too!," and "The Greatest of All Great MGM Musicals ... Bigger, Better Blushin-er than the famed Broadway Smash Hit."

The film was praised by *Variety*, Bosley Crowther in *The New York Times*, who wrote that Miller was a splay of nimble legs and amusingly casual inclinations in handling some of the film's better songs, and John Douglas Eames in *The MGM Story* but received a mixed reaction from Pauline Kael who did say that the star came off as lively and amusing. It was not a box office success, though nominated for the Academy Award for Best Music Scoring of a Musical Picture. The film was remade as made-for-TV movies broadcast on November 20, 1958, March 25, 1968, and a Dutch made-for-TV movie broadcast on October 4, 1975, and the February 26, 2003, episode of the television series *Great Performances*.

She considered this film one of her best, being proud to be a part of it, with Lois perhaps her favorite part as she had so much to do. Miller claimed she was considered so good that there was talk of a Best Supporting Actress Academy Award nomination, which did not happen. The first 3-D musical had to be shot twice—once for the 3-D camera and once for the regular ones for theaters not equipped for innovation. The star loved the 3-D effects, finding them exciting, and wished she could have done another film like it. Cole Porter visited the cast and was photographed with Miller on the set. She said he was such a darling.

The star also loved George Sidney, the film's director, whom she described as a big teddy bear. He had seen Miller when she was 12 at a benefit at the Pantages Theatre and thought the girl was the greatest young tap dancer with the greatest legs. The director reported that Miller did "Too Darn Hot" without perspiring and from then he called her the Iron Lady out of admiration, though her heart was really made of gold. She said the number had had multiple takes due to mishaps that occurred as the star climbed around Grayson and Keel sitting on the couch, like her shoe buckle snagging on Grayson's wig and knocking it askew, or jolting Keel to one side. He reported in his memoir *Only*

Make Believe that in one take Miller threw a bracelet at Grayson which also got caught in her wig. But the one Keel most enjoyed was his kissing scene with the star. She gave him and Grayson the nicknames "Tangle Foot" and "Twinkle Toes" because neither were good dancers, which Miller thought was apparent in the "We Open in Venice" number.

She had known Bob Fosse as another M-G-M contract player. The star credits herself for discovering the eccentric dancing he created for his part of "From This Moment On," and claimed Fosse always credited her for giving him his first break as a choreographer and director. She gives two versions of the story. One has her seeing Fosse and Carol Haney rehearsing the number in a style that Miller had never seen before so she ran and got Hermes Pan and George Sidney, who allowed it to be put in the film. The other version had Pan and the star finding Fosse and Haney when Haney, who was Pan's dance assistant, was not in their rehearsal room. The "noodling" they discovered was described by Miller as in the Jack Cole style and she said Sidney had to see it and put it in the film. When Sidney came and saw the dance, he agreed.

While making the film the Shah of Iran contacted Pan and asked him to persuade the star to go on a date with him. She had previously stood up the Shah when he was last in California because of a misunderstanding over a misquoted newspaper story. Miller had met the Shah's half-brother, Prince Hamid Reza Pahlavi, at a party given by Sir Charles and Lady Mendl, the reigning hosts of Hollywood. The Prince told her the Shah was coming to Hollywood and wanted a date, since he loved to dance and tall brunettes were his type. She was thrilled and read in the paper that he had arrived and was staying at the Ambassador Hotel. The Prince called to confirm the next night for dinner and dancing at a black-tie party at the Mocambo, with a limousine to pick her up at 8 p.m. The star bought a new dress from Saks, which cost a week's salary, had her hair coiffed, nails manicured, and took out the best jewels from her bank vault to wear.

While waiting, she read the front-page story about the Shah in the evening paper, which had a quote from him saying he was not in Los Angeles to date the fleshpots of the West but to buy farm machinery for his country. Miller was outraged and when the doorbell rang 10 minutes later she saw the limousine waiting from her bedroom window and the Prince as the door. She refused to even go downstairs to greet him and instead wrote a note and sent it down with the maid, saying the star was unable to dine with the Shah but gave no excuse. When the half-brother Prince telephoned the next day for an explanation Miller told him she had seen the Shah's interview and did not want to be considered a fleshpot. Miller felt if this fleshpot had kept the date it would have made a liar out of his half-brother, although the Prince claimed the Shah had been misquoted. After that he married but now he was separated and thought he might have better luck this time by approaching Pan, who was close to the Iranian royal family and who the Shan knew was a friend of the star.

She was invited to be a guest at the palace in Tehran for one week, where there was to be a festival climaxed by a ball, and Pan suggested Miller ask George Sidney for the time off. Being away for only a week was not a huge problem, since there were often filming delays due to actor's illnesses or injuries. She wanted to go but Sidney refused, saying shooting around her would waste millions of dollars, so Pan had to report back that the star was unavailable.

After shooting was done, Dore Schary was so impressed with her work that M-G-M sent Miller on a three week publicity tour with the film, though she was not allowed to do any dancing in her personal appearances. The studio had insured the star's legs for $1 million and she was now signed to a new contract, though with a cut in salary. *The Hollywood Reporter* of October wrote that Miller was to be in the cast of the musical comedy *Athena.*

She made her first foray into television as a guest on the November 1 episode of the musical comedy series *Toast of the Town*, filmed at the CBS New York Studios and broadcast on CBS. The show's directors were Robert Bleyer and John Moffitt. Miller joined Julius La Rosa to show him some dance steps. She was the intermission guest on the December 10 episode of the live series *Lux Video Theatre* entitled "Three Just Men" which was broadcast on CBS. The show was written by Elliott Street and directed by Richard Goode, and filmed at the CBS Studios in Hollywood.

It was reported that Miller was the top contender for Joe Pasternak's film of the book *The Life of Eva Peron*, to be called "Woman with a Whip." She was no doubt considered because the First Lady of Argentina had started out as a dancer, but the film would not be made.

In 1953 a source claimed the star admitted to being a terrible actress, which seems unlikely. She supposedly gave context by adding that if Lana Turner and Ava Gardner could act under a good director, Miller still had a good chance.

M-G-M celebrated its 30th anniversary on January 29, 1954, and Ann was among the surviving contract players who appeared in footage taken for the occasion, seen wearing a white short-sleeved suit in a crowd with Dore Schary around a cake. The stars also appeared in a photograph for *Look* magazine, where Miller wears a beautiful gray and white low-cut floor-length gown. The studio was now in trouble, despite the success of films like the musical romances *An American in Paris* (1951) and *Singin' in the Rain*. Expenses were up and profits down and the New York office demanded they rein in operations with financial retrenchment, cutting deep into production budgets, technical departments and personnel. The order came to prune the dead weight and the worst hit were the collection of stars. In 1949 there had been 58 of them, but the *Look* photograph showed 36 and the film footage has only a dozen. Within a space of two years every single one would be released from their contracts.

Miller returned as a guest to *Toast of the Town* for the February 14 episode, which was their "MGM's 30th Anniversary Tribute" broadcast on CBS. Shot at the Television City in Hollywood the show was directed by Robert Bleyer and John Moffitt. It had Ed Sullivan hosting and featured some of the studio's biggest stars, with clips of their most popular films, and recreated scenes and songs from their films.

Athena (1954) was shot from late March to early June but the star was not in the cast. Instead her next film was the Technicolor biographical musical comedy *Deep in My Heart* (1954), produced by Roger Edens. It was shot with the working title "The Romberg Story" from late April to late June at the M-G-M Hollywood Studios. The screenplay was by Leonard Spigelgass, based on the book by Elliott Arnold, and the director was Stanley Donen. The story centered on American composer Sigmund Romberg (Jose Ferrer). Miller is billed after the title as one of the Guest Stars, who are listed in order of appearance. She is only in one scene, singing and dancing as part of the number "It" with music by Romberg and lyrics by Oscar Hammerstein II and Otto A. Harbach, said to be from the show *Artists and Models*.

She wears a Helen Rose orange and black-fur knee-length coat that she removes to reveal an orange satin beaded 1920s flapper dress which was said to have 23,000 beads, with spaghetti straps and a matching hair ribbon. Director Donen uses some medium shots and the multi-colored costumes of the chorus drew attention from her, but she does non-tap dancing and impressive twirls. The choreographer was Eugene Loring and the set behind Miller was a giant mural drawn by John Held, Jr., the famous cartoonist chronicler of the twenties area.

The film was released on December 9 with the tagline "M-G-M's Finest Musical in Color." It received a mixed reaction from Douglas Eames in *The MGM Story* but was lambasted by Bosley Crowther in *The New York Times*. The film was a box office success.

Joe Pasternak now produced a color remake of the 1929 RKO musical comedy *Hit the Deck* with the same title (1955), which was shot from late August to late October on locations in San Francisco and at the M-G-M Hollywood studios. The screenplay was by Sonya Levien and William Ludwig based on the musical by Herbert Fields from *Shore Leave* by Hubert Osborne, and the director was Roy Rowland. The story centered on three sailors, Danny Xavier Smith (Russ Tamblyn), Chief Boatswain's Mate William "Bill" F. Clark (Tony Martin) and Rico Ferrari (Vic Damone) on shore leave in San Francisco.

Miller is billed seventh after the title playing the supporting role of Sirocco Club showgirl Ginger who is Bill's fiancée. She sings and dances in four numbers: "Keepin' Myself for You," with music by Vincent Youmans and lyrics by Sidney Clare, "The Lady from the Bayou," with music by Youmans and lyrics by Leo Robin, and as part of "Why, Oh Why?" and "Hallelujah," with music by Youmans and lyrics by Leo Robin and Clifford Grey. Her best is "The Lady from the Bayou," despite director Rowland's use of some medium shots. This mambo number has her first heard screaming before she is seen, though the screams that also end the number were provided by Kitty White. After one of the chorus boys is pushed out of a doorway, presumably by the star, she appears behind a beaded curtain and stands against a street lamp before kicking off her shoes to dance barefoot.

Miller wears a Helen Rose red low-cut knee-length sleeveless dress with a split skirt and a yellow and red feather in her long black Sydney Guilaroff wig. The dance has a walk over the boys' backs at one point and ends with the star returning to the doorway and disappearing behind the curtain in red light. The film's musical numbers were staged by Hermes Pan. Helen Rose also gives Miller flattering civilian outfits, especially a gray circle-necked knee-length white-patterned dress with a full skirt and worn with a white hat and white fur throw. She makes Ginger's anger at Bill funny, and gets some funny lines. When he gives her a baby turtle as a present, the star says "First a parrot, now a turtle—always another mouth to feed." When Bill tells her he worships the ground she walks on, Miller replies, "Now he's talking real estate." She also gets a cute moment telling the sailors she has to get changed for her next number at the Club, and unzips from a floor-length robe to a leotard. In addition, the star has a dramatic scene where she has tears in her eyes when Ginger admits she loves Bill.

The film premiered in Maryland on February 24, 1955, and then opened on March 3 with the taglines "Broadway's hit musical hits the screen splashed with COLOR and sensational CINEMASCOPE" and "MGM's star-sparkling, laugh-loaded, song-splashed musical!" It was praised by *Variety* but received a mixed reaction from A.H. Weiler in *The New York Times*, who wrote that Miller earned her keep in a fast rattling climactic tap routine. Sources differ as to whether the film was or was not a box office success.

A torrid, tantalizing dance by Ann Miller, "Lady From the Bayou", to a great Vincent Youmans song lately discovered.

M-G-M's CINEMASCOPE "HIT THE DECK" In COLOR

Copyright 1955 Loew's Incorporated   COUNTRY OF ORIGIN U. S. A.   8   Property of National Screen Service Corp. Licensed for display only in connection with the exhibition of this picture in your theatre. Must be returned immediately thereafter.   59-73

Lobby card showing Miller and chorus boys in "The Lady from the Bayou" from *Hit the Deck* (1955).

Jane Powell, who played Susan Smith, reportedly dubbed the false start for her in "Keepin' Myself for You," once the dance break ends where Bill steals his way into the song from an off-stage microphone. Ann liked the numbers choreographed by Pan, "Hallelujah!" in particular. She said she had a chorus of 100 sailors (the real number was reportedly 46), marching behind her keeping time while Miller did a staccato tap to the rhythm of their feet on a recreation of the main fore deck of a U.S. battleship. She reported "The Lady from the Bayou" was her first time dancing barefoot on film in a style that was influenced by Jack Cole. It replaced a song called "Loo Loo," a little shindig that made "Too Darn Hot" look cold.

Columnist Harrison Carroll visited the set when "The Lady from the Bayou" was shot, and reported that before a take the star did kicks to tone up her muscles. She wanted the character to have an evil smile to match what Miller called her evil dress, but Pan disagreed. A pillar on the set of row houses in the New Orleans French Quarter was pulled loose as one of the chorus boys grabbed it and Pan called cut. She cried "Oh, murder! Now we're going to have trouble with this bit." But in less than a minute they were ready for another take which went all the way to the end of the number. Pan was pleased but his star was not. After calling for a towel to wipe her brow, she wanted to go again. Being a perfectionist, Miller said she could do it better since her evil woman had come across as more like Shirley Temple. On the film she became friends with Debbie Reynolds who played Carol Pace, who described the star as a kick in the pants—so funny and silly.

It had been reported on October 16 that Miller would co-star with Howard Keel in M-G-M's "International Review," a revue type musical then in the script-writing stage. This film, planned to be shot in countries throughout the world, was however not made. On October 24 she attended a gala testimonial dinner honoring Joe Pasternak for 50 years of motion picture achievement and the nonsectarian Mount Sinai Hospital for 30 years of community service. The event was held at the Cocoanut Grove of the Ambassador Hotel where stars of Pasternak's films entertained, though it is not known whether that included her. She had been photographed accepting her invitation from Dore Schary on an unknown date with Pasternak standing with her.

Miller was photographed on January 7, 1955, for the Do Your Hands Match Your Face campaign, with the press lines reading that she and Cyd Charisse knew that hands were as important as one's face in expressing lovely, well-cared-for femininity, and that both required daily attention. On February 28 the star attended the annual Red Cross rally held at Boston's Symphony Hall.

She was sent to Australia by M-G-M to promote *Hit the Deck* and for the April 20 Melbourne opening of the musical biography of Australian opera star Marjorie Lawrence *Interrupted Melody* (1955), replacing the ill star of the film Eleanor Parker. Miller was the first U.S. movie star to appear in the country, receiving red carpet treatment and given the car that Queen Elizabeth rode in. She got to see her first platypus at the zoo and said the Australians were fabulous.

After the success of the trip the star was made an ambassador by the studio's foreign department who would send her all over the world as their representative. The movie junkets had become more important with M-G-M's dwindling profits and they were also a way to use stars that were not working on a film. Miller was considered a good choice for many reasons—she could be counted on to behave, got along with people, took her career seriously and was always reliable. Also the star loved travelling and saw it as the education she had missed since choosing a life in show business. Despite her lessons, Miller had only gotten to the 10th grade and still couldn't add or spell well, and her handwriting was appalling. The star hadn't known how to write a check before marrying

Reese Milner and she had always turned her money over to her mother for safekeeping. Miller wanted to be able to converse with people intelligently and the price was right, since the studio picked up the tab on all the expenses for herself and Clara.

For her first junket in South America she was a good sport about doing whatever was asked of her, signing autographs, posing for pictures, and riding in parades. She danced the tango with the Argentine dictator Juan Perón, who stepped on her feet, ruining the white satin shoes Clara had bought her, and held Miller so close she couldn't breathe. Irene Dunne was on the same junket and went to the American Embassy to help her leave, when Perón tried to prevent this because of his crush on the star. She reportedly received huge ovations wherever Miller went, including Germany, Italy, France, England, Turkey, Egypt, Lebanon, Jordan, and Spain.

In Madrid, Miller met Spanish bullfighter Mario Cabre, who saved her life from a switch-hitting bull. He had invited the star to his birthday fiesta at the ranch of a wealthy Spaniard who entertained his guests with a celebrity bullfight. Cabre filled her with wine, then dressed Miller up in a toreador outfit with a white satin cape lined in red and decorated with beads and embroidery, and hat. She was unaware that Ava Gardner had recently had the same experience but ended up with 12 stitches to her face after the encounter with the baby bull. The star went out into the middle of the bull ring, carrying the cape and the other guests sat around the tall fence. The corral gate was opened and out came the 2000 pound bull, which made her drop the cape and run to hide behind one of the escape boards. The bull chased her and hit the board so hard it made the star shake with fear. Realizing she was in real danger, Cabre leapt into the ring, grabbed the cape and fought the bull away, with the crowd laughing hysterically. But Miller didn't see the humor.

In Paris she met Claude Terrail, owner of the Tour d'Argent restaurant, and Andre Dubonnet, the aperitif king. Dubonnet invited her to be his guest at the annual Red Cross Gala at the palace in Monte Carlo, where she met Prince Rainier and Aly Khan who flirted like mad. Financier Frank Ryan took the star to a small dinner party at the home of J. Paul Getty, whose other guests included Aristotle Onassis, a man she thought had a great animal vitality, a love of life, and marvelous sense of humor.

On June 7 Miller was photographed arriving in New York on a Trans World Airlines flight from the west coast. She was reportedly bound for the opening of the Hilton hotel in Istanbul having been invited by Conrad Hilton, and planned to tour other parts of the Far East. When the star had told M-G-M of her plans they added a new junket. She was to be accompanied by two older star ladies, both Oscar winners and married to wealthy men, but not M-G-M contract players, and Louella Parsons. In *Miller's High Life* she does not name the ladies but the one that was said to be a devout Catholic may have been Loretta Young.

The devout Catholic planned to trek to the Holy Land and Ann to join her. Though there was a war going on in Jerusalem they would be permitted to fly to the Arab side. She wanted to go to impress Bill O'Connor since the place was where Christ had lived. Just before the party arrived in Lebanon at 2 a.m. Miller touched up her lipstick and combed her hair, preparing for who would be there to meet them. The star ladies didn't bother doing this, presumably figuring there would be no one at this time of the morning. But there was a battery of photographers when the plane door opened to capture the star ladies with cold cream on their faces and their hair in rollers. The M-G-M representative helped Miller through customs and pushed her into a limousine, where more photographers and reporters were waited at the hotel. In her room the exhausted star took off her makeup, tucked herself into bed, and was about to fall asleep when the telephone rang. It was the devout Catholic, livid and abusive. She un-invited her to the trek to the Holy Land, feeling Miller was such a publicity hound that they would be followed by photographers and this was not done when you went to the Holy Land. Miller was crushed and spent the morning crying and unable to sleep. She knew it was a bad idea to go there alone but later told the M-G-M representative about it.

He drove the star to the airport and put her on the first plane out to Jerusalem. He persuaded her to purchase a switchblade knife for protection before she left, since guns were not permitted, which Miller put in her makeup kit. Halfway through the flight she went to the ladies room and upon her return noticed the kit was open and the contents awry. The only thing missing was the knife, which the star took as a bad omen. She was met by a car at the Jerusalem airport but the two men in it did not take her to the American Hotel. They drove 20 or 30 miles beyond the city and stopped at a small dark Arab hotel. Brusquely told to get out of the car, Miller was scared. When she asked where they were one of the men replied that the star had a lot of explaining to do. They escorted the star to a room and locked her in. There was no electricity, just a small candle, and a pitcher of water which she was afraid to drink.

Miller reflected that this was not the adventure she had always wanted, thinking about her mother and the life the star might have led if she had stayed in Texas. A man arrived with a tray of food and she ate. Another man appeared and told how they believed Miller was a spy for the American Jews. The star explained the junket and how M-G-M had sent her to get frozen funds out for the Jewish people who owned their theaters. And also that she had come for personal reasons to study to be a Catholic. Miller begged to use the telephone to contact the theater distributor in Cairo who would verify the story, and the men took her to the downstairs desk where the operator located the manager of the one theater in Jerusalem. He offered to call M-G-M, and she was locked into the room again. After waiting what seemed like an eternity the theater manager arrived with the police to free her. Later the star would said she had been kidnapped and kept for two nights, and the manager came for her with Irene Dunne and Merle Oberon, who were also in Jerusalem.

After saving her from the Arab jail, the man took her to the head of the Catholic archdiocese. He assigned Miller a priest to conduct her tour of the Holy Land which followed the life of Christ step by step. On her last night the theater manager gave a party to honor the star in front of the Arab hotel where she had been locked up. The 200 guests sat on the ground and ate spicy Arabian lamb with rice and fine wine as soft Arab music played. The next day she was to leave for Cairo, just as the star ladies were to arrive in Jerusalem from Lebanon, and the manager arranged to have photographers meet the plane. He and Miller watched from a commissary that overlooked the airfield and saw the star ladies de-board, posing with their hair and makeup done. She guessed they had learned from the previous incident, but the man had played a trick—the photographers had no film in their cameras. When the ladies spotted him and Miller they looked mortified. She had to walk past them to get on the plane and it was quite a moment, with only Louella Parsons saying she had been terribly worried about her. Miller had come to believe that, although the devout Catholic was the one to make the abusive telephone call, it was really the other older star who had put her up to it, and karma would get her. This became true when, after years of ruling the roost in international jet-set society, her billionaire husband went broke and she had to hang up the For Sale sign on their palatial digs.

In Cairo she stayed at the Menna House Hotel near the Pyramid of Gaza, but before the star could see all the pyramids and the Sphinx and everything that had fascinated her about Egypt, Miller had to do publicity for M-G-M. One of her movies was playing at the biggest theater in the city and she was introduced on stage and spoke a few words in Arabic to the audience. The star was introduced to King Farouk's favorite dancer who taught her the belly dance and gave her a pair of finger cymbals. One of the most important pashas arranged a dinner party for Miller in a big hotel. They were served okra in little tureens which the pasha said was one of the most ancient dishes in the world. However she had been brought up on okra in Texas so did not find it as exotic or exciting as everyone else.

The star wanted to consult an Egyptian seer and the M-G-M representative brought a woman to her suite, and he translated. The woman, who had a good reputation, claimed to not know who Miller was. She began by taking her hand and looking into it. She saw the star's name up in lights and that she would be very famous, then suddenly wanted to leave without needing payment. This petrified Miller who feared this meant she was going to die soon or something awful would happen and begged her to stay. Reluctantly the woman consented and saw the star would have many men come into her life but most of them would die premature unusual deaths. This was her karma for being the Egyptian Queen Hatshepsut who had had many men killed in her lifetime. The karma would also inflict personal hardships upon Miller, though she would survive. What the seer saw about the men on her life came true. Bill O'Connor would have a heart attack, Charles Isaacs an incurable blood disease, her O.B. doctor complications from an operation on polyps in his nose, and her last husband, Arthur Cameron, a stroke. The star herself would also experience physical injuries and emotional turmoil.

In addition to the reading haunting her, the last days in Cairo saw Miller get a virus but she recovered. Before leaving the city the star met an archaeologist named Kamal who took her on a tour of the museums, tombs and pyramids, riding a camel at the Giza Pyramid. In a Cairo antique jewelry shop she spotted a beautiful bracelet and matching clips that had rose-cut diamonds, emeralds, rubies and Egyptian hieroglyphics. They were said to have once belonged to the royal family and were part of the Farouk collection. Miller didn't believe the claim but wanted them anyway, but she was not allowed to take the jewels out of the country. The jeweler was going to be in New York soon and later the star was able to have them. She would wear the jewels to a party in Hollywood that the exiled Egyptian Queen Mother Nazerlie attended. The woman recognized them as once as having belonged to her. Miller was sympathetic, but not enough to want to hand the jewels over, instead saying she would treasure them forever. Despite this, the star formed a great friendship with the Queen.

On August 24 she was photographed with a new poodle crop coiffure and a new black poodle named Robert, pronounced "Row-bear." In the week of October 28 Miller was photographed having dinner at Hollywood's Moulin Rouge with world-famous Metropolitan Opera Star Lauritz Melchior.

By the end of the year she was on another studio junket in the Caribbean, which involved a Hilton Hotel ground-breaking in Trinidad, then spent two weeks island hopping over Trinidad, Barbados, and Bermuda. Conrad Hilton had arranged a free pass to his entire hotel chain around the world and she flew back to New York on November 6. The star reported replacing her beloved tap shoes "Moe and Joe" with a pair called "Frick and Frack."

A South American junket saw her accompanied by Errol Flynn, his wife Patrice Wymore and their six weeks old baby, though Flynn was not an M-G-M contract player. Miller found Flynn to be a paradox—a flamboyant man who had old fashioned ideas, like insisting his wife breast-feed. Although he asked Wymore to join him for martinis at the cocktail hour as Flynn hated to drink alone, she disappeared to feed the baby which the star had never heard cry. She would reason this was because it was probably happily tranquilized on martini milk, an idea the man found to be hilarious. The same junket had her joined by Anita Ekberg and her husband Robert, a British actor. Unfortunately when he drank Robert was violent, something Miller became aware of in Rio de Janeiro. At 4 a.m. the badly bruised Ekberg came to the star's bungalow door and begged for sanctuary. She hid her in the closet until Robert pounded on the door, making Miller join her, and waited for him to retreat. This occurrence would be repeated until Ekberg thought it was safe to return to her bungalow where her husband was sleeping it off.

Ekberg said she could do something to repay the star. A jeweler had shown them some semi-precious stones said to be the biggest of their kind in the world—a 363 carat aquamarine and a 300-carat pink tourmaline as well as amethysts and topazes. She was told they were not for sale and to be presented to the President of Brazil who in turn would present them to President Eisenhower as gifts from Brazil. Miller wanted the aquamarine and had offered $800 to the jeweler as all the cash she had on hand, which was far less than its worth. Miller was heartbroken at the man's laughter but saw Ekberg wink at her.

That night Ekberg went to dinner with him, so when Robert came looking for her, the star could honestly say his wife was not in her room. The next day Ekberg appeared, saying she was leaving for Sweden to begin divorce proceedings, and handed Miller an envelope. Inside was a note that Ekberg had arranged for the star to have the aquamarine for the $800. She didn't know what her friend had done to swing the deal but Eisenhower never saw the stones. Miller had it made into a necklace which became one of her prized possessions, and though the Maharajah of Baroda would try to buy it for his wife, the star wouldn't sell.

She was not the only M-G-M contract player chosen to go on junkets but, if Miller heard about a new one coming up and she had no movie to make, the star would make her interest known. If she *was* making a movie, Miller would rehearse twice as long and work twice as hard to finish early and be available. On the junkets she would be the first one up and out sightseeing or looking at shops while other stars were asleep. Miller would go out alone when the others never left their hotel rooms except when they had to, spending hours in the beauty shop to prepare for the night ahead. With people in the street she was gracious and friendly, and ask *them* questions. The star would try to learn as much as she could in the short time there was, which made her very popular with the natives of whatever country as well as the local press corps whose photographers followed her everywhere. At this time Miller reportedly dated actors Dan Dailey and Philip Reed, producer Edmund Grainger, Charles Isaacs, Bill O'Connor, and Arthur Cameron.

Her next film was for Joe Pasternak: the Metrocolor musical comedy *The Opposite Sex* (1956), shot from 6 February to May 23, 1956, on location in New York and at the M-G-M Hollywood Studios. The screenplay was by Fay Kanin and Michael Kanin adapted from the play by Clare Boothe. It was a remake of the M-G-M comedy "*The Women*" (1939) that had also been remade as the February 7, 1955, episode of the dramatic musical and comedy television series *Producer's Showcase* that was broadcast on NBC. The film's director was David Miller. The story centered on former popular radio singer Kay (June Allyson), whose ten year marriage to New York theater producer Steve Hilliard (Leslie Nielson) is ended because of his marital indiscretion with Crystal Allen (Joan Collins), a gold-digging chorus girl in one of his shows.

Miller is billed fifth after title, playing the supporting role of Gloria who had been essayed by Paulette Goddard in the original film as Miriam Aarons. The new film makes Gloria a nightclub entertainer, though she only gets to sing a variation of the traditional folk song "The Yellow Rose of Texas" with Allyson and Agnes Moorehead who plays the Countess. Miller makes the character funny and uses a broad Texan accent when Gloria makes fun of the accent of Buck Winston (Jeff Richards), with her best scene the catfight with Sylvia (Dolores Gray). Helen Rose provides a becoming black low-cut suit with a matching white fur-lined throw, white hat and white gloves.

The film was released on October 26 with the taglines "Fast, frank, funny!," " M-G-M's fun-filled girlie show—with music!," " A screenful of fun!," "M-G-M presents the bare facts about ... the opposite sex," and "Listen in on the low-down on dames (with music!)" It was praised by *Variety* and Bosley Crowther in *The New York Times* but the film was not a box office success. It was remade as the West German made-for-TV movie *Women in New York* (1977), the made-for-TV movie *Stage on Screen: The Women* (2002), and *The Women* (2008).

Miller had reduced her weight for the role in the film, according to the September 20, 1958, edition of the *Saturday Evening Post Magazine*. An article titled "How do you measure up to the stars? Here's Hollywood's secret of weight control" by Jean Manning said the star had learned she had gained some pounds, though it was not enough for the camera to show. But David Miller agreed Miller should reduce as Vista-Vision played nasty tricks. Finding exercise not enough, she used a special low-calorie, vitamin-and-mineral enriched candy called Ayds, which worked as an appetite suppressant. A professional boxer was hired to demonstrate fast uppercuts and body blows to the star and Dolores Gray for the catfight, and the two remained good friends. She also befriended Ann Sheridan who plays Amanda. Another Texan, Miller described Sheridan as the most big-hearted girl she had ever met, and a real champion among women.

Her next film was for producer Henry Berman: the black and white sports comedy *The Great American Pastime* (1956), aka "Father's Little Leaguer" and "Little Leaguer," shot from late June to late July at the M-G-M Hollywood Studios. The screenplay was by Nathaniel Benchley and the director was Herman Hoffman. The story centered on Bruce Hallerton (Tom Ewell) a New York lawyer who becomes coach of a little league baseball team in Willow Falls on his summer vacation. Miller is billed third after the title, playing the supporting role of Doris Patterson, a former stage actress and the widowed mother of team member Herbie (Raymond Winston). This is another straight role for her and she makes Doris funny. The star looks smashing in a costume by the uncredited designer of dark pants with a sheer, dotted, light-colored, long-sleeved blouse, and the film is the first where we see her smoke. Miller's performance is naturalistic despite her playing someone who could be theatrical, and this continues when Doris performs in the play "Yellow Gold" with Bruce in her home. She is good in the dramatic scene, reacting to Bruce's romantic rejection by first laughing and then being angry at his assumption of her interest in him.

The film was released on November 28 with the taglines "Star of 'Seven Year Itch'—Tom Ewell is a RIOT," "The funny star of 7 YEAR ITCH's back to keep us all in STITCHES," and "It Ain't Pinochle!" It was praised by *Variety* but lambasted by John Douglas Eames in "The MGM Story." The film played as a second feature on release and it was not a box office success.

Miller was shocked to be asked to play a mother in the film, feeling that was an unsuitable role, but finally agreed and was glad. She got lots of fan mail and believed the role widened her career.

The star was the mystery guest on the October 7 episode of the black and white television family game-show *What's My Line?* filmed in New York and broadcast on CBS. Directed by Franklin Heller, she signs in right-handed and uses a Spanish accent to disguise her voice, with her identity not guessed by the panelists.

Miller reported producer Arthur Freed initially wanted her for the supporting part of Peggy Dayton in the musical comedy *Silk Stockings* (1957), which began production in November. This was the film version of the Broadway show that had run at the Imperial Theatre from February 24, 1955, to April 14, 1956, which itself was an adaptation of the M-G-M romantic comedy *Ninotchka* (1939). Gretchen Wyler had played Peggy in the show. Miller was told she was going to do it, and then Freed changed his mind, because both Miller and Cyd Charisse playing the leading role were brunettes. Janis Paige was cast instead and wore a red/lighter shade of brown hair color. She was a very good friend of Ann, who said the loss broke her heart. She so wanted to work with Charisse again, but felt Paige was wonderful in it. Miller was so hurt by the slight that she asked for a release from her contract, which was denied. The star said the situation had to do with the king's court where one pet would be in for a moment and then out and a new pet was in favor.

She flew to the Nouasseur Air Base in Morocco in July 1957 to appear with Bob Hope on the Timex TV Hour, which was broadcast on NBC on October 6 as the family comedy television series *The Bob Hope Show*. Miller entertained 5,000 troops in 120 degree weather as she sang "Too Darn Hot" and also appeared with Hope and Eddie Fisher in a sketch about a sheik. The star appeared as a guest on the October 16 episode of the music television series *The Big Record* which was broadcast on CBS. Louis B Mayer died on October 20. She saw irony in how her so-called reign at M-G-M started after the courtship with Mayer was over, and her time was coming to an end soon after his death. Those years were the happiest of her life because Miller's career was in full bloom but now the studio was no longer making as many musicals. Dore Schary, as brilliant as he may have been in his own right, was not as interested in them. She predicted her leaving M-G-M, observing the feeling of gloom around her, with Schary himself fired that year after the three films he personally produced all lost money.

On November 9 the star was photographed dancing with sportsman and manufacturer Jim Kimberly at an after-dinner party at the Beverly Hills Hotel.

She was a guest on the December 29 episode of the music television series *The Dinah Shore Chevy Show* which was broadcast on NBC. It was directed by Bob Banner and the musical numbers were staged by Tony Charmoli. Miller sings and dances in three numbers: "Baby, It's

Cold Outside" with Shore and fellow guest Fred MacMurray, which is reprised for the show's finale, the solo "I'm Gonna Live 'Til I Die," and the "Muskrat Ramble" duet with Shore. Despite director Banner's use of some medium shots, her best number is "I'm Gonna Live 'Til I Die" where the star dances to the bongo of Jack Constanzo. She wears a Robert Carlton sparkly low-cut floor-length dress with split skirt revealed under a gray-colored coat, and the dance sees her also beat a drum and tap on a table.

In 1957 Miller was photographed with Maurice Chevalier at a performance of the Ice Follies in Hollywood.

She appeared in the documentary short *Screen Snapshots: Salute to Hollywood* which was shot at the Columbia Hollywood Studios and released on March 29, 1958. It was written and directed by Ralph Staub and had him attending a big awards show and party by *The Saturday Evening Post* magazine.

The star asked for a release from her M-G-M contract and it was granted in 1958. Although this is what she wanted, Miller cried because it was leaving another studio family. Her love affair with Hollywood was like a bumpy marriage. It had ups and downs but Miller still hung in there, not to be found on a street corner with a dancing bear and a tin cup. She was proud to have never played politics or slept with producers, and was never on call to entertain the bankers from New York. The star had kept her legs crossed when not dancing and so she ended up neither a Big Star nor a little one, but a happy medium. Except for the *George White Scandals* the career had been in films and principally as a dancer, since no one thought of her seriously as a singer or actress. Being a dancer was a handicap now that the era of movie musicals was over and it seemed Miller had few options left.

CHAPTER 6

· · · · · · · · · · · · · · ·

A New Marriage

*T*he timing of Miller's leaving M-G-M seemed perfect since now Bill O'Connor finally gave her an engagement ring, a beautiful star sapphire in a gold basket weave setting of 20 large diamonds. The man thought he had found a way to have his Catholic marriage annulled and went to Rome, but his wife refused to sign the necessary papers. So when O'Connor returned to California the star gave him back the ring knowing they would never marry.

Then Bill Moss came into her life, the Texan former husband of Jane Withers who looked like Reese Milner. He was reddish-blond, blue-eyed, tall, handsome and virile. He smoked cigars, had an eye for women and loved expensive clothes. Also like Milner he wanted her to give up her career. His pet name for Miller was Twinkle Toes or Twink for short and she had it embroidered on shortie night gowns to wear for him. The engagement was announced on August 12, 1958. Jane Withers warned her that the marriage would not be a happy one, but her friend didn't believe it. It happened on August 22 at the Union Congregational church by the sea in La Jolla, California. The star's bridesmaids were Linda Darnell, Margaret Pereira whose husband Bill gave the bride away, Cobina Wright, and Betty Bloomingdale. Moss' best man was the Texas oilman Gordon Guiberson, and one of his ushers was Arthur Cameron. The wedding's guests read like a Who's Who of Hollywood and Texas oil millionaires, among them Conrad and Nicky Hilton, Ginger Rogers, and June Haver and Fred MacMurray, and the reception was to be held at the home of the Guibersons. When Ve Guiberson was helping the star into her wedding gown—a Ceil Champman sheath of champagne lace over satin—the telephone rang. It was Bill O'Connor begging her not to proceed, saying he would leave the Catholic Church and marry her. She had been waiting 12 years to hear this but it was now too late so Miller hung up the phone. The call made her heartsick because the star knew she really belonged to O'Connor. As Miller walked down the aisle holding a bouquet of lilies, then took her wedding vows all she could hear was the phone ringing and ringing, like an omen. The Moss' walked out of the church to the sound of the song "Around the World in Eighty Days" chosen by the groom, and as they were showered with rice and confetti, she could still hear the telephone ringing.

The star said the marriage might have worked had it not been for Bill O'Connor, Arthur Cameron, a Dallas heiress, too many drinking parties, and a few other hindrances. Although she had been born in Texas and lived there as a child, Miller had never been initiated into the wild and woolly world of Texan oil men until she married Moss. The star adored him but the union was stormy, though never as violent as her previous one. The fights were sometimes her fault as the star simply couldn't keep up with the pace of her husband and his friends. Hollywood wild parties were tame compared to the binges that lasted for days.

She didn't know Texas oil men travelled so much. They had a house on Summit Ridge Drive in Beverly Hills and an apartment in Dallas and were constantly commuting between the two. As the wife of an oil man Miller was expected to entertain lavishly and she did so but the star simply didn't have the energy or patience for the parties, despite her love of parties and Texans. The bashes usually began at a friend's house, where the drinks flowed like water and everyone whooped it up, and they would wind up two or three days later at a nightclub in Dallas. She would ask to go home especially when Moss was drinking too much, which is when the trouble started, though in between their battles they had some marvelous times.

Miller was a guest on the November 8, 1958, episode of the black and white music television series *The Perry Como Show*, shot at the Vitagraph Studios in New York and broadcast on NBC. It featured her singing and dancing "The Great Lady Interview (Madame Crematante)" surround by a troupe of male dancers, the number that had been originated by Judy Garland in the M-G-M musical comedy *The Ziegfeld Follies* (1945). It had been devised for Greer Garson to play a movie star who does Oscar-winning dramas but who really wants to play sexy and do her acting with her torso. Miller doing this number doesn't make sense since she is already known for her torso. The star waves a large feathered fan in a doorway, shows a leg, and then emerges wearing a sparkly low-cut dark-colored floor-length dress with a split skirt and jewel on the left hip, using rhinestone comic eyeglasses and a feather boa as props. She was also a guest on the November 17 episode of the family music television series *The Arthur Murray Party* which was broadcast on ABC. On November 24 Miller was photographed with Conrad Hilton at the Hollywood premiere of the Icecapades.

She and Moss travelled all over the world together and were invited to the opening of the Cairo Hilton Hotel in March 1959. The star discovered that none of the electrical outlets worked for American equipment and she was unable to dry her hair after washing it to prepare for the opening night ball. Her friend Zsa Zsa Gabor was staying in the suite next door, and having the same problem, they decided to use the hot weather to their advantage. The women went out onto the balcony and swung their wet locks over the Nile River to get it to dry. Miller met President Gamal Abdel Nasser whose edict that all belly dancers wear mesh netting between their bras and their skirts to cover the belly buttons she found ridiculous, as the dance could not be done right with the body wrapped up in this way.

Moss arranged for them to sail up the Nile in a private boat which had once belonged to King Farouk to visit the Valley of the Kings, but his wife became ill and had to be flown out of Cairo before they could make the trip. In Athens they were scheduled for another hotel ground-breaking, but Ann was put to bed with a high fever. The star was seen by the doctor of King Paul I but insisted on getting out of bed to see the Acropolis, though she practically had to be carried. Her temperature shot up to 103 and Miller was flown out on a special plane to the American Hospital in Paris with a severe case of pneumonia. She almost died but when the star had recovered enough to be moved again she was taken to St. Moritz in Switzerland where Miller was bedded down in the Palace Hotel for five weeks before returning home.

She was a guest on the August 1 episode of the music television series *The Juke Box Jury* which was shot in Hollywood and broadcast on CBS.

The Moss's made it through the first year of their marriage, which was better batting than the star had with her first one, and they returned to La Jolla to stay at the El Charro Inn. Suddenly one night she awakened with a psychic flash that something terrible had happened to Bill O'Connor. Their psychic rapport told her that he was going to die and the star woke up her husband and said they had to go to him. Moss was furious but when she began weeping and wailing and begging he agreed, perhaps knowing that his wife was still in love with this man. On the radio they heard O'Connor had died of a heart attack on August 27 before the pair could arrive. Miller visited her neighbor Cobina Wright, sobbing in her friend's arms over the loss of her beloved. Wright warned her not to let her husband know how deeply O'Connor's death hurt her or she would lose him too. He agreed to take her to the funeral but he didn't want to see his wife crying any more. First she went to the funeral home to see O'Connor. The star had never seen a loved one deceased before and she thought he looked peaceful. Miller remembered his always combing a wisp of black hair that tumbled down on his right eye back into place and she took a comb out of her purse and stuck it in his pocket. Now in Heaven he would have it to fix his hair. She didn't cry then or at the funeral, probably because of the half a bottle of Miltowns she had taken to get through it.

On November 15 Miller was photographed attending the circus and going for gobs of cotton candy. On February 8, 1960, she was given a star on the Hollywood Walk of Fame on Hollywood Boulevard for her contribution to the motion picture industry.

Every Easter Bill O'Connor had sent her two dozen red roses and the couple had gone to Palm Springs for the weekend at the home of Nat and Valerie Dumont. This Easter Valerie again invited Miller, who bought a lily plant at a florist on the way to give to the Dumonts. On Easter morning they reminisced about O'Connor, and she noticed that nestled between the green leaves of the lily plant was a single red rose, which was not there when she bought it. The star believed the rose was a message from her great love, saying they were together in spirit in another dimension.

Her solo trip to Palm Springs began a period where her husband went off on *his* own. He would sometimes call her but she was mostly alone and soon the couple decided upon a temporary separation. Miller accompanied Ve Guiberson, who had her own marriage woes, on a trip to Hawaii. They stayed at the Royal Hawaiian Hotel in a huge suite with all the luxuries, but instead of having fun, the pair was sad and miserable over missing their spouses. One night Miller's psychic antennae sent her a vision of Moss with a beautiful blonde in a red dress at a nightclub in Dallas. The star told Ve and wanted to call the club, which her friend thought was a bad idea. However she made the call and found her husband, asking who the blonde was. He was silent for a moment then asked if Miller had had him followed, admitting to being with the Dallas heiress in the red dress. But she had something better than a detective and hung up on him. Strangely the star now did not care about the affairs of her husband, who stayed in Texas and said he wouldn't be back.

She returned to television's "Toast of the Town" aka "The Ed Sullivan Show" for the June 19 episode shot in New York and broadcast on CBS. The show was directed by John Moffitt and Robert Bleyer. Miller reprised a performance of "I've Gotta Hear that Beat" from *Small Town Girl*.

The star was now pursued by another man, her husband's usher, Arthur Cameron, who heard about the trouble in her marriage. She had known him for 20 years and considered him an old family friend, as he was a friend of Bill Moss, Reese Milner, and Bill O'Connor. But unlike her husbands, the man had a wonderful sense of humor. He was another millionaire, with real estate holdings and oil wells, and lived at the house that Louis B. Mayer once owned in Benedict Canyon. Cameron had two Cadillacs painted "Cameron-white," and owned a six-acre walled-in paradise estate in Palm Springs. He was older, 60 to her 37, though he looked and acted much younger. Cameron was handsome like Cary Grant, though to Miller he most resembled O'Connor, which was probably not a good sign. She described him as the most colorful and flamboyant off all her men, the comic opera of her life. He had an irresistible charm and was like a big black panther, able to mesmerize a woman merely by staring with his dark eyes before pouncing.

The star was surprised when one day Cameron came to the house and told Clara and herself that they should marry because he had always been in love with her. The man felt she had made two mistakes and he had made five in marriage, all failing because of the philandering that no longer interested him. Cameron had recently gone to court for an interlocutory decree from his latest wife, Jean Lawrence, and Miller had planned on divorcing Moss but Cameron proposed before she had even gone to court for her decree. This meant that neither of them was free to marry at the time, both having to wait a year for their divorces to become final in California. The couple began dating but were constantly trailed by detectives hired by Moss, and when they found out, Cameron hired his own men to trail the detectives. The star called this the Max Sennett comedy days and when she had to leave the house Miller would look to see that the gang was ready to go with her.

Cameron invited her and Clara to Mexico City, and when they went sightseeing he proposed every 10 minutes and told anyone who would listen that they were going to marry. Moss tracked them to the Tecali Hotel, where Cameron and the Millers had separate suites, and appeared at dinner. The two men tangled and the star retreated to her room, but the fight was quickly over when the men realized it was silly and then ended up drinking together to talk it out. An agreement was reached and Miller now agreed to marry Cameron when it was possible. He said they didn't have to wait because the divorces could be finalized in Mexico. She wasn't sure about the idea but assumed that Cameron's money meant he could manage anything.

One day Arthur Crowley, a friend of his, came to see her, begging the star not to marry him here because it would not be legal in the United States. They would have to do it again in California after the year was up, but that was fine with her. But Crowley's real zinger was that he didn't think Cameron would marry her again in California because he was notoriously unpredictable and got bored fast with women. If Miller wanted to marry him she should wait to see if the man was still interested after their American divorce decrees were final. The star promised to take Crowley's advice.

She filed for divorce on Valentine's Day, 1961, on the grounds of extreme cruelty. On May 11 at the Santa Monica Supreme Court, Miller testified that he had frequently struck her and once broke her hand. On May 12 she got the interlocutory decree and received a settlement of the Summit Ridge house, a car and $30,000 cash over a period of three years, though another source states the star received $43,000. Miller said she planned to resume her career. The star also said there would always be a soft spot in her heart for Moss, who saw her through the grand finale of the one great love of her life. The couple would socialize after their divorce, getting got along better as friends than man and wife.

She agreed to marry Cameron in Mexico but when her friend Cobina Wright heard about it she begged Miller not to. The star knew Wright had had a crush on the man for years and just assumed she was jealous. Miller and Cameron flew to Mexico City with Valerie and Nat Dumont as their matron of honor and best man. Former President of Mexico Miguel Aleman helped arrange the Mexican divorces and sent the star a bouquet of flowers and a letter for her wedding day, wishing Miller much happiness. They married on May 25 in their suite in the Tecali Hotel, with the service performed by a Mexican justice of the peace, and a dinner following at the Villa Fontana where the groom had gypsy violins and Mexican music played. The star said he was a haven in a storm of unhappiness and she admitted to being in love, a bird-brained state where her heart ruled her head and Miller never listened to anyone else's advice.

If she was angry at Cobina Wright it was forgiven as the star had her and Clara join the married couple on the first lap of their honeymoon tour of Europe. The first stop was the Niehans La Prairie Clinic in Lausanne, Switzerland, where the women were eager to take the rejuvenation shots of Dr. Niehans that were supposed to prolong your life and restore the fountain of youth. Called cellular therapy, or CT, it was an injection of liquefied animal glands, with men getting those from bulls and women from lambs. Many of the famous had been injected, such as Hedda Hopper, Pope Pius XII, and Somerset Maugham.

Cameron saw the five inch needle and declined, suggesting his wife be the guinea pig. If it didn't hurt her then he would take one. She thought her husband was joking but he was not, and even after Niehans said Miller was too young and active to need the shot, she agreed to take it. This was because the star felt it was important that Cameron have treatment after having suffered a mild stroke a few years earlier. She wasn't afraid of needles and after taking three of them, her husband submitted to the ordeal. Clara and Cobina Wright also took the shots and they seemed to help, though Cameron refused to comply with the rules of no liquor or sex for two months during the treatment. Two days after his shots he was chasing the chambermaids, and his wife.

One night in bed half-asleep, Miller had a vision of Bill O'Connor, sitting in a chair and laughing. She woke up her husband for him to also see the man. When Cameron asked what he wanted, the vision faded away, and after then the man stopped sneaking in bourbon for the rest of the stay at the clinic. Clara and Wright went back to California and the Camerons moved to the Beau Rivage Hotel in Lausanne. She developed a belated allergic reaction to her shots with a fever and had to stay in bed, so he decided to comfort her with a diamond ring. Cameron had Harry Winston of New York send a missionary but he was unhappy with the selection.

The weakened star had overheard the conversation and crawled downstairs on her hands and knees to see the diamonds, telling her husband she would be happy with any of them. But he wanted a virgin stone cut especially for her long tapering finger which Winston supplied—a 20-carat blue-white diamond with a tiny flaw that cost $125,000 and would have been worth $650,000 if it was perfect. Miller called the stone her Arthur Cameron diamond and kept it in her jewelry bank vault to wear only on special occasions, costing $15,000 a year in insurance. He said the ring was the star's security against the future, to be sold only if she became desperate.

After Miller's fever lifted, the couple went on to Paris to see friends, the couture collections, and the famed Lido. Then it was on to Rome to stay at the Grand Hotel, where they had an argument. At the Villa Camilluccia were two Moscatelli chandeliers that so took Cameron's eye that he wanted to get some from Milan where they were made for the Benedict Canyon home. He had Texas bourbon at dinner, which angered his wife, since Cameron was not supposed to drink liquor so soon after the Niehans shots. Smashed and annoyed about the star's nagging, he raced ahead of her on the way back to their suite and locked Miller out. She had a bellboy open the door and went to bed in her separate rooms, but the star had a plan for revenge. In the morning she took a cab to Balestra, Rome's top fashion designer, and charged $10,000 worth of clothes to her husband. Back at the hotel Miller presented with the bill and at first he was furious. But then he laughed, admitting to being a bad boy and paid for the clothes. They would fill one huge closet and she labeled them her Arthur Cameron dynasty.

The Camerons returned to Paris where she got a special hairdo from Alexandre. The dresser named it Romance of the Seventeenth Century, and the styling took an entire day. It was upswept and it wrapped a bunch of little braids wound with ribbons in the shape of a heart, with spit curls. Everyone else in the salon applauded when it was done and a photographer took photos, but when her husband appeared, he laughed. It was the funniest damn hairdo Cameron had ever seen, and though the $150 bill for it was less amusing, he also gave a generous tip. The star thought her husband would find the hairdo less ludicrous with the proper dress and jewelry, and had Alexandre put lots of spray on because she wasn't going to take it down for a week.

The "Romance of the Seventeenth Century" became, however, a sticky mess. They travelled to Venice and stayed at the Bauer-Grunwald Hotel but, when it came to undo the hairdo, the beauty salon operators could not get a comb or brush through it. They would have to cut the heart off which made Miller cry. Before it was set she was like a French poodle in drag but afterwards it wasn't so bad, and though the experience was awful, the story became of the star's favorites.

She noticed how kind her husband was to her in Venice, affectionately calling Miller his little duck and having a little glass duck blown for the star at a factory in Murano. In Milan he purchased two Moscatelli chandeliers for $5,000 each, and Cameron liked them at home so much he had two more shipped from Italy. (The little glass duck and the chandeliers had a sad ending, when after the man died, they were sold at auction.)

When the couple returned to California they divided their time between Benedict Canyon and Palm Springs, though she still had the Summit Ridge Drive house which the star sometimes used when he was away on business. Cameron wanted the Benedict Canyon property redecorated, perhaps because his wife believed it was haunted by the ghosts of Louis B. Mayer, William Randolph Hearst and Marion Davies. She refurnished the bedroom and had her closet filled with $10,000 worth of lingerie from Saks Fifth Avenue, but then her husband hated nightgowns so she could not wear them. However he did like to see the star in only a negligee and a ribbon in her hair for breakfast. Cameron had all the seats ripped out of Mayer's beloved projection room and converted into a storeroom for the antiques he was constantly collecting and a business office. The man conducted most of his oil and real estate business from home, though he also had a suite in the Kirkeby Building on Wilshire Boulevard with four secretaries who were never busy. Together the Camerons entertained frequently and she found him to be charming and gracious, thoroughly enjoying living like a king and treating her like his queen. But things began to change when it seemed the warning that Arthur Crowley had given Miller was becoming true, that her husband was bored.

He spent more and more time away, claiming to be golfing or just going for a walk for hours. She was suspicious the man was seeing other women, and the telephone calls the star listened in on confirmed it. She issued an ultimatum that either they go or she would and, to her horror, he told his wife to pack her bags. She moved back to the Summit Ridge house and two days later got a call from her mother that all the star's belongings had been left at Clara's Alta Drive Beverly Hills house that her daughter had purchased for her. Miller said she was ready for a nervous breakdown but then, inexplicably, the star went back to Cameron. He was irrepressible and irresistible and she believed that love sprang eternal. But the feeling didn't last long. One day the man sent word via a maid that he wanted his wife down at the pool. There she found a party going on, and for a moment thought it was in her honor. Cameron sat like a potentate watching 17 bikini-clad beauties in the pool who were strangers to Miller. He said they were her little sisters, but she didn't have to worry as the star was the one the man had married. Not wanting to be the queen of a harem she stalked out of the house and never went back.

The star wanted a divorce but would have to go to Mexico to file for it. The divorce from Bill Moss would not be final for nearly two months and Miller feared that she could be arrested in California as a bigamist. The star telephoned Cameron's secretaries repeatedly but her messages went unanswered. She went to the Benedict Canyon house, to be told the man was not there. Miller even telephoned hotels in Mexico where he wasn't registered. Finally she received a telegram from Arthur Crowley, saying he could not reveal where her husband was and that Cameron denied marrying her, despite the witnesses. The star consulted the lawyer Jacques Leslie, who said she would have to file suit against Cameron claiming he had led her into a fraudulent marriage.

The story hit the press, with the *Los Angeles Times* of April 5, 1962, headlining "Actress Ann Miller Sues LA Oilman for $7 Million." She was claiming damage to her career, loss of valuable marital rights, pain and mental suffering and mortification, and punitive damages. In a separate maintenance suit the star asked for $10,000 monthly expenses plus lawyer fees and court costs. She was stunned by the article as Miller didn't want Cameron or his money—all she did want was for him to acknowledge their marriage. Cameron called her from Mexico to say she wasn't going to get away with it but hung up on her before she could respond. Miller learned he hired detectives to have his wife followed the day the suit was filed.

On May 3 Miller appeared at the Santa Monica courthouse, expecting her husband to appear, with a news article reporting she was asking for $10 million in temporary alimony. This was the first of several meetings held by the couple with their lawyers, where strangely but perhaps not surprisingly the Camerons became on friendly terms again. The star even brought a snack of bananas and cookies for him, knowing the man was not accustomed to being up at 9 a.m. Their amicability had the lawyers suggest a reconciliation, as did Judge Edward R. Brand. But even though Valerie and Nat Dumont testified that they had attended the wedding, the fact that Cameron had apparently made the official documentation disappear bothered Miller. She refused to reconcile and would only drop the suit if the marriage was acknowledged by her husband, which he finally did when the man agreed to an annulment. He let her keep the ring and gave Clara $50,000. When the couple went back into the Judge's chambers Cameron is said to have swooped up the star, turned her over his knee and gave Miller a spanking, with the Judge looking on.

The *Los Angeles Herald-Examiner* of May 10 had the star say she was glad it was all over and that the former married couple were still the best of friends. All Miller had wanted was to clear her good name, though she admitted to asking for $7 million and $10,000 a month temporary support and alimony when he had got her Irish up. The star was still in love with the man whom she found kind and generous. On May 13 Miller was photographed with Valerie Dumont at the courthouse, and she and Cameron walked out arm in arm, going to dinner together that night. Their friendship was sustained until the day he died, and the man did many nice things for the star and her mother, like paying the hospital bills and a stay at the Beverly Hill Hotel when she broke her leg. Cameron gave his ex-wife a $50,000 diamond necklace, a floor-length white mink coat and a sable stole, which like the 20-carat diamond ring, he felt were part of the nest egg.

She put her Summit Ridge furnished house up for sale for $80,000 but accepted $65,000 needing the money. The real estate agent reported that the seller didn't want their name revealed and Miller learned later that it was Cameron, who wanted it for one of his other women. This burned up the star, who said if she had known of his interest, the price would have been tripled. Nonetheless this did not end the friendship. They often went to the Monseigneur Room at the Beverly Hilton to dance, and to the Bistro, which was the place of their last date. Miller knew the man was not well as it had become more difficult for him to walk without being dizzy. On their last night Cameron asked her to take him to Acapulco to recover, with a nurse and doctor, and she agreed, but he would die before they could make the trip. She was sad that the man had to die alone in his Benedict Canyon house, and the star had hoped that they would eventually get together again if she had been able to get him well. But it wasn't to be.

Now with her marriage annulled and the divorce from Bill Moss finalized Miller was a free woman. She blew the Cameron settlement on art objects at auctions, though "Auction Annie" as the star was known in the trade, was actually glad because that money made her feel cheap. She moved in with her mother on Alta Drive and did some self-reflection. Miller couldn't keep marrying the wrong men, and wondered why her psychic powers couldn't help her find the right one. She had had madcap adventures that ended in sadness and divorce and the star could no longer afford the same loss of time, tears and energy. So she decided to stop dating and concentrate on the one and only thing in her life that Miller seemed to handle well—her career.

The Golden Years of movies were over, so a return was out, even for one to be made in Lebanon where she was expected to appear with her nude body covered in gold paint. The new Hollywood was pornographic, like watching someone go to the bathroom, and Louis B Mayer would have turned over in his grave. The star didn't want to try to hang on where she was no longer wanted, like an extra or bit player in their later years, and she well knew The Looks. When you were on top, it was one of admiration and awe, but there was the other look for those who had slipped from the top or who weren't working. Miller had never gotten that look when she was at M-G-M or when married to Bill Moss or Arthur Cameron because everyone knew they were rich and money bred respect in the jungle. But after her marriage to Cameron had been annulled, people the star had known at M-G-M might now smile and shake hands and then look away or look through her or at her with that expression of polite dullness in their eyes that hurt. There were exceptions since she had made some real friends in the business, like the Nat Dumonts, the Bill Pereiras, the Art Linkletters, the John Tylers, and Kathryn Grayson, all of whom helped each other through some of their bad mutual bad marriages. These Miller called her funeral friends because if they outlived her they would give a good, old-fashioned Irish wake, as she wanted everybody to be happy at her funeral. But the star wasn't ready to die yet and though she had retired to pasture three times in marriage, Miller always jumped the corral and went back to the welcome clamor of show biz. Her dilemma was to find where she could still fit in, something that would be resolved in a totally unexpected way.

CHAPTER 7
· · · · · · · · · · · · · · · · ·
New Management

*O*ut of the blue Miller received a telephone call from the producers of the prestigious live family comedy and music television series *The Hollywood Palace* asking her to make a guest appearance. She chose the song "It Had Better Be Tonight," which Nick Castle staged as a Latin number with a tropical background. Louis De Pron helped her on the tap steps and Bob Mackie designed the costume. The star would sing in English and Spanish and dance on big drums while Jack Costanza played the bongos on stage with her, with Miller rehearsing for two months. The show was filmed at the Hollywood Palace Theater in Los Angeles and broadcast in black and white on December 12, 1964, on ABC. The show was directed by Grey Lockwood. She is first seen as legs and the camera tilts up to show her dressed in a dark-colored, low-cut, sparkly leotard with spaghetti straps, a tail feather, long dark-colored gloves and a flower in her hair. Lockwood uses some medium shots but mostly covers the dance in long shots.

The response to the Miller's appearance was so sensational that the producers invited her back three more times. She enjoyed doing the show because they knew how to treat a star correctly and knew how to film a dancer.

She made two appearances on the television music talk show *That Regis Philbin Show* that was shot in Los Angeles, on February 4 and March 4, 1965. On one of the shows a psychic predicted Miler would meet a man in whom she would become seriously interested.

For the star's second appearance on *The Hollywood Palace* broadcast on May 22 she sang and danced "Won't You Come Home Bill Bailey" with chorus boys and featured dancer Dante de Paulo, a number again staged by Nick Castle. She wore a sparkly dark-colored fringed leotard with a feather boa, long dark-colored gloves, and a large sparkly necklace. The number has her standing and dancing on tables and the show was directed by Grey Lockwood.

Miller was a guest on the October 6 episode of the television comedy talk show *Late Night with Johnny Carson* aka *The Tonight Show* that was shot at the NBC Studios in Hollywood and broadcast on NBC. On October 15 she threw a party for Maurice Chevalier to celebrate his 66th anniversary in show business at the Beverly Hilton Hotel. It had a menu of all French foods and vintage wines, and a huge cake in the shape of the singer's signature straw hat. He paid tribute to the star, saying she had legs just like Mistinguett, his French dancing partner and the great romance of his life who had died in 1956. The same month Miller attended a screening of the M-G-M drama *The Sandpiper* (1965) in Hollywood.

In 1965 she replaced her tap shoes "Frick and Frack" with a new pair she named "Tip and Tap" and they never left her side when she travelled or went to the rehearsal studio.

The star was a guest on the March 13, 1966, episode of the color music television series *The Bell Telephone Hour* entitled "Music of the Movies" on NBC. The show was directed by Dave Geisel with Miller billed third after the title. She sang and danced in five numbers: "Latin from Manhattan," "Saturday Night (is the Loneliest Night of the Week)" with Gloria de Haven and Constance Towers, "Puttin on the Ritz" with Ray Bolger, where she appeared in drag in top hat and tails, as part of the chorus of "The Stanley Steamer," and in the finale medley of Oscar winning songs. Although the duet with Bolger is spectacular, her best solo showcase is "Latin from Manhattan" with the star dressed in a red sequin fringed leotard with long-sleeves, a feathered floor-length removable back skirt, and a red flower in her hair.

For the third appearance on *The Hollywood Palace* on the April 2 episode now in color she sang and danced "Slap That Bass," a number Fred Astaire had done in the RKO musical comedy *Shall We Dance* (1937). Louis De Pron staged it with two male dancers and three upright bass players, and again the show's director was Grey Lockwood. Miller is first seen with her back to the camera in a sparkly black suit, removing the jacket to reveal a sparkly blue fringed leotard. After the performance the host says to a soldier in the audience, "Will you look at her face once in a while!" which makes the star put her hand to her face in embarrassment.

She was a guest on the January 19, 1967, episode of the television talk show *Girl Talk* broadcast on ABC.

Miller developed a blood clot in the right leg that became swollen and painful and her doctor sent her to the hospital for three weeks. She was told not to dance until the vein had healed and to wear a tight rubber stocking on the leg to avoid permanent injury, but when *The Hollywood*

Palace called again the star accepted. The star had Bob Mackie make a strapless beaded leotard with a big red heart-shaped spot in the middle, rubber tights embroidered with sequins and beads to conceal the rubber, and long black gloves. The wild design reflected Miller's character of a black widow spider for the song "Trapped in the Web of Love." Louis De Pron staged the number which had her begin in a pink Little Miss Muffett costume, with four boy dancers dressed in long-tailed suits as big black spiders hanging on a web of rhinestones who rip off the Muffett disguise. They come down from the web to dance with the star, who ends up being lifted to the ceiling in the chair of the web's white spider. The show was broadcast on March 11.

Her leg eventually healed though of course she caught hell from her doctor who called her afterwards to say what a terrible risk she had taken.

She was a guest on the May 4 episode of the family daytime variety television series *House Party* which was broadcast on CBS. The star made her first guest appearance on the June 29 episode of the comedy and music talk show *The Mike Douglas Show*, which was shot in Cleveland, Ohio, and broadcast on the Westinghouse Broadcast Company.

She was asked to take over Gwen Verdon's part in *Sweet Charity* on Broadway when Verdon was to leave on June 30, but refused. Miller felt it had been tailored for Verdon and she couldn't do a carbon copy, which is what the producers wanted. Some day the star hoped to play it in summer stock, her way, but that would never happen. Sonja Henie attended Ann's annual Christmas Eve party. In 1967, though the date is unknown, Miller was a guest on the country music television series *The John Gary Show*.

She returned to *The Mike Douglas Show* to co-host from January 22 to 25, 1968. On January 24 the star and Douglas danced together and did a medley of songs from *Kiss Me Kate* including her singing "Too Darn Hot," "Why Can't You Behave?" and "Always True to You in My Fashion" solo. For this appearance she wore a green and black patterned sleeveless layered knee-length dress. Miller also did a go-go dance at the end of the performance of the Lemon Pipers, wearing a shimmery silver knee-length dress and matching high boots. She was a guest on the television talk show *The Woody Woodbury Show*, which was shot in Hollywood (with one source giving the date as January 28 and another as June 4).

On February 20 the star attended the Hollywood premiere of the British film musical *Half a Sixpence* (1967). She was a panelist on the family comedy game-show *The Hollywood Squares* from March 4 to 8, shot at the NBC Studios in Hollywood and broadcast on NBC. It was directed by Jerome Shaw. Miller was a guest on the March 8 episode of the musical comedy television series *The Pat Boone Show*, shot at the NBC Studios in Hollywood and broadcast on NBC.

She was back on *The Hollywood Squares* for the episodes broadcast from July 1 to 5, and then was on the August 20 episode of the television talk show *The Joey Bishop Show* which was shot at the Vine Street Theater in Hollywood and broadcast on ABC. She was a guest on the September 15 episode of the comedy television series *George Jessel's Here Come the Stars*. The show was directed by Dick Ross.

Miller was a guest on the October 2 episode of the television comedy series *The Jonathan Winters Show* which was shot at CBS Television City in Hollywood and broadcast on CBS. In October she also played a straight supporting role in Chicago in a comic play called *Glad Tidings* written by Edward Mabley and produced at the Pheasant Run Theatre. It had originally run on Broadway from October 11, 1951, to January 5, 1952. The star presumably played Maude Abbott, originated by Signe Hasso, and despite the city's reputation for rip-'em-up critics the reviews were good. But Miller was robbed of furs, clothes and jewels one night during the stay. She sued the hotel for compensation but even winning couldn't salvage the Chicago experience for her.

Friends asked the star to Sun Valley for a skiing weekend. She was not a skier, fearing a leg injury, but enjoyed the après-ski parties, clothes and especially the good-looking ski instructors. The party got snowed in for 10 days but were rescued.

In 1968 though the date is unknown Miller was a guest on an unsold pilot for the television game show *Talking Pictures* that was shot at CBS Television City in Hollywood and broadcast on CBS. She was one of 10 famous people where contestants had to remember what numbered picture frame the stars were seated behind and what they revealed about themselves. In the first round she said that her father worked for Bonnie and Clyde, and in the second that the one thing Miller would change about herself was to get rid of her Irish temper. The show was directed by Joe Behar.

The star now decided to take singing and drama lessons in the hope of getting a book musical on stage. The singing teacher was Harriet Lee and the drama coach Bill Tregoe. She also hired a new agent, Don Wortman, who got her a stock engagement of the Cole Porter musical *Can-Can* in Houston, her home town. The show was reportedly produced in early 1969 and ran for two weeks, incorporating a tap number so Miller could do what she did best. It was a great success and made her love live theater again.

Her old friend Red Skelton offered $10,000 to appear on his

comedy television series for CBS, but another offer was more intriguing. New York producer John Bowab wanted to sign the star for a Palm Beach, Florida, run of the Broadway smash hit *Mame* which he was directing. She had auditioned when it was to be done in Las Vegas in December but lost out to red-haired Susan Hayward (Miller claimed that the producers were only thinking blondes). The show's appeal had diminished so that it was now on two-fers, meaning two tickets for the price of one, but Bowab thought she could bring new life to it. He had seen her in *Can-Can*, but there was skepticism about her casting as others still believed the star couldn't hack playing Mame and that she had been dubbed in her movies. Miller herself was hesitant about following Angela Lansbury who had originated the role and won the Tony Award for it, even if it is was to be in Florida. Also, though she had played a comedic role on stage in *Glad Tidings*, this was something that required real acting talent, apart from an ability to sing and dance. The star could not afford to get bad reviews in this new phase of her career. The Red Skelton show was perhaps the safer bet, where she would only need to dance, but she chose instead the challenge of *Mame*. Miller asked that a tap number be written in and Bowab agreed, bringing in New York choreographer Diana Baffa.

The show was at the Palm Beach Playhouse, notorious for attracting the bored, rich, top-hat society crowd who went just to be seen, get their names in the society columns, and left the shows at intermission. But this time they stayed to the very end, and gave a standing ovation. The show was a sell-out smash, with the *Miami Beach Reporter* flabbergasted by the star's performance, showing talents they never knew she had. Composer Jerry Herman and producer Bobby Fryer flew out to see her and approved a Broadway transfer, after seasons in Miami Beach and at the Parker Playhouse in Fort Lauderdale for six weeks.

Miller made a guest appearance on the March 3, 1969, episode of the comedy music television series *Laugh-In*, shot at the NBC studios in Hollywood and broadcast on NBC. The show was written by Paul W. Keyes, Hugh Wedlock, Jr., Allan Manings, Chris Beard, David Panich, Coslough Johnson, Marc London, Dave Cox, Jim Carlson, Jack Mendelsohn, Jim Mulligan, Lorne Michaels, and Hart Pomerantz, and was directed by Gordon Wiles. She also returned for the March 17 episode of the show which was written and directed by the same team.

The Broadway run of *Mame* had begun on May 18, 1966, and was ending its third year, with the current star Jane Morgan being the sixth "Mame." To prepare for Miller's engagement, director Gene Saks did a polish, though Miller claimed she had no onstage rehearsal at all before opening night. Onna White choreographed a new tap section for the song "That's How Young I Feel" in the second act where before only the chorus boys danced. Miller said some of the veteran members of the company were a problem—bored with the repetition of doing the show and blasé about the changing leading lady. But they had a special antagonism to her, since she was perceived as a Hollywood person taking over a Broadway show. Miller made it worse by demanding changes, ordering the title number be re-done faster and with the new tap number. But she was determined to put some life and excitement back into something that everyone knew was dying. Miller told the cast if they were not happy with her they could leave and the message worked, and though she had to work at it, the star won the company's friendship and respect.

The opening night was May 26, 1969, at the Winter Garden Theatre. Backstage she was nervous with dark and dread thoughts, like Miller would inevitably be compared to Lansbury and following someone in an award-winning role in a big Broadway hit was one of the roughest things in show business. She peeked through the curtains, and panicked, feeling the urge to run away but didn't. The star got into position so when the curtain opened there she was, poised up high on the staircase in her gold-beaded pajama costume and with a gold bugle in her hand, ready to sing "It's Today." The audience went wild with a standing ovation before Miller had even begun. The applause must have lasted several minutes and she finally held up her hand to stop it so she could sing. The frenzy continued throughout the show and she got another standing ovation after the title number, but it

Miller as *Mame* on Broadway (May 26, 1969, to January 3, 1970).

was her tapping on "How Young I Feel" that brought the house down. At the show's end there was another standing ovation and people swarmed to the footlights, throwing flowers and love beads onto the stage.

The show again was praised by *Variety* who wrote that Miller was probably the best Mame since Angela Lansbury and she projected warmth and sincerity and looked smashing, Clive Barnes in *The New York Times* said the star brought zest and a real shot in the arm to the part even if she was rather less sophisticated than her predecessors. The show was a hit and ran till January 3, 1970, though it appears no original cast recording was made.

Miller said the hardest thing about the show was the costume changes, since she had so many and they had to done with split-second timing. The star had three dressers and the stage manager to help her cope, since she was also half blind without her glasses and was always bumping into something backstage. Also difficult was the Christmas scene, which reminded Miller of her baby's death so she inevitably cried. But the star said *Mame* fitted her to a T and doing it was the biggest love affair of her life. It was exciting wooing a new audience every night, and Angela Lansbury sent congratulations, saying the tap number had given the show a whole new dimension. Miller had seen Lansbury do the part twice but felt she herself was different in it. Essentially the star played herself because there was a lot of Mame in her, and felt she couldn't play it any other way.

Long lines of fans, many of them young and only newly aware of Miller, waited at the stage door to see her. She graciously and patiently signed autographs and talked to as many people as her time and energy would allow. Even one of the Lebanon star ladies came, though Miller didn't mention the long-ago incident that she knew they both remembered. But offstage the star was lonely, going to Rumpelmayers for a hot chocolate and a sandwich at the counter. She lived in the Essex House Hotel on Central Park South and treated herself by buying stuffed toys, mostly dogs.

One Miller named Mamie guarded the sofa, and she felt the dogs were substitutes for her toy poodle Pooshay who was back in Beverly Hills because the animal was too nervous to fly. But toys meant something else to the star who felt she had no childhood, though at the end of the show's run they were all given to the Children's Hospital.

Miller returned to television's *What's My Line?* though the broadcast date for the color episode is unknown. For the appearance she wears her hair uncharacteristically loose and long down her back, with a watermelon-colored long-sleeved dress with a large gold necklace and bracelets. The star uses a little girl voice to hide her identity, which is guessed by the panelists. Miller reports she was recently made a junior member of Actors Equity, which she had not been when she did the *George White Scandals*, though the star assumed she had belonged to another union then in order to allow her onstage.

Rita Hayworth and Miller had remained friends and she saw how in the 1960s Hayworth became like a dual personality. When she drank, out would come this spitting gypsy, who got angry if somebody said something her friend didn't like.

She also reflected on Judy Garland who died on June 22, 1969, at the age of 47, the woman who had on stage what psychics called an electric force field in her body and around her. It was so powerful that when she turned it on, it would reach the back of that house. Another thing that astounded the star was how Garland had spent five hours with members of her British fan club when she had to perform at the London Palladium that night. But now that beautiful light had been turned off, with the drugs being the thing that had torn her apart. Miller wasn't shocked by her friend's death (they were born a year apart), since she knew Garland was fated to die young, and maybe God had done her a favor by ending the drug problem.

Ann was a guest on the July 9 episode of the television talk show *Allen Ludden's Gallery.*

She was interviewed by David Johnson for the October issue of *After Dark* magazine. Miller reported that on the way to the interview she had had her first hot dog with sauerkraut on it. The star spoke about doing *Mame* and her career, claiming that she was like a cat with nine lives only with her it was careers, and this was about her fourth phase. It had taken 30 years to get back to Broadway, and New York had been good to her, with the opening night of *Mame* being the most thrilling experience of her life. Miller reported that a new musical was being written expressly for her, based on Patrick Dennis' story *Good Good Friends.* It appears this show was never produced.

The star's run with *Mame* came to an end in January when she contracted flu and double pneumonia, collapsing with fatigue and a 104-degree temperature, which Miller said was a rather inglorious finale. She was flown back to California and in bed for weeks, but had recovered by April to be able to do the show at Jimmy Doolittle's Huntington Hartford Theatre in Hollywood. In some ways being invited to perform there was the most gratifying of the season. Hollywood was her adopted home town and the toughest in the world, with some of the star's peers who were out of work hoping she would fail. But on opening night they too gave a standing ovation; the party afterwards was attended by Lucille Ball, and the Lebanon star lady.

At this time she heard from Howard Hughes for the last time, when Miller went to Palm Springs and he telephoned at 2 a.m. for a brief chat.

She was a guest on the April 24 episode of the television talk show *Philbin's People* which was shot in Hollywood. On May 23 the star was a guest on the comedy music television talk show *The Rosey Grier Show*, which was also shot in Hollywood, and directed by Wes Butler. In May she also attended the public auction held at M-G-M. Miller cried watching her costumes from *Easter Parade, Kiss Me Kate, On the Town, Texas Carnival*, and *Hit the Deck* being sold. Debbie Reynolds bought them and other costumes and props and planned to preserve them in a Hollywood Museum she planned to establish. Miller *did* buy Esther Williams' bull fighter suit from *Fiesta* and a cape of Eleanor Powell's for $7. She was a guest on the June 1 episode of the television game-show *It's Your Bet*, which was broadcast on NBC. The show teamed her with John Bowab to bet on their partner's ability to answer questions.

In the week of September 1 1970, Miller played *Mame* to standing ovations and packed houses on the John Kenley circuit at the Packard Music Hall in Warren, Ohio, and the Memorial Hall in Dayton, Ohio.

In early November she did her first television commercial, said to be the most expensive ever shot, a one-minute musical extravaganza for Heinz' Great American Soups. The director was Stan Freberg, whom the star said was something of a wild genius, and the choreography was by Hermes Pan. Shot at the Samuel Goldwyn Studio soundstages in Hollywood, sources also differ as to how long it took to film—four weeks or one week of rehearsals and three days with an additional scoring session of synchronized music and vocals and tap sounds done on November 10.

The commercial has Miller as Emily, the housewife of Dave Willock, serving soup for dinner. She tosses off a blue apron to reveal a red satin leotard decorated with iridescent red sequins and a glittering white rhinestone filigree pattern, trim around the hips and top of the bust, made by the Berman Costume Company. As the kitchen set is pulled away we see a stage of 5,000 square feet of mirror-like black tile, with a 24 piece orchestra, a bevy of blonde chorines, and a 20 foot high dancing waters special effect with spurting red, white, and blue fountains and a staircase.

The star stands on top of an eight foot high cylinder designed to look like a giant soup can, also wearing a bright red silk top hat decorated with a silver band and blue stars, and taps on the floor back to Willock. The kitchen returns and he gets the button line, "Why do you have to make such a big production out of everything?" She said that commercial gave her more exposure than being in *Mame*, and the costume would later be on display in the National Museum of American History.

Ava Astaire McKenzie reported that when Miller accompanied Hermes Pan to a tribute to Oscar Hammerstein on an unknown date that year she asked if the composer would be there, not knowing he was dead. When informed of this, the star replied that she had been in New York, with a variation of her response being, ""Well, how should I know? I've been touring in *Mame*." That year on another unknown date Miller also attended the opening night party for the national touring company of *Butterflies Are Free*, which starred Eve Arden at the Los Angeles Huntington Hartford Theater.

She read that someone was producing a Broadway musical called *Ari*, and the star asked her agent to get her an audition for the part of a tap-dancing Jackie Onassis, since they both were tall brunettes who loved horses and knew Onassis. His reaction differs according to sources—one has him laughing and the other, not revealing the musical was actually an adaptation of the Leon Uris novel *Exodus* that would run at the Mark Hellinger Theatre from January 15 to 30, 1971, but Miller maintained that a play about Jackie and Ari would have been fabulous.

The star was back as a panelist on the June 7 episode of *The Hollywood Squares*. She was a guest on the June 29 episode of the television talk show *The Virginia Graham Show*, which was shot in Chicago.

In the summer Miller played Dolly Gallagher Levy in *Hello, Dolly!* on the John Kenley circuit at the Packard Music Hall Theatre in Warren, Ohio, the Veterans Memorial Theatre in Columbus and Memorial Hall in Dayton, Ohio. The seasons ran for one week only and Kenley added a tap number to the show for her. Afterwards she got shingles and had to give away her low-necked dresses, crying when seeing them leaving the house.

In the fall Arlene Dahl arranged for President Nixon's adviser Henry Kissinger to be a dinner companion for the star at a party in Newport Beach. She had heard the man had dated many starlets and had previously spotted him at Trader Vic's in Beverly Hills necking with one quite openly. Miller did not consider herself a prude but felt that since Kissinger was someone of political stature and prominence, he should do his canoodling in private. So at the party she told him so in a quiet and lady-like manner. The man thanked her for the friendly advice but the star was sure this had squelched any chances with him, despite her claim that he wasn't her type.

She was back on *The Mike Douglas Show* on the episode broadcast on September 14, 1971, which also had Janet Leigh as a guest. Leigh wrote in *There Really Was a Hollywood* about the appearance, where

Miller spoke about having just returned from India. Her prattling about maharajas and the exquisite silks and the starving peasants made Leigh fall off her chair in spasms of silent laughter. When the show was aired it was apparent that a camera operator had caught this, and Leigh was distressed at appearing to be derogatory or hurting her friend. Miller was just being herself and her beguiling humor always made Leigh laugh.

She next appeared in the made-for-TV movie musical *Dames at Sea* which was broadcast on NBC as a Bell System Family Theater Special on November 15. Shot in New York it was an adaptation of the 1966 Off Broadway musical with book and lyrics by George Haimsohn and Robin Miller and music by Jim Wise. The new directors were Walter C. Miller and Martin Charnin. The story centered on Ruby (Ann-Margret), a dancer from Utah who comes to New York to appear in a Broadway show. Miller is billed seventh after the title, playing the supporting role of Mona Kent. She sings in three numbers: "Wall Street" also dancing, "That Mister Man of Mine", and as part of "Let's Have a Simple Wedding." The star delivers a sensational vocal for "That Mister of Man" but her best number is "Wall Street" wearing a Theoni V. Aldridge dark-red, glittery, high-colored, fringed leotard with matching long gloves and top hat. Despite some medium shots, the number also has an aerial shot of her tapping in the pattern of a dollar sign around the chorus. Miller's Mona is funny as when she clicks her fingers trying to remember Ruby's name and when she's seasick. Choreography was by Alan Johnson. The show received a mixed reaction from John J. O'Connor in *The New York Times* who wrote that it was not without its moments, particularly when Miller was allowed to tap out her brassy impersonation of the temperamental star. A soundtrack album was recorded and released.

She reported that the producers cut 24 bars out of her opening number for time and a complete other number. The former upset her but the latter the star understood, since she claimed the producers did so because it made her part more important than that of Ann-Margret.

The New York Times of November 30 reported that negotiations were under way for Miller to appear in a new musical in the new year. "The Eighth Wonder," with book by Noel Gerson and songs by Bill Snyder and Stanley Allen Baum. However the show was not staged.

In 1971 her friend Rita Hayworth asked for help. She had been hired to replace Lauren Bacall in the stage show *Applause*, on Ann's recommendation according to Miller. But Hayworth was having a hard time learning lines—peculiar since she never had this problem before. Together they worked on the script for a week, with Ann prompting her friend until she did well. But when Hayworth got to New York her memory failed her again, and the producers let her go. Flu was given as the

Miller in the made-for-TV special *Dames at Sea* broadcast on November 15, 1971.

official reason for her withdrawal from the show, and she was replaced by Anne Baxter.

Hayworth's loss of memory may have been an indication of the Alzheimer's disease with which she was later diagnosed. This was to cause more aggressive behavior, which alienated friends who had attributed it to drunkenness. One night at dinner with Miller and Hermes Pan, Hayworth suddenly announced that her friends must leave, refusing to say why. Another night when they arrived she threatened them with a butcher knife. The star told two versions of this story—one had a Spanish woman answering the door saying she would get Hayworth and another that nobody answered for a long time until she herself appeared with the knife. Hayworth didn't recognize her friends; an inability to recognize otherwise familiar people or things is a common symptom of the disease. Miller stated they were close friends whom she had invited to dinner, but Hayworth saw them as fans. She wasn't going to sign autographs and demanded they leave her courtyard. The star and Pan must have hesitated because Hayworth then chased them with the knife and they got to their car to get as she was screaming. Then the next day or two days later Hayworth called Miller or Pan to ask why they hadn't come for dinner.

Miller was to appear in the made-for-TV comedy movie and unsold television pilot *Call Her Mom*, which was broadcast on ABC on February 15, 1972. The teleplay was by Gail Parent and Ken Solms and the director was Jerry Paris. The story centered on Angie Bianco, a sexy waitress who becomes the house mother in a fraternity house. The star replaced Cyd Charisse in the supporting role of Helen Hardgrove, but she in turn was replaced by Gloria DeHaven.

Miller went to Munich for a Sheraton Hotel opening, and then planned to go to Tehran for the Iranian Film Festival, accompanied by her latest beau, Henry Berger. After getting painful shots the trip was cancelled because of an earthquake on April 10. So to cheer herself up she went out and bought books on Persia, peacock feathers, and Kenneth Lane jewelry. Hermes Pan also cooked the couple a Persian dinner.

The star was a guest on the June 29, 1972, episode of the television talk show *The Bob Braun Show* which was shot in Cincinnati, Ohio, and directed by Dick Murgatroyd.

She did a John Kenley summer circuit tour of *Can-Can* at the Packard Music Hall Theatre in Warren, the Veterans Memorial Theatre in Columbus and Memorial Hall in Dayton, Ohio. In August Miller went to St. Louis to do the Cole Porter musical *Anything Goes* at the Municipal Opera House, playing the part of Reno Sweeney, an evangelist turned nightclub singer. When she walked into the open-air theater the star had a premonition of disaster, which did occur on opening night. In the first act the star finished a number called "Friendship" when the lights went out and, as she turned to leave the stage, Miller was hit in the head. One report said it was a big mechanical boom but she said it was a steel studded curtain or elevator doors on a track moved by accident which knocked her down and dragged her four feet before the star blacked out. When she came to and tried to sit up Miller saw there was blood on her wig and the rest of her, but the wig had saved her from a protruding nail that might have gone right into her brain. The star's vision was one-sided and she was in great pain. The rest of the performance was cancelled and it was announced on August 16 Miller could not continue in the show. An examination revealed vertical vertigo and a concussion of the inner ear, which also affected her vision, with bruises on her back and legs.

The star's version of how long she was in the Deaconess Hospital in St. Louis differs, saying three weeks in one interview and a solid month in another, but the doctors said Miller would not dance again. She went back home to Los Angeles heartbroken with her career halted, with the hopes of the show being transferred to Lincoln Center in New York dashed. The star now had to walk with assistance, and this would continue for two years, and it took three years to receive an out of court settlement of $4,651.78 from the Opera Company. Wanting desperately to dance again, she prayed hard and worked in a rehearsal hall. It would take many months but Miller would dance with her balance restored.

She appeared in the November 17, 1972, episode of the comedy romance television series *Love, American Style* which was shot at the Paramount Hollywood Studios and broadcast on ABC. The star was in the segment "Love and the Christmas Punch," written by Gene Thompson and directed by Charles R. Rondeau. It was a straight acting role, and Miller said she could almost hear her dancing feet saying, "Thank God, she's going to let us rest in this one. Let's hope this dizzy dame lets us cool it more often." In November it was announced that Lucille Ball would play the title role in the film version of *Mame*, released on March 4, 1974.

The star was a guest on the December 5, 1972, episode of the television news and talk show *Today*, shot at the NBC Studios in New York and broadcast on NBC. She was there to promote her memoir *Miller's High Life*, co-written with Norma Lee Browning, published by Doubleday. It was dedicated to her mother, the greatest friend Miller said she ever had. On the same date the star was photographed gleefully receiving the present of a gold bracelet from John A. Murphy, president of the Miller Brewing Company, while a guest in his home.

She felt the book came out at a very good time, because if it had done so when Miller was in a show, there wouldn't have been time to promote it with television appearances. She had initially planned to call it "Lucky Legs," though then considered that tacky, and then "Native Dancer," which was the name of her favorite race horse. He was a champion whose record was remembered, and the star wanted the same thing. But she decided upon *Miller's High Life* as a bond with Murphy's advertising label Miller High Life, and as the book was selling so well, a sequel was proposed to be called "Miller on Tap."

She couldn't dance at the present time because of the *Anything Goes* injury and needed another six months or a year to get over it. The star was not involved romantically with anyone but hoped to be again someday. Miller's biggest regret was losing her child, and she considered adopting one, or if the star met a man who was also a father, it would give her the chance to be a mother. The saddest sound in the world was the tinkling music of the Good Humor ice cream truck coming down the street, something she had had heard after each divorce, and at the baby shower her friends had given. It was as if the music was mocking her, but the star realized that this thinking was just her unhappiness at the situation and now she didn't want to waste time dwelling on the past. Miller had good old-fashioned Texas horse sense and values that Clara had installed in her and that Hollywood hadn't been able to take away.

Miller was told she looked younger than her age, which the star attributed to never smoking or drinking hard liquor, and taking care of her skin. She took vitamins, ate healthy, and exercised. Miller was not perfect—admitting to being a clothesaholic, a spendaholic, and a hoarder—afraid to let go of mementoes and hundreds of racks of clothes. There were the stuffed toys and jar of bubble gum and candy by her bed, and a Walter Keane print of an orphan with big eyes sitting alone on steps in the moonlight looking cold and thin and hungry. The print reminded her of what the star she had once been and feared would be again, and Miller always looked at before going out gussied up in furs and feathers and finery.

She considered herself down to earth, but some people thought her beliefs in Ouija boards and reincarnation made her some sort of a ding-a-ling. But she had visions of experiences in past lives and two recurring and disturbing dreams which were actually nightmares. One had a woman with long black hair dressed in gold and jewels in an Arab tent who whipped a chained man senseless then danced to drums. The other had Miller herself as a Pharaoh Queen bound in chains on a golden slab and carried into a pyramid at night to be buried alive, which caused the star to wake up screaming. The dreams confirmed what the Egyptian seer had said about having to repay a karmic debt, and Miller hoped the debt had now been paid in full. A psychic predicted her next husband would be in politics, and that a new career was unfolding with a vision of a rainbow in front of the star which she would swing from. Miller saw a rainbow in her garden one day with the vision of herself as a little girl swinging on it, with a voice that told the star there was a brand new future ahead of her.

She appeared as a guest on the December 18, 1972, episode of the comedy family and music television show *The Merv Griffin Show* which was shot at the Hollywood Palace Theater in Los Angeles and broadcast on NBC. On December 20 Miller represented the United States at a gala benefit for UNICEF held at the Paris Opera. She introduced ballet companies from all over the world for the event that was televised throughout Europe.

The star was back on *The Mike Douglas Show* for the January 1, 1973, outing. She was a guest on the January 17 episode of the syndicate television talk show *Joanne Carson's VIPs*. Miller was a guest on the January 26 episode of the television talk show *Dinah's Place*, though another source gives the date as March 3. It was shot at the NBC Studios in Hollywood and broadcast on NBC. On the show she displayed a collection of antique jewelry including some that once belonged to Queen Mother Farouk. On April 23 the star attended the After Dark Annual Ruby Awards held at New York's Delmonico Hotel. In April she also visited Paris with Henry Berger, surprising friends and being photographed with another jet-setter, Juliet Prowse.

Miller returned to *The Merv Griffin Show* for the September 4 episode. On September 7 she attended a dinner in the presidential suite for the opening of the Los Angeles Marriott Hotel. From September 18 to 30 the star appeared in *Blithe Spirit* by Noel Coward at the Little Theatre on the Square in Sullivan, Illinois. She was directed by Stuart Bishop in her first stage appearance after the *Anything Goes* injury. Miller played Elvira, and while she had to learn to walk and talk again, the psychic star said it was appropriate to be playing a ghost.

In *Photoplay* of 1973 she was photographed in some of her Indian jewelry. Miller was an enthusiastic collector, having acquired a beautiful turquoise bracelet as a gift from the governor of New Mexico when she made a personal appearance there. When dining with friends from Chicago Beach, the star admired the squash blossom necklace and bracelet on a companion's wife, which the woman then gave to her. At her Beverly Hills home they also showed Miller and her mother a dazzling sterling silver belt lined with turquoise. Clara was allowed to try it on but not to keep the item.

She was seen wearing Halloween garb in a photograph with Ann-Margret and Michael Hayes in the February 1974 edition of *Photoplay*. The star returned to *The Merv Griffin Show* that was broadcast on March 12. She appeared in a production of *Anything Goes* at the Paper Mill Playhouse in Millburn, New Jersey, from March 27 to

May 12 directed by Lawrence Kasha. Miller was a guest on the CBS special *Grammy Salutes Oscar*, broadcast on March 30, which highlighted music from the movies. The show was written by Ann Elder and Rod Warren and directed by John Moffitt.

She attended *The 46th Annual Academy Awards* held on April 2 at the Dorothy Chandler Pavilion in Hollywood and televised by NBC in a show directed by Marty Pasetta.

The M-G-M family musical documentary *That's Entertainment!* (1974) written and directed by Jack Haley, Jr., was released on May 23. Although Miller was not one of the stars who narrated or co-hosted segments she was seen in it, in footage from the 1949 silver anniversary luncheon, doing "I've Gotta Hear that Beat" in *Small Town Girl* and in the "Hallelujah" finale of *Hit the Deck*. The star reported she saw the film several times and it brought back great memories, though one thing annoyed her. All you saw Miller do in clips was turn, like she was the village idiot, with none of the intricate footwork or any of the other things the star did well. Despite this misgiving, she agreed to promote the film internationally and travelled to Hawaii, London, Spain, France, Puerto Rico, and Australia.

In London, Miller had another psychic experience. Staying at the Dorchester Hotel she was in bed reading at 3 a.m. when the star heard German speaking voices, laughter, the clinking of boots and the clanking of glasses. Fearing someone had gotten into her suite the star had the night manager check, but he found no one there. Still frightened, she finally got to sleep. That day, Fred Sill, the M-G-M foreign press representative came with people from BBC-TV to do an interview. When Miller relayed what had happened he reported that Nazi spies had occupied the suite during the war.

In June she again did *Anything Goes* at the Westchester Playhouse in Yonkers, New York, directed by Bill Guske. The star was back on *The Merv Griffin Show* on July 23. On August 6 it was reported she had signed to appear in a revival of the musical *Girl Crazy* on Broadway with Michael Kidd directing, though this did not eventuate. Miller was scheduled to do *Anything Goes* once more at the Detroit Music Hall. She was back on *The Merv Griffin Show* on November 20, 1974, where the star reported that she had recently been to an archaeological dig in Egypt but had stayed at the Cairo Hilton Hotel rather on site overnight.

Miller was in Australia in December for the release of *That's Entertainment!* and interviewed for the ABC news and current affairs television show *This Day Tonight*. She spoke about being named Ann Miller and being a star in Hollywood's golden years. Some of them liked to tell stories of being ruined by the machine, which she considered a bunch of blarney. To her they were lucky since most of them came from nowhere and otherwise would have been nobodies. Miller resented the ones who became spoiled, where success went to their head, citing Frank Sinatra as an example. He had recently been to Australia and caused a scandal which she was sorry about because it was not good for her country.

In March to May 1974 the star played *Anything Goes* at a Paramus shopping mall in New Jersey as a benefit for a gay liberation movement group. In the show she wore a bra button with an "A" in the shape of a lambda, which was the national emblem of the movement. Afterwards Miller went to a special champagne party held in her honor at a nearby church, but was disappointed that the boys did not dress up as her which they had promised they would.

She was a guest on the television special *At Long Last Cole* aka "At Long Last Cole: What a Swell Party It Was!" broadcast on April 10 on ABC. Shot on the 20th Century–Fox Studios in Hollywood and directed by Ronald Lyon, it was a delightful, delicious, delovely tribute to Cole Porter filmed for the premiere of the comedy musical *At Long Last Love* (1975).

The star was profiled by Arthur Bell in the June 1 edition of *Esquire* magazine in an article entitled "The Lady of the Taps." She was in New York staying at the Hilton Hotel and rehearsing *Anything Goes* at the Broadway Arts Rehearsal Studios for a summer stock tour. The tour would incorporate the Candlewood Theatre in New Fairfield, Connecticut, and the Summer Star Theater in Miami in August. Her injuries left Miller unable to pirouette well and with no depth perception so she had to make new demands, which had a director nickname her Miss PITA, meaning Miss Pain-In-The-Ass. The stage floors needed to have their lacquer removed to make them less slippery, and they and the staircase entranceway needed to be lined with phosphorous white binding. The star also needed to be led on and off the stage as she was afraid of falling into the orchestra pit as Marlene Dietrich had recently done when bowing. But Miller saw the demands as less about being a diva and more about herself as Mrs. Magoo.

Esquire's Bell thought she was like Minnie Mouse with a slab of Billie Dawn—and it was difficult to figure out whether it was self or self-parody and where the star began and caricature ended. He observed her as totally dependent on others, as she couldn't cook or do laundry or drive a car—and Miller became a veritable basket case when friends or strangers weren't around to help. What Bell found fascinating about the star was that, under the brass, she was puritanical about sex. She only tolerated a smutty joke or a hot rumor when it involved others. Even a kiss on the mouth was taboo. Miller might allow someone to kiss her on the cheek but never kissed back. She had a general terror of touch, dating back to her days in the 1930s dancing for nickels and dimes at the Black Cat Café in Los Angeles, where drunks grabbed her and propositioned her.

This scar on the psyche meant the star had a fear of playing Vegas because of the close proximity of the audience, and she had recently declined an offer to dance there. However this decision may have been influenced by another factor. They had wanted her to include a revival of "Shakin' the Blues Away" from *Easter Parade*, with the movie version projected on a backdrop, and the 52-year-old Miller didn't want to be compared with her younger self in this way.

She made a return to movies with a cameo in the Paramount comedy *Won Ton Ton: The Dog Who Saved Hollywood* (1976) which had the original title of "Won Ton Ton, the Dog Who Saved Warner Brothers." It was shot from August 25 to October on locations in California. The screenplay was by Arnold Schulman and Cy Howard with uncredited work by Jane Wagner, and the director was Michael Winner. The story centered on Estie Del Ruth (Madeline Kahn) who in 1924 comes to Hollywood to become an actress, but the German shepherd dog that followed her, Won Ton Ton (Augustus Von Schumacher), becomes the star.

Miller is billed 44th after the title among the guest stars listed in alphabetical order, and credited in the end credits as President's Girl 2. She appears in one scene as the date of J.J. Fromberg (Art Carney) at the National Film Society Awards, wearing a white beaded gown and a white fur, and has no lines. The film was released on May 26, 1976, with the taglines "Introducing the Dog Who Launched 1000 Stars" and "When Movies Were Silent—His Was the Bark Heard 'Round the World." It was lambasted by Arthur D. Murphy in *Variety*, and received a mixed reaction from Richard Eder in *The New York Times*. The film was not a box office success. The star commented about it that Hollywood was going to the DOGS!

She was interviewed by Roy Pickard in the December edition of *Photoplay* for an article entitled "Ann Miller and Her Metro Musical Memories." The interview was conducted at London's Dorchester Hotel as Miller was in town to promote the West End re-run of *That's Entertainment!* Pickard believed she was a good choice for a promotional star since she laughed a lot, enjoyed life and enthused warmly about the great days of M-G-M. Miller said the M-G-M ladies got on well together all the time because the studio was so strict. They could get touchy if someone else's part was bigger but by the time they got on the set all they cared about was the script. Esther Williams, Kathryn Grayson, Debbie Reynolds, Jane Powell and Cyd Charisse all remained great friends.

Lobby card for *Won Ton Ton: The Dog Who Saved Hollywood* (1976), in which Miller has a cameo.

She took a celebrity cruise where her films were screened and the star answered questions from passengers but the time when Rita Hayworth was on the same cruise was a heartbreaking experience. Her friend needed a companion to do makeup, hair and dress her but sometimes she appeared disheveled and her words were slurred, which the star attributed to drink.

Miller was a guest on February 20, 1976, episode of *The Mike Douglas Show* held at the M-G-M Studios to promote the sequel to *That's Entertainment!* (the family musical documentary): *That's Entertainment: Part II* (1976). The film was written by Leonard Gershe and directed by Gene Kelly and released on May 16. She was seen in it doing "From This Moment On" from *Kiss Me Kate.* For the show the star wore a brown floor-length long-sleeved dress with a red feather boa and her stage wig, and joined the other former M-G-M stars in doing a time-step. She bemoaned that the days of glamour and mystique were gone, as the modern stars walked around in blue jeans and sloppy hair, and commented that Hermes Pan was the world's greatest choreographer.

From June 9 to 27, 1976, Miller played in the musical *Panama*

Hattie at the Paper Mill Playhouse in Milburn. She was on a summer tour of the show that included a Kenley Players production at the Packard Music Hall Theatre in Warren; the Veterans Memorial Theatre in Columbus, and Memorial Hall in Dayton, Ohio. From August 3 to 8 the star played *Panama Hattie* at the Syracuse Symphony Famous Artists Playhouse in New York in the "Summer Festival of Stars," and from August 9 to 21 at the Westchester Playhouse in Yonkers. She saw the same man in the audience at her shows, believing he had seen *Anything Goes* 18 times and *Panama Hattie* 10 times. So when the man asked for a dinner date, Miller agreed. He was very charming and gave her a beautiful book.

It was reported by Rona Barrett in September that the star's Beverly Hills neighborhood had been plagued by muggers and burglars. She and her neighbors hired a private security patrol to safeguard the area, though Miller had her own pistol nearby. On October 10 she was back on *The Mike Douglas Show*. The same month the star attended an event for George Burns in Beverly Hills and was photographed with Ann-Margret.

She was sent by M-G-M to Vienna for the Salsburg Film Festival to promote *That's Entertainment: Part II* and to act as their good will ambassador. When Miller appeared on stage for the opening night she was given a five minute standing ovation, which made her cry. As the star had never been to the city before, she did three days of sightseeing but refused dance offers because of her injury. This was a strategy as Miller had previously been worn out by every man wanting to dance with her since she was known to love to dance.

The star was back on *The Merv Griffin Show* in 1977 although some sources claim this occurred in 1979, with the date unknown. Wearing a black, high-necked, long-sleeved floor-length dress with a fur trim on the base and a jeweled broach on the left shoulder, she sang three numbers. Miller is part of the Broadway belters doing "There's No Business Like Show Business," and solo performs "Anything Goes" and "I Get a Kick Out of You." She is best in "Anything Goes" displaying a leg for the glimpse of stocking line in the song. The star reported she was about to do another season of *Anything Goes* and hoped this would lead to a new tour, and being on Griffin's show with Ethel Merman was a thrill as Merman had originated *Anything Goes*.

Miller gave Griffin a super star paper weight for his 25th anniversary in show business, a late present since she had been out of town on the date. The star had never danced on his show claiming it was because of her injury but promised to do so in the future with 6 or 8 chorus boys. She was grateful for Griffin for having her on his show as a singer, and told how a little boy in the street had recognized Miller as such because he had never seen her dance on television.

From June 2 to 15, 1977, she appeared in *The 24th Annual Milliken Breakfast Show* in New York at the Waldorf-Astoria Hotel's grand ballroom. The author was Tom Eyen and the director was Frank Dunlop. Its story was "Who Dunnit" about a designer, Falston, murdered at his own fashion show and the suspects included Miller as a beauty contest winner, who did a rousing tap-dance routine. In *The New York Times* of June 12 Tony Cabot, director of operations of the Nanuet Star Theater in Rockland County was in talks to co-produce a Miller show. The *Times* reported that she had recently been interviewed on the New York television talk show *The Joe Franklin Show*. June also saw her return to *Anything Goes* for John Kenley in a production directed by Leslie B. Cutler. The star was back in the show from August 22 to 27 at the Sikithville Theatre in New Jersey, followed by seasons at the Connecticut Star Players at the American Shakespeare Theater in Stratford, Connecticut, from September 6 to 11 and from September 13 to 28. She returned to *The Mike Douglas Show* on October 10.

In 1977 Miller was photographed with Rita Hayworth, June Allyson and Peter Lawford on a trip to an unknown destination. This time Hayworth was in better spirits and the star reported that one beautiful night the group had just had dinner and came to the hotel swimming pool where her friend impulsively jumped in with her clothes on. Hayworth did it because of the wonderful time she was having on the trip, and then, out of the pool and dripping wet, suggested they go for a drink. Miller found this hilarious.

In the February 1978 it was reported that she wanted people to know that there was no truth to the rumor that the star had started a hairspray panic at her local Rexall store. The April edition of *Photoplay* said the touring production of *Anything Goes* was headed to Broadway.

She was again in the *Milliken Breakfast Show* to June 8 to 21, 1978, tapping down a platform and belting out Visa lyrics to "Anything Goes" and with a tap-dancing chorus singing and dancing to "Ridin' High." The produces presented Miller with a 52 carat amethyst and diamond ring in appreciation of her work. On June 13 she attended the New York premiere of the musical romance *Grease* (1978). In October the star was photographed at New York's Christo's Steak House, with an observer noting that she managed to eat and still get her foot in her mouth.

Miller appeared in a 52 week tour of the Abe Burrows play *Cactus Flower*, presumably played the part of Stephanie, the shy spinster assistant to dentist Julian who is having an affair with a younger woman. For the show a tap number was inserted by producer Harry Rigby, which made the run a huge success. When she did it in Dallas, Texas, the star saw her first UFO. At mid-afternoon when the sun was on the wane a silver disk moved through the sky, hovered for a minute or two and then took off fast.

While doing the play in Scottsdale Miller had her first glimpse of Sedona, Arizona. On a Sunday off she travelled there, staying in a villa at the Poco Diablo Resort. When the star walked out onto the golf course and saw the red mountains, she decided to have a home there someday. Miller was accompanied by her two dogs, Cinderella and Jasmine, and her secretary and assistant, Debbie Zehnder, who had come to the star in an unusual way. One day her mother had a vision as she stood on the house's staircase of the girl on the landing below. By the time Miller came to see, the vision was gone but Clara predicted this girl would become her daughter's companion. Debbie was hired a year before Clara's death, partly because she shared the star's interest in metaphysics.

CHAPTER 8

· · · · · · · · · · · · · · · · ·

Sugar Babies

*H*arry Rigby changed his mind about the Broadway revival of *Anything Goes*, instead choosing to sign Miller to co-star with Mickey Rooney in a new musical burlesque called *Sugar Babies*. The songs were by Jimmy McHugh, which she said was her idea, and the lyrics by Arthur Malvin. The book material was by Ralph G. Allen and the sketches directed by Norman Abbott, the nephew of the late Bud Abbott. The choreography was by Ernest O. Flatt, with Raoul Pene du Bois doing sets and costumes. The show's title derived from the 14 showgirls, who were accompanied by six comics, a dog act, and pigeons. Rehearsals began in March 1979 with the company to open at the Curran Theater in San Francisco in May, go on to the Pantages in Los Angeles in June, and then skip through a few more cities until it opened in New York in the fall.

The star had known Rooney after they met in professional school as children in Hollywood, and the pair were an odd couple and a study in contrasts. She had height, a soft offstage Texas drawl and careful manner and he was short, had a rasping delivery and mercurial behavior. Miller said Rooney was wonderful to work with because he was an old pro, and felt the actor would have been a good director where he would have his greatest success, though Rooney didn't want to do that. He could get angry and scream and yell, wanting things done his way which he almost always got. He had a thirst at all times to be heard and listened to, and his mind was restless and never at peace. But Rooney had a great sense of humor, and it was never dull around him. Miller was a slow, methodical worker who carefully memorized the role and stuck to the script unlike her co-star who liked to improvise and ad-lib. She coped with this by keeping her lines no matter what he was doing, which made Rooney say she was as tough as nails and frightening.

The company joked about Miller's stage wig, saying one day she tripped, fell and broke it, but the show had serious conflicts too. Harry Rigby found Norman Abbot wrong for the assignment and after two weeks he was replaced with Rudy Tronto, a onetime burlesque actor and director. Miller said she nearly left the show in rehearsal when made to feel like a chorus girl, rather than a glamourous star with great numbers, but things changed when Rooney also threatened to leave. Then she twisted her ankle and Miller's numbers were temporarily given to Ann Jillian, who was in the supporting cast, until the star could recover. She had no fear that Jillian would want to replace her permanently since the women were friends, having dinners together and Miller driving her home.

In fact Ann said she had saved her friend from being fired three times. But a rumor of a feud began after Jillian claimed the healed Miller had taken away her part, which she dismissed as not nice since Miller was hired as the female star of the show. Jillian would stay after it opened in New York but for only five months, and get a form of revenge upon her friend and Mickey Rooney when neither was mentioned in the coverage of the show in her biographical television movie *The Ann Jillian Story* (1988). In that version, with a teleplay by Audrey Davis Levin and directed by Corey Allen, Jillian describes herself as the young female lead in the show.

While in rehearsal on March 27 Miller attended a performance of the Broadway play *Deathtrap* at the Music Box Theatre. On April 29 the star attended a lunch at Katja thrown by Arlene Dahl for the musical alumni of M-G-M. She was photographed with Van Johnson.

The San Francisco tryout began on May 13, 1979, with the first performance sold out and the audience giving the cast a standing ovation. The *San Francisco Progress* raved that the show was the fun musical comedy entertainment of the decade, the *Chronicle* said it was exhilarating, and the *Examiner* found it vastly entertaining and an obvious crowd pleaser. When Rooney injured his hip a roller skating number was replaced with a medley of songs sung by him and Miller. Moving to Los Angeles in June she was said to have developed into a first-class "straight man," despite the fact that her heart belonged to the big musical numbers with the feathers and beads and glamour. She had two disappointments, with a huge number called "Julius Squeezer" dropped and half of her dance routine in the big military finale cut, which the team later regretted.

For the finale, Miller had wanted a big Shirley Bassey–style entrance, coming down a flight of stairs in a cape, but they refused. She threatened to leave the show but was placated by being allowed to create her own tap routines with the choreographer working them into the dance numbers. But the *Los Angeles Herald Examiner* wrote that *Sugar Babies* delivered. In Hollywood the star returned to *The Mike*

Douglas Show on August 8 with Rooney, to publicize the show. In Chicago the *Sun Times* wrote that the sassy, classy, burlesque-style hit had first-nighters in ecstasy and the show was just what the country needed at the moment. The *Tribune* proclaimed that it was a magical musical trip down burlesque's memory lane that everyone should take. By Detroit, Miller felt the show was still not good enough after what she considered bad shows in San Francisco and Los Angeles, and it was reimagined. The Detroit *News* said it was a pocketful of miracles and such miracles were darn hard to come by. But in Philadelphia in September it was panned by two of the three major reviewers, though still broke box-office records.

The star said the six month road tour had been like having a baby, with labor pains that she hoped to never have to go through again. Opening night at the Mark Hellinger Theatre in New York was October 8, 1979, and Miller had the jitters, with wet palms, shaking knees, and a dry mouth. Rooney told her to have fun and relax because that was what it was all about. In her dressing room she got into her first costume with her stomach in knots, warming up her feet on the tap dance board. The star stood in the wings waiting for the opening train number's opening music and for four chorus boys to roll her onstage atop a luggage cart. When the spotlight hit her a force field of energy took over Miller's body and the shakes and nerves and upset stomach were all gone. Out came the professional singer and dancer and the applause was deafening.

In the second act she and Rooney did a medley of songs ending with "Sunny Side of the Street." The star had to grab a straw hat off the piano and whip off the long black satin skirt to reveal her in tuxedo jacket and black stockings with the hat in her hand. As she moved to the front of the stage to join Rooney, Ann felt a presence with a force so strong that it almost knocked the hat out of her hand. Something took over the star's body and she had never sung better in her life. The strange look that her co-star gave to Miller made her know he had felt the same phenomenon. The pair came offstage like two steam engines. She ran to the dressing room, with an earring falling off, which was odd (the star had adhesive on the back of the earrings to hold them in place while she danced). When Miller bent to pick up the earring it rolled away from her and she noticed a piece of scenery with the letters JUD in white tape. The earring rolled to the lettering and the star heard a voice, and stagehands appeared and said the scenery piece had been moved, so when they pushed it back, the letters JUD became JUDGE, COURTROOM SET. She was frozen in reaction until the dresser tugged at her arm for her to change into the finale costume.

After the show the star told Rooney that she believed Judy Garland had been on stage with them that night. He looked at her with wonderment and smiled, though he told *The New York Times* that the two of them had been rotten that night. After the incident Miller kept a picture of Garland on her dressing room wall all during the 8½ years the show ran, feeling that somehow her friend approved of the enormous success Rooney had in it, since it was the kind of show business entertainment she loved. Years later after the show had closed, Rooney told her many people thought the star was the best partner he had had since Garland, which made Miller smile with wonderment and a quiet sense of knowing.

Sugar Babies was praised by *Variety* who wrote that Miller was a tremendous tapster who knew how to belt a song and deliver lines with the best of them, and Walter Kerr in *The New York Times* who said that the star was in stunning shape and strode through sketches with a hammer-and-tongs authority. The show received Tony Award nominations for Miller for Best Leading Actress in a Musical as well as nominations for Best Leading Actor in a Musical, Best Direction in a Musical, Best Original Score, Best Costume Design, Best Choreography, Best Book of a Musical and Best Musical. Regrettably it won none of them.

Miller said *Sugar Babies* came at a good time because Clara had become very ill and needed round the clock nursing, but it also gave her the stardom she yearned for. At M-G-M she had always played the second feminine lead, never the star role with a big moment on the screen. The show had something for everyone, and although it was thought to be a family show, it wasn't; some of the jokes were very raunchy. But it was a success because people wanted to see a leading lady who was still glamourous and who could wear good clothes. Miller admitted to having had to become tougher to survive, no longer the M-G-M hothouse flower, who hustled and did her own interviews rather than pay for a $1,000 a week press agent. She had no time for the tidal wave of nostalgia for the so-called Golden Age of films and didn't get excited by revivals of her musicals, but the star wanted people to look at what she was doing now.

Commenting on Rooney, the perennial bad boy of show business, Miller would roll her eyes. He would go to her dressing room every day and ask if she wanted to make money with new inventions, like spray-on hair or a square hot dog or Mickey Melon soda pop, or the miracle diet and ask for a $50,000 investment. The star didn't have that kind of money, though she thought the hot dog and miracle diet were dumb ideas and the pop tasted awful. There was nobody like him. To Miller, Rooney was a midget Lionel Barrymore, a genius who could write, direct and sing, with 27 little people running around inside him so

Miller and Mickey Rooney in the Broadway musical *Sugar Babies* (October 8, 1979, to August 28, 1982).

that you never knew which one you were talking to. She could get mad at her co-star, as when in the Madame Gazaza sketch he improvised his monologue and kept the star waiting for her cue. She finally pronounced that Madame Gazaza quits and walked offstage, intending to leave the theater. Rooney ran after her, promising never to do that again, and he never did. Miller felt the man could be a naughty brat who wanted to see how much he could get away with. However Rooney admired the star, saying that show business and pleasing people was her life, and that there would never be anyone greater or more lovely and gracious than she.

On October 26, 1979, Miller participated in a celebration of the 2,000th episode of *The Merv Griffin Show* held at the Vivian Beaumont Theater, followed by a backstage party. She was interviewed in her hotel room by Moira Hodgson for *The New York Times* of October 28. The star looked younger than her 56 years, now rarely taking dance classes and simply warming up for half an hour before going on stage. She had a one year contract to do *Sugar Babies*, which Miller wished was not described as burlesque since many thought that meant bumps, grinds and tassel-twirlers. They were doing 1900s burlesque which wasn't cheap and sleazy, and was just for laughs, which the world needed. Her beloved mother Clara was the victim of strokes and now lived in a rest home. The star still held a fascination for Egypt, and had two unsuccessful attempts to get to Luxor but was taken ill in Cairo and had to turn back both times. The third time she finally made it and cried uncontrollably when she arrived, even though Miller felt a scorpion bite was a sign by the spirits to stay away. But she planned to go back and hoped to build a house close to the Valley of the Tombs.

The star wanted to do a musical version of the RKO romantic comedy *Ball of Fire* (1941) with her as the nightclub performer Sugarpuss O'Shea and Rock Hudson as Professor Bertram Potts. But most of all she wanted to see a revival of the grand style of Hollywood musical, thinking they could do another *Ziegfeld Follies*.

Miller had many backstage visitors, including Larry Hagman, Helen Hayes, Cary Grant, and Ethel Merman. One night she heard the familiar husky voice of Katharine Hepburn calling outside her dressing room, asking for String Bean, which was what the star was named on *Stage Door*. On another night Henry Kissinger came, depressed about his political future with the Carter administration. She had a vision he would be called upon to return to Washington to advise the president on the Middle East, and when Ronald Reagan was made president, this came true.

Living at the Mayflower Hotel, which overlooked Central Park, Miller saw another UFO early one morning—a big white light that moved away fast. That day the newspapers reported on the event, saying it was possibly a planet or a star. The occurrence would be repeated and she believed the Air Force's denial was the government withholding information from the public.

Miller said that she only had one day off from the show and then just wanted to sleep, have a good dinner in her hotel room, and start the week again. But the star also reported that she frequently travelled. There was the Center Bridge Inn in Buck's County, Pennsylvania, where one time Miller arrived at 1 a.m. to see a strange phenomenon. Being helped with her luggage by the owner she saw a Victorian looking red-headed young man in a pin-striped suit walking in the hotel. The owner had not seen the man and, when questioned, reported that he had no other guests. This so disturbed the star that she moved to a house in Lumberville down the road, learning that many men had been killed in the area in the Revolutionary War.

Miller also flew to Los Angeles to go on to Sedona, which the famous white Indian trader Don Hoel said was a healing place. She had a strong sense of déjà vu there and many psychics and sensitives called it home because of the powerful force fields of energy that came from the iron ore content in the mountains. Normally the star awoke at 9 a.m. but in Sedona it was 6. She lived in a Mexican designed abode which sat in the middle of 13 and ¾ acres and was formerly owned by a Hopi chief and blessed by a Hopi medicine man. Miller had felt a deep sadness and a strong sense of the Indian people when she first walked inside, perhaps because the builder had placed a prayer house away from the main house where he went to meditate over his dead young son. The star used this as her own meditation room and felt the psychic antennae worked overtime there.

On November 1 she attended the Ziegfeld Ball at the Pierre Hotel and was crowned Miss Ziegfeld of 1980. The event was organized by the Ziegfeld Club Inc., an organization founded to help theater women in need and perpetuate the name of Florenz Ziegfeld. On November 22 Miller appeared in the Macy's Thanksgiving Day Parade in New York which was televised and broadcast on NBC. The show was directed by Dick Schneider who won the Emmy Award for Special Events Coverage.

When winter came, she had the *Sugar Babies* backstage heat turned off because the footlights were so hot, and the stage manager dispensed aspirin, scarves and humor to a shivering crew.

On December 2 the star participated in *The Kennedy Center Honors: A Celebration of the Performing Arts* held at the John F. Kennedy Center for the Performing Arts in Washington. It was broadcast on December 29 as a television special by CBS. The show was directed by Don Mischer, and that year it honored Aaron Copeland, Ella Fitzgerald, Henry Fonda, Martha Graham and Tennessee Williams. Although strangely unrelated to any of the honorees, Miller and Mickey Rooney did the McHugh medley from *Sugar Babies*. The show was nominated for the Outstanding Program Achievement–Special Events Emmy Award. The pair also hosted a company Christmas party for *Sugar Babies.*

In an article in *The New York Times* of January 25, 1980, she commented on a film festival at the Regency Theater entitled "Dancing Ladies," to run from January 27 for six weeks. The star felt that Ruby Keeler and Eleanor Powell had started it all, with Keeler pointing the way and Powell being one of the great ladies of Hollywood. One of the titles to be shown was *Reveille with Beverly* which Miller said she would love to see.

On February 3 an Ann Miller look-alike contest was held at a Manhattan discotheque to benefit the theater-equipment fund of the Cherry Grove Arts Association, with help from the Islanders social club of Fire Island. She was honored that 13 contenders wanted to look like her and, for them, wore a new wig and white mink coat. The star also posed for a photograph with five of the look-alikes.

Miller participated in the March 5 episode of the biographical documentary television series *This Is Your Life* which focused on Stewart Granger and was broadcast on Thames Television. This was written by Tom Brennand and Roy Bottomley, and directed by Terry Yarwood and Paul Stewart Laing. She was seen via satellite from backstage at *Sugar Babies* and told how Granger wanted to meet her because he had a yen for women who wore long black stockings when they danced. Miller reported that the couple dated and she found him to be a great actor and a wonderful person.

The star was photographed backstage at *Sugar Babies* for the *Daily News* of April 8 with Raquel Welch. A pre-show 57th birthday bash was held on April 12 at New York's Bruno's restaurant with guests including Ethel Merman, Carol Channing, Dina Merrill, Dolores Gray, Arlene Dahl and Rock Hudson. Miller was photographed with Hudson and Channing and her cake for the *Daily News* of April 9.

She and Rooney were presenters at *The 52nd Annual Academy Awards* held on April 14 at the Dorothy Chandler Pavilion and televised on ABC. The star was photographed at the show's rehearsal on April 12, and for the show, did a turn as she entered the stage, before they gave the Best Art Direction award to Philip Rosenberg and Tony Walton for Art Direction and Edward Stewart and Gary Brink double-dagger for Set Decoration for the musical *All That Jazz* (1979). The show was directed by Marty Passetta and was nominated for the Outstanding Program Achievement–Special Events Emmy Award. On April 24 Miller and Rooney and "Sugar Baby" chorus girls posed for a photograph for *Life* magazine.

The *Times* of June 6, 1980, reported that she was now signed to a 2 year contract for *Sugar Babies* keeping her in the show until October 8, 1981. Miller attended the 34th Annual (1980) Tony Awards held on June 8 at the Mark Hellinger Theatre and televised by CBS. She and Rooney sang and danced the McHugh medley from *Sugar Babies*, with the star wearing a black suit with sparkly blue and purple lapels and sleeves, blue blouse and split skirt which she pulled off in the number. Director Clark Jones uses some medium shots for coverage, and regrettably Rooney seems to constantly attempt to upstage her. She was also seen later in the audience in a gold jacket over black when her name was announced as one of those nominated for Best Leading Actress in a Musical Tony Award. Miller lost to Patti Lupone for *Evita*. The show won the Outstanding Program Achievement–Special Events Emmy Award. On July 23 she was photographed with Rooney, Robert Morse and Carol Channing backstage at *Sugar Babies*, since Morse and Channing were to take the show on the road.

On September 2 the star was photographed backstage with Charlene Tilton, and in the week of September 19 she and Rooney were photographed under the marquee exhorting moviegoers to give money to the Will Rogers Foundation. On the afternoon of September 28 Miller travelled to Short Hills, New Jersey, to appear in a two hour musical revue in the Temple B'nai Jeshurun. This benefit for the Paper Mill Playhouse in Milburn was to start a fund drive to rebuild the burned out playhouse. She was back on *The Merv Griffin Show* that was shot in New York and broadcast on October 21. It had the theme of "A Salute to Legendary Women" and was directed by Dick Carson.

On an unknown date in 1980 the star was photographed by Bill King wearing a Blackglama fur for the "What becomes a Legend most?" campaign. She was also interviewed backstage at *Sugar Babies* for the television show *New York Live at 5*. Miller had several wigs for the stage show since they took a terrible beating from perspiration and hair spray, with one called Miss Pinta. Her whole life was ruled by her wigs—if they didn't look good, she just wouldn't go on stage, and her secretary planned to take them out after the show had ended its run and shoot them. That year the psychic Char came to see the star backstage, saying Miller's spirit guide and guardian angel was John the Baptist. After the meeting Char moved to Los Angeles and stayed in touch, having visions like the Indian chief White Eagle behind the star. The psychic had not been to the Sedona house so could not have known that it had an oil painting of White Eagle hanging over Miller's bed.

In the early 1980s friend Rita Hayworth in her final years was cared for in her Beverly Hills apartment by medical staff provided by her daughter Yasmin, whom the star admired. Yasmin always had someone come in to set Hayworth's hair, do makeup and dress her, so that she was kept just like a big French doll.

She was thrilled that 22 of the 52 American diplomats and citizens who were held for 444 days as part of the Iran hostage crisis and feted in New York City saw *Sugar Babies* on January 29, 1981. In their honor Miller and the cast sang "God Bless America" and the audience joined in.

Joey Bishop replaced Mickey Rooney in the show from February 2 to March 2 when Rooney went on vacation. Bishop commented that he got a strained left knee trying to keep up with the star, who gave him notes after every performance. She said Rooney was like one long scream compared to Bishop, who worked very low-key, like a sleek cool cat. Miller was used to shouting to be heard over Rooney but now toned it down, and the difference in co-stars was like going from the North Pole to the South Pole. When Rooney returned it was as if they had been sleepwalking and were awakened with a bang. But despite his being on vacation Rooney was photographed on February 11 backstage with his co-star, trying to tempt her with a sweet from his Valentine gift box of candy.

On February 18 she attended a luncheon at the Helmsley Palace Hotel in New York where the Actor's Fund of America announced it would mark its centennial with an ABC television special called *Night of 100 Stars*. The star reportedly spotted Elizabeth Taylor, noticing that her friend had lost weight and Miller had to tell her how envious she was. The star was also photographed with Gina Lollobrigida.

She was photographed with Rooney and President and Mrs. Reagan backstage at *Sugar Babies* after the March 13 performance, though another source says the date was March 14. The star presented them with a jar of jellybeans as a memento from the cast. She had known the couple for 35 years. To celebrate her 58th birthday on April 12 the company gave a look-alike doll dressed in a shiny white top hat and tails.

A party was also held in Bloomingdale's executive board room which coincided with the release of the new biography *Ann Miller Taps: An Authorized Pictorial History* by Jim Connor published by Franklin Watts. Miller wore a black skirt and black blouse with black mink collar, and welcomed old friends Ethel Merman, Benay Venuta, Father Thomas Donlan and Jane Pickens Hoving. In the introduction to the book Hermes Pan wrote that he had recently given a small party to unveil a painting of the star by a prominent portrait artist. When the covering was drawn aside a surprised and bewildered quiet settled over the select group present as the life-size painting showed a serious-faced Miller.

Her hair was pulled back severely and parted down the middle, and she had a sad wistful expression. There was no stage wig or false eyelashes, and no jewelry or furs or frills, and people could not believe this was the real star. Perhaps this reaction unnerved her because Pan later heard she persuaded the artist to touch up the portrait by adding a few baubles, blue eyeshadow, longer lashes, and lipstick.

In an article in *The New York Times* of the same date, Mickey Rooney reported that early in the run of *Sugar Babies* there was a mishap in a skit where Miller took aim at his hat and swatted a wig off as well. Rooney the irresistible force enjoyed doing well-meaning pranks to his immovable object co-star to keep the show loose. He ate an onion before going on, wore the worst cologne, perverted her name with whispered obscenities, passed mash notes, and tickled when she sang. With his back to the audience Rooney stuck out his tongue but if the star didn't laugh he would get mad. But though he could be annoying, she did find him funny and couldn't help but love the man Miller called her little brat and a juvenile delinquent. He may have been unpredictable but Rooney was also generous, giving the star the last bow which he didn't have to do because of his top billing.

In an article about coping with keys in the *Times* of April 12, she reported being a lugger of dozens of keys on a metal key ring including those for her New York hotel room, four closets and a perfume cabinet; also 30 suitcases packed with clothes and shoes and the like, and another 20 suitcases with the tools of the trade. They were a universal irritant, ruining her pockets and purses and her solution was to have a huge purse just for keys, but it could be so heavy as to nearly break the arm.

On May 5, 1981, Miller participated in an *Eyewitness News* Special Report by Doug Johnson entitled "Nothing's higher than being on top," commenting on being famous. On the same night a one-woman show by Barbara Perry entitled *Passionate Ladies* opened at New York's Bijou Theater. Written by Perry and directed by Edmund Balin, it included her doing an impersonation of the star. Mel Gussow in the *Times* wrote that Perry demonstrated a certain talent for mimicry and for hoofing. The show ran until May 10. The *Times* of May 20 reported that she had contributed a pair of her tap-dancing shoes to the "Shoe Wall of Fame" at Roseland Ballroom. These were her standbys, the pair Miller used for rehearsals, since she was saving her regulars to leave to a museum. Already hanging at Roseland were shoes worn by Adele Astaire, Ruby Keeler, Anna Held and Bill Robinson. On May 31 the star participated in a Philly Popps Gala Concert at the Academy of Music in Philadelphia to benefit the All Star Forum.

She attended the 35th Annual (1981) Tony Awards on June 7 held at the Mark Hellinger Theatre which was televised by CBS and directed by Clark Jones. Footage of Miller singing from the previous year's broadcast was part of a montage under the song "There Is Nothing Like a Dame," which demonstrated this year's theme of "A Salute to Women in the Theater." After host Ellen Burstyn introduced her as "the indefatigable Ann Miller," director Jones gave a shot of the star's legs as she came onstage and did a turn. Miller presented the Outstanding Choreography award to Greg Champion, the son of the late Gower Champion who won for *42nd Street*. The television show was nominated for the Outstanding Achievement in Lighting Direction Emmy Award. The *Times* of June 12 reported that while Mickey Rooney had signed a new contract for *Sugar Babies*, extending his engagement for a year from next October, Miller was still negotiating.

When Rooney went on vacation again from June 29 to July 8 he was replaced by Rip Taylor, the comedian who was known for throwing confetti. Rehearsals were directed by Debbie Reynolds with Jane Summerhays who had replaced Ann Jillian and Anita Morris in the musical as standby for the star. When Miller came in to work with Taylor she brought the stenographer's notebook with a record of the changes introduced by Rooney and Joey Bishop. However the star was concerned about the confetti which might cause her to slip, and he agreed not to use it, since there was no confetti in the script. Taylor cried at the opportunity to dance with "that big M-G-M star" and as he pranced smoothly but clench-teethed by her side, Miller told him to stop worrying or she would kick him.

On August 10 the star attended a dinner dance hosted by Halston honoring "New York, New York" at Olympic Towers in New York. The *Times* of August 15, 1981, reported that she had met with a group of Californians at Roseland Dance City. When Vera-Ellen was hospitalized in August with cancer Miller sent flowers to the UCLA Medical Center. August also saw the death of her mother, which was a terrible blow.

Sugar Babies had given the star a new costume with a stole of real peacock feathers and the superstition about wearing real peacock feathers causing a death in the family proved to be true when Clara died the night after Miller wore it. But the show's producers and Mickey Rooney were wonderful about her loss, letting the star fly to the coast. Her mother had been Miller's guiding light, wearing "10 hats" as her driver, house cleaner, cook, secretary, manager, and publicist. Once when she was living in New York at Christmas, the star had asked her to send the Christmas card mailing list and Clara sent two California phone books.

But osteoarthritis, three strokes and three hip operations had nearly ended it all for the 89 year old.

Finally Clara fell into a coma from which her doctors said she would not recover and recommended the life support be shut off. Miller called upon her psychic spirits to ask for advice but they told her no. So she held her mother's hand for two hours, feeling the subconscious mind working and after the star had repeated a cry to come back to her, Clara responded. She opened her eyes and said hello and lived for six more months. After her mother died Miller would still feel her energy around her, smelling roses when there were no roses in the room. She believed Clara would be waiting for her when she died, which made her unafraid.

On September 9 she was photographed backstage with Jaye P. Morgan who was to play the star's role in the eight month national tour starting September 17 while Miller continued on Broadway. On September 29 she was photographed backstage with Pat Nixon.

The star took a few weeks off to make a segment of the two-hour episode of the television romantic comedy *The Love Boat* entitled "The Musical/My Ex-Mom/The Show Must Go On/The Pest/My Aunt, the Worrier" which was broadcast by ABC on February 27, 1982. Shot at the 20th Century–Fox Studios in Hollywood the show was written by Art Baer, Ray Jessel, Ben Joelson, and Tony Webster, developed by W.L. Baumes and suggested by Jeraldine Saunders. The director was Roger Duchowny. Miller is billed third alphabetically among the guest stars, playing Connie Carruthers, the former mother-in-law of Doctor Adam Bricker (Bernie Kopell) who is to take part in a musical revue "Love Boat Follies." Costumes are by Nolan Miller and the choreographer is Carl Jablonski.

The whole show is unavailable for viewing but excerpts make it appear that the star sings and dances in two numbers, Cole Porter's "It's All Right with Me" and as part of "I'm the Greatest Star" in the "Follies" with Ros Smith (Ethel Merman), Aunt Sylvia (Carol Channing) and Millie Washington (Della Reese). She also sings "You Were Meant for Me" at a rehearsal, and is part of the "Follies" finale as Miss Panama Canal. For "It's All Right with Me" Miller enters the ship's dining room wearing a sparkly pink floor-length split skirt dress with one long-sleeve and one shoulder bare, floor-length silk scarf and her stage wig. The number has her leaping onto tables to tap and having the skirt pulled off by chorus boys, with director Duchowny using a cutaway to the audience and a shot of the star's feet as she dances.

She appears to make her entrance in the show leading two wolfhounds, recalling Miller in *Easter Parade*, and when told the dogs are not allowed on board tells a steward to "give them each a glass of champagne and send them home." Connie gets another funny line in the rehearsal scene. Millie asks her if she is trying to sabotage her act as Connie plays the piano, and she replies, "Oh honey, you can do that all by yourself." When Purser "Gopher" Smith (Fred Grandy) announces the entrance of his mother, Ros, Connie replies, "There goes my hearing" in regard to Merman's loud voice. And in another scene the incomparably modest Connie tells one impressed bystander of her past: "I just danced a little—you know, the way Luciano Pavarotti sings a little." The show received a mixed reaction from John J. O'Connor in *The New York Times*.

On her United Airlines flight back to New York she lost a million-dollar 30-carat diamond ring and gained Van Johnson, whom the star had met on the show, as a frequent escort. The ring had disappeared when she had used the washroom and officials searched the plane for nearly 24 hours without success.

Miller was back onstage on October 12, 1981, and the same night there was a party at Astor's celebrating two years of *Sugar Babies*. The actual anniversary was October 4 but the party had been postponed until she had returned to the cast. The star signed a contract for her third year, saying she was not at all bored with it. The audience was different every performance, sometimes great, sometimes awful. If they sat on their hands Miller assumed they were New Yorkers since tourists and out-of-towners loved the show. If the audience didn't laugh at Mickey Rooney's first couple of jokes he got mad and stayed that way for the rest of the performance, not having learned to woo a bad audience like a lover, which is what she did.

Miller had heard that Miss Piggy had done a takeoff of her in the adventure crime comedy *The Great Muppet Caper* (1981) but had yet to see the film, directed by Jim Henson, which had been released on June 26. The takeoff was presumably when Miss Piggy does a tap dance on a nightclub table for the song "The First Time It Happens" by Joe Raposo, though Miller's name is not referenced. The star loved Miss Piggy and had a huge poster in her dressing room, thinking their eyes were alike. She would have loved a tap-off with her so that the papers could headline "MISS PIGGY MEETS MISS WIGGY."

On October 26 Miller participated in "Broadway Salutes the New York City Opera," a benefit held at Lincoln Center's New York State Theater. A supper dance on the Grand Promenade was held after the salute.

On November 13, 1981, it was reported that she had turned down a chance to perform for the Queen at the Royal Variety Performance later in the month. Organizer Louis Benjamin had wanted the star to make a surprise appearance and dance briefly with a chorus line behind her, but she preferred a solo spot. Benjamin spent two hours negotiating with Miller in her Broadway dressing room but failed to persuade her. On November 26 she participated in the Macy's Thanksgiving Day Parade in New York which was televised by NBC, with the show directed by Dick Schneider. It was nominated for the Outstanding Achievement in Coverage of Special Events Emmy Award. *The New York Times* reported that along one section of the route the star was greeted with more cheers than Donny Osmond or Snoopy.

In the *Times* article of December 17 about Christmas tipping, Miller's habits were explained. She tipped in all the cities the star had residences, giving $5 to her Manhattan hotel housekeeper, doormen and bellmen and the California mail carrier and gardener. The star was also a big sender of expensive Christmas cards, lined in velvet and suitable for framing. On the week of the 18th she and Mickey Rooney followed the *Sugar Babies* cast ritual for the third year, trimming the Christmas tree in the lobby of the Mark Hellinger Theater, and posing for publicity shots draped with decoration.

In 1981 Miller was interviewed in her dressing room for an article for *Playbill* and commented on the myth started by Henry Youngman that she was bald, having the interviewer tug on her hair to prove that it was real and not a stage wig.

The star appeared on the January 12, 1982, episode of the family television talk show *Hour Magazine*.

She had become friends with Eleanor Powell, who after leaving films had become a minister in the Church of Religious Science. The ailing Powell wanted to see her in *Sugar Babies* but couldn't afford it so Miller paid for her and her secretary, Eleanor Debus, to come to New York. But before they could get there Powell died on February 11. The star didn't think she could do the show that night but was motivated by a paranormal experience: she tells two versions of this story. One had her television off because of a cable failure in the hotel then suddenly coming on for Miller to see Powell tapping the "Pin Ball" number from the United Artists musical *Sensations of 1945* (1944). The other version had the television working and suddenly changing channels for the number, without the star touching the dial. She liked to think that her friend did come to New York on the screen to say goodbye.

Miller was satirized in the Broadway revue *Forbidden Broadway*, written by Gerard Alessandrini and directed by Michael Chapman, playing at Palsson's supper club. Wendee Winters voiced her, singing "I'm Entertainment" to the tune of "That's Entertainment," wearing an ebony bird's nest on her head and leaping and bouncing through a jumping dance. She wailed, "My smile is constructed of stone" and admitted to killing Louis B. Mayer by hitting him with her hair. Alessandrini reported that the star had come to see the show and stopped backstage afterward.

She and Mickey Rooney participated in the Music Hall Ball *Night of 100 Stars*, which was a fundraising event for the Actor's Fund. It was filmed on Valentine's Day at Radio City Music Hall and broadcast on March 6, 1982, on ABC. The show was directed by Clark Jones and won the Outstanding Variety, Music or Comedy Program Emmy Award. On March 8 there was a party at the Red Parrot nightclub to celebrate the 1,000th performance of *Sugar Babies*. There Rooney announced that he and Miller would be leaving "sometime after September" for a national tour that will last through most of 1983. On March 31 she presented Ruby Keeler with a Lalique crystal bowl at Studio 54, as part of the dinner that was given to honor her. The star said she watched her movies as a child of nine and Keeler replied that Miller had certainly caught up fast.

Eddie Bracken was her new co-star in *Sugar Babies* when Mickey Rooney had his vacation from May 31 to June 13. In *Newsday* of June 4, the show's 88-year-old doorman Albert Stern reported that in the three years he and the star had become buddies, often having a post-show bite to eat or Miller giving him a ride home in her limousine. Stern would do anything for the star who he felt was like a mother(!) to him. If she needed something he would get it, and if Miller didn't feel like facing fans the man brought Playbills to her dressing room to sign for them.

On June 6 she was a performer on the 36th Annual (1982) Tony Awards, held at the Imperial Theatre in New York televised by CBS and directed by Clark Jones. As part of a tribute to the musical history of the Imperial, the star sang "No Time at All" from *Pippin* and danced in front of the words to the song to encourage the audience to sing along.

She appeared on the Ben Bagley–produced record *Kurt Weill Revisited*, singing "This Time Next Year," "Moon-faced, Starry-Eyed" and "Is It Him or Is It Me?"

On June 16 Miller attended Les Mouches to celebrate the first annual Astaire Awards to dancers and choreographers on the New York stage and to accept an award. On July 9 she attended a reunion at the Russian Tea Room of former RKO stars now living in New York, to mark RKO's donation of its film archives to the University of California at Los Angeles. On August 24 the star was the host of a birthday party for Lee Roy Reams at the cabaret the Palace.

August 28, 1982, was the closing night of *Sugar Babies* after 12,008 performances, with Miller dissolving into giggles when she accidentally whacked Mickey Rooney's wig off. The cast also sang a song written for the occasion by Rooney that included the lyric "We're sorry we have to leave." The star cried, saying she felt like someone jerked her heart out, and was incredulous the producers wanted to close the show when they were still getting full houses. But Rooney wanted to go, feeling it was better to leave with their flags flying, and she agreed.

Backstage Miller dried her tears and posed for photographers, showing off her famous legs. She also posed hugging a huge stuffed tiger that had been sent by a couple from White Plains the star didn't know, and treasured the telegram from new friend Helen Hayes which read, "The lights would be dimmer till you come back to Broadway." At an after-show party at Luchow's restaurant, Lee Roy Reams praised the two stars as real professionals who had been through many eras and did things with real craft. A lot of people had talent, but they were survivors.

She and Rooney began the national tour of the show in Chicago on November 8, having a contract that allowed Miller two weeks off at a time so she could return to Sedona. There the star could walk her dogs, read books, and look at television, and this double life made her feel like a split personality.

Miller participated in a promotional 20 minute short film conceived by the New York Convention and Visitors Bureau entitled "Taste of the Big Apple" which had its premiere on November 23 in the McGraw-Hill Building auditorium.

But in January 1983 she tore an Achilles tendon and when doctors ordered her not to dance the star had to withdraw from the show temporarily.

She was interviewed for the March 13 edition of the newspaper *Grit*, for an article by Reba and Bonnie Churchill entitled "Broadway's Ann Miller: Expert in Art of Preservation." Her talent for preservation included having a walk-in closet where Miller had squeezed 35 years of clothing, like the costume she had worn at the Bal Tabarin at 15. What was more amazing was that the star could still fit into the clothes, having maintained her waistline partly by taking her dogs for long walks. She had spent three-quarters of her life travelling and there were few places Miller had not seen. She loved being a gypsy at heart and always travelled with her dogs as companions. The life had not been one happy chorus line but when the star had a problem she sat down and talked with God.

Miller had gone to Santa Fe to recuperate and made a pilgrimage to a church built around a spring in Chimayo, near Taos, where the Indians went to pray. It was like Lourdes with crutches and canes hanging on the walls from people who claimed that the holy mud and sand had cured them. She filled two large coffee cans with mud and put a picture of Jesus on the hotel suite fireplace, praying and rubbing the mud on her heel. While it did not appease the pain, somehow the star could walk easier.

She met with choreographer Ernie Flatt in Florida, telling him it was too soon for her to dance, but he wanted Miller to try. So she put on her tap shoes and made a silent prayer. The muscles were tight and painful but slowly she was able to dance, which the star credited to the power of mind energy, determination and God's will. Another motivation was the show's producers who threatened to sue her, saying if she could walk around Santa Fe or Beverly Hills then Miller could walk on stage.

While the star had been out she had been replaced by Jane Summerhays, whom Miller had befriended. After the show they would have margaritas together before Summerhays got a lift home in the limousine. She described the star as a "dame" and unique, having an M-G-M bubble world around her. Summerhays observed that the timing of Miller and Mickey Rooney was like an Elgin clock, and though they had a lot of respect for each other, the pair didn't always get along. The rumor was that they never spoke offstage but Summerhays felt it was more that the stars went their separate ways.

Miller re-joined *Sugar Babies* in June after four months' medical leave, hoping that doing so did not cause any permanent damage. The venue was the Miami Beach Theater of the Performing Arts before the company would move on to New Orleans at the Saenger Performing Arts Center. She said her dancing wasn't up to full throttle and wouldn't be for another four or five months, but the producers wanted the star back even if meant no dancing. She tried to give audiences a little teaser feeling they expected some token from her but the heel was very painful. Miller insisted that a pre-show announcement be made about the broken heel and that she would do the best she could. On July 5 a press conference was held in Boston to announce a four-week engagement at the Met Center. On July 19 the stars got together at the RCA studio in New York to make the cast album which was to be released in September on Original Cast Records. During the recording they danced, and Rooney was writing a play for her called "Agnes, Mabel and Becky." He felt that Stephen Sondheim should write a play for Miller called Style, with her as the empress of the fashion industry, all deco and gorgeous. She reported being offered a revival of *Anything Goes*.

The tour continued at the Shubert Theater in Philadelphia from August 9 to September 3, 1983. According to the August 10 *Newsday* the star's opening night gems were fakes and not her originals. Sometime during the week thieves entered her dressing room and stole them.

She participated in the February 4, 1984, episode of the television show *This Is Your Life*, which was devoted to Rooney. On February 28 Miller appeared at *The 26th Annual Grammy Awards* which were held at the Shrine Auditorium in Hollywood. The show was televised by CBS and directed by Walter C. Miller. She was back on the *Hour Magazine* television show broadcast on March 13. On March 15 the star was photographed backstage at *Sugar Babies* at the Pantages Theater in Los Angeles with Rooney and Michael Jackson.

On April 13 she was back on *The Tonight Show Starring Johnny Carson* aka "Late Night with Johnny Carson" with guest hostess Joan Rivers. Miller wore her natural hair in an uncharacteristic loose style with a sparkly black pants suit with sheer long sleeves. She confirmed *The Hollywood* Reporter story of wanting to have a face lift but didn't know who to go to, so Rivers said she would give her names. The star talked about the bad review *Sugar Babies* had received from Sylvia Drake in the *Los Angeles Times*, who had hated the revival as much as she had the out-of-town tryout. Drake in particular was critical of Miller for no longer dancing 500 taps a minute, and the star responded by wiring the reviewer's boss that she danced 1000 taps a minute. But despite bad reviews Miller and Rooney had been made multi-millionaires from the show. The producers had initially decided to close the revival in Los Angeles but now had decided to continue the tour onto Cleveland and Detroit. Rivers asked to do a time-step with the star, and she did. The Carson show was directed by Bob Ostberg.

Miller was back on *The Merv Griffin Show* broadcast on May 27, 1984, which was directed by Dick Carson. On June 5 she and Rooney received the Canadian Club's Break-A-Leg award at the Actor's Fund of America luncheon for their work on *Sugar Babies*. The June 19 *New York Times* reported that the star had made $4.6 million on the show. It had two more years on the road to go and either London or Australia as an encore, with a film version planned. From July 3 to 11 *Sugar Babies* performed at the San Jose Center for the Performing Arts. The cast recording was released by Broadway Entertainment on August 12 and was praised by Paul Kresh in *The Times*, who wrote that Miller was a woman whom age seemed not to have withered in the slightest.

The Griswold's Cabaret in New York featured an impersonation of the star in their show entitled *Lavender Follies*. The *New York Post* of November 6 reported that she was glad the presidential campaign was over, since politicians kept trying to run her out of hotel rooms in Indianapolis and Memphis in October of that election year. Miller had refused to move for George Bush at the Indianapolis Hilton and Walter Mondale at the Peabody Hotel in Memphis. The *Times* of November 11 reported that a charcoal sketch portrait of the star by Ben Solowey was one of those on display at the Palace Theater in New Haven. On November 15 her 35-year-old tap shoes were presented to the Smithsonian Institution in Washington, while she was appearing in the capital in *Sugar Babies*. The *Times* of December 23 reported that Miller had advised John Raitt on his possible casting in the forthcoming Broadway musical *La Cage aux Folles*. He had been turned down to play one of the homosexual lovers, and she couldn't have imagined him playing the part.

The *Sugar Babies* tour continued into 1985 with shows at the Shubert Performing Arts Center in New Haven from January 8 to 13, a week at Norfolk, Virginia, and then a return to New Haven from January 29 to February 3. A chapter was devoted to the star in the Tony Thomas book *That's Dancing* that was released by Harry N. Abrams in February. Miller was quoted as saying that she was born to dance and "I Could Have Danced All Night" might have been written for her. *Sugar Babies* moved to the Riverside Theatre in Milwaukee, Wisconsin, from March 19 to 24, the Music Fair Theater in Valley Forge, Pennsylvania, in June and then moved to the Westbury Music Fair from July 7 to 21 with Jane Summerhays replacing the star who was out injured.

On December 2, 1985, she attended the *All-Star Party for "Dutch" Reagan* that was taped at an NBC studio in Hollywood and broadcast on December 8 on NBC. It was sponsored by Variety Clubs International with proceeds to be used for a Ronald Reagan Wing for children at the University of Nebraska hospital in Omaha. The musical comedy television special was written by Paul W. Keyes and directed by Dick McDonough. It honored Reagan being sworn in for his second term of office as the American president.

In 1986 *Sugar Babies* opened in Fort Lauderdale, Florida, on February 25. Miller performed at *The 58th Annual Academy Awards* held at the Dorothy Chandler Pavilion in Hollywood on March 24. Wearing a Nolan Miller emerald green chiffon dress with an emerald green ostrich feather boa she was part of the tribute to M-G-M musicals and tapped to the song "Once a Star, Always a Star." The show was directed by Marty Pasetta.

Sugar Babies continued on to the Sunrise Musical Theatre in Sunrise, Florida, to April 5, where it ended its record run of 8½ years. After the last show the star went to a party given by the producers in a small restaurant, where she made a farewell speech. While thanking the talented company, Miller also predicted she would do the show again.

In the June 22 edition of the *Los Angeles Times* the star commented on the heartbreaking current state of M-G-M, where ghosts had to be flying around after turning over in their graves. She had just bought 200

M-G-M movies that were on sale, most of them musicals, for preservation. On June 27 Miller was photographed at the 21 Club in the *New York Post*, back in town for the first time in four years.

In an August 3, 1986, article in *The New York Times* about diaries and journals public relations worker Terry Lilly told of having met the star when she was doing *Sugar Babies* on Broadway. Learning he kept a diary of the famous the man had met, Miller told Lilly she hated people who wrote books about famous people. On August 15 the star was photographed with Morgan Woodward on a date at the fifth annual Golden Boots Awards at the Los Angeles Equestrian Center.

On November 12 the *Post* included in their advice column her low opinion about blue jeans worn in public, saying that people only wore them in Texas for rounding up and milking cattle. The star appeared on the November 18 episode of the comedy music television talk show *Late Night with David Letterman* which was shot in New York at the NBC Studios and broadcast on NBC. On November 22 the *Post* reported that the star attended the newly renovated Roseland on November 19. She was photographed dancing with Tom Wopat and holding up a T-shirt decorated with foxtrot steps.

In 1986 Miller appeared in a print ad for Rose's Lime Juice, wearing a costume from *Sugar Babies*, and standing over Michael Clark with a raised right hand holding a glass. The ad read "What do a sugar baby and dance's post-punk prince have in common? One classic step. Rose's."

On March 28, 1987, she attended a tribute to M-G-M's Dancing Ladies held at the Filmland Corporate Center in Hollywood. The star was photographed in front of an enlarged still of herself doing "I've Gotta Hear That Beat" from *Small Town Girl*, as well as with Esther Williams, Betty Garrett, Leslie Caron, Debbie Reynolds and Cyd Charisse.

On May 16 she attended the SHARE Boomtown Party held at the Santa Monica Civic Auditorium. Miller participated in the television documentary *Happy 100th Birthday, Hollywood* which was broadcast on May 18 on ABC. The show was written by Jack Haley, Jr., William Moritz and Hildy Parks and directed by Jeff Margolis. Her taps are heard before she is seen wearing an Alvin Colt pink tailed jacket with black fringed sash, black leotard, pink top hat with a black feather, and pink gloves. She sang and danced "Shakin' the Blues Away" with Lee Roy Reams, Don Correia, Greg Burge, and Hinton Battle leading a chorus. The star appears to repeat the original choreography from *Easter Parade* but choreographer Walter Painter has the chorus swamp her and director Margolis' coverage includes camera angles that pull the focus away from Miller.

On July 17 she attended the 17th Annual Nosotros Awards held at the Beverly Hilton Hotel.

The New York Times of January 1, 1988, reported a plan had been abandoned to unite the star with Alexis Smith for a Broadway revival of *Legends*, the James Kirkwood comedy about two aging battling stars. The original show had run on Broadway from January 7, 1986, to January 18, 1987, and starred Carol Channing and Mary Martin.

On March 19 she attended an event held at the Beverly Hilton Hotel which honored Bob Hope with the Humanitarian Award from the Myasthenia Gravis Foundation.

In April of 1988 Miller's foretelling of doing *Sugar Babies* again came true in a production at Sedona. After the show closed she had another psychic feeling and arriving back in Los Angeles, received a telephone call from Ernest Flatt. He wanted to see her to discuss a London production at the Savoy Theatre on the West End, to open in August.

CHAPTER 9

· · · · · · · · · · · · · · · ·

Sugar Babies
in London

*R*ehearsals began in May 1988 in a dance studio and the star was in great shape for London. She appeared on *The18th Annual Nosotros Golden Eagle Awards* held at the Beverly Hilton Hotel which was televised and broadcast on May 13 on NBC. On July 4 she was photographed with Cyd Charisse, Kathryn Grayson, Betty Garrett, Donald O'Connor, Margaret O'Brien, June Allyson, and Esther Williams at Chasen's Restaurant in Beverly Hills for a party thrown by MGM/UA Home Video to salute the Hollywood stars of yesterday.

She decided to go shopping in Beverly Hills for some new clothes with Debbie Zehnder, and saw some shoes she liked. But as the star started towards them she slipped on the newly-waxed and polished marble tile floor and landed on her right knee and left buttock. Debbie helped Miller to a chair and someone gave her a glass of water until she felt better. But when Debbie was trying on a skirt, the star felt faint and had to sit down again. She refused an offered ambulance and was driven home by Debbie but Miller knew she had sustained an injury. A doctor confirmed that the star had fractured her pelvis and had a swollen knee. She telephoned producer David Martin in London and broke the news, hoping to recover in time for the planned opening date but fearful of being replaced since Miller knew attendance would drop if the show opened at Christmas time. Martin promised to wait for her to heal, which meant paying Mickey Rooney to stay in London, since he was already there. The producer checked the star's progress every week and healing was slow. You couldn't put a pelvic bone in a cast and dance but after six weeks she was back in the rehearsal room regaining her strength and endurance. Miller felt recovered enough to leave for London and the dogs were flown to Cincinnati to stay with Debbie's aunt, not being allowed to go with the star.

167

When she arrived in London there was a press reception at the Savoy Hotel, which noted that Miller had lost 10 pounds. Ernest Flatt and Rooney agreed Miller had never looked or danced better, and spirits were high in the company though she remained worried about the show's late opening and that perhaps it was too bawdy for the Brits. The star had new costumes made for her in New York by Barbra Matera, and also found a wonderful new dresser. Opening night came in September at the Savoy Theatre, though at the stage door a fan accidently pushed Miller which hurt her ankle. There was a post-show party held at the Ritz Hotel and the reviews were wonderful. The company had a hit, which pleased the star who had planned to stay for a year. But when she had the ankle examined it was discovered Miller had stress fractures in each foot across the instep. But she couldn't rest to let them heal because of her contract and the star's desire to not let the team down.

Rhonda Burchmore had been her stand-in while the show was in rehearsal and remained as Miller's understudy in the run and wrote about her experience in the book *Legs 11: My Life in Front of the Lights and Backstage*. Burchmore reported that the star greeted her with trepidation and cool charm and she was pleasant if somewhat distant. Miller sized up the younger and taller girl as competition, like Muhammad Ali viewing Joe Frazier before the opening bell, after the producers had said how good Burchmore had been. It was clear that any friendship would have to be earned and come out of a mutual respect. Burchmore felt the star played the prima donna both on stage and off, being fully aware of exactly who she was and sensitive to anyone who tried to disrespect her.

The girl reported on Miller's idiosyncratic way of working, arriving at 5 p.m. for the 8 p.m. show to check the stage. She would carry a box of tissues and drop a crumpled one on any danger points, scanning the floor for bobby pins, a raised board, a paint bubble, hardened bird excrement, or a groove. On any given day the stage manager would find up to 20 crumpled tissues on parts of the floor that needed immediate attention so as not to hinder the star's performance. Burchmore also reported that Miller wore five pairs of tights to hold her legs in place and it was a wonder that she didn't melt under the lights and the legs didn't turn to butter. The multiple pairs were not apparent to the audience from their distance, with the gussets removed from the tights so that there was no seamline.

No male member of the cast was allowed to wear jewelry, like a watch, in case it wore the stockings. When a male understudy forgot

Opposite: **Flyer for the London production of *Sugar Babies* (September to December 31, 1987).**

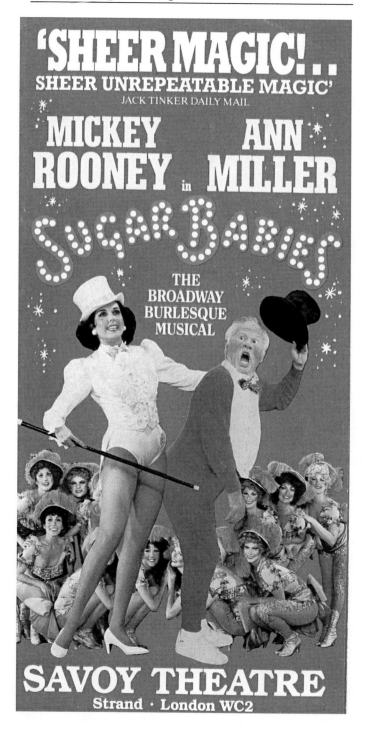

this and his timepiece snagged the star's stockings on a lift, he received a dressing down. She was particularly incensed that he had attempted to poke back the sausage of flesh during the number, and needless to say, was fired from the show. Burchmore said that Miller was put off by some of the girl's costumes, like a silver gown worn with silver body glitter in the finale. The star said the glitter in the air interfered with her singing voice so it was no longer used, though Burchmore also felt Miller would have been happier to not have the girl in the finale at all.

It appeared that the star only spoke to Burchmore if she had to, preferring the chorus boys because they were no threat. Burchmore tried to open conversations with her, one day saying she dreaded having to go on stage in Miller's place if that became necessary since the girl was not who the audience came to see. Slowly the star's guard came down and they became pals, with Burchmore finding her adorable. She would stop into Miller's dressing room before a show to display the bargains she had purchased that day in Covent Garden.

One night the girl had a blue and purple cashmere sweater, which the star fell in love with. Burchmore volunteered to get her one too but gingerly asked if Miller would pay her for it, since it was expensive and the girl was not pulling in the same huge salary. The star looked stunned and said she would think about it and after an interval Burchmore was summoned back to the dressing room. Miller produced a Platinum Amex card and told the girl to practice copying her signed name. The next day the sweater was purchased with the card and the forged signature. It seemed to Burchmore that now the star loved her, and the girl would no longer be frozen on the spot with Miller's disapproving look.

The star's guard was understandable since she was a person who had survived the dog-eat-dog world of show business, navigating her way past all the time wasters and phonies and users and thieves and bullies. A tough guard was needed since any display of warmth or vulnerability would have been preyed upon and exploited, and only revealed to those Miller trusted. When Burchmore's parents visited from Australia, the star entertained them in her dressing room and took them all out to dinner at her expense. One night when the girl and Miller were walking through a market a pair of hoop earrings going for 20 pounds were spotted that the star wanted and asked Burchmore to borrow the money. Miller insisted on writing an IOU and the next day the money was repaid, and as a thank you came a giant bottle of Chanel concentrate with a note saying "With love from Annie."

Burchmore reported that while the star and Rooney had the utmost respect for each other as performers, offstage they hated each other intensely. The couple refused to socialize together, and if at the same event when one walked into a room the other would leave immediately. Burchmore said the conflict was due to their opposing personalities, though she admitted that of the two, Rooney was the hardest to like. Onstage they were magic together, though Miller got mad at him when he wasn't in the mood to do the show and just walked through it. Sometimes at Saturday matinees Rooney would wait backstage listening to horse races which left her alone in a sketch they were meant to do together. She and the audience just had to wait until the race was over for the co-star to appear.

Rooney would also resent the audience if they gave him a lackluster response and on one occasion was caught verbalizing his contempt for them, whining about the energy he gave to try to entertain them. Rooney's tirade had been broadcast to the auditorium when he had left his radio microphone on and the incident was reported in the next day's newspapers which led to bookings falling off. Burchmore felt it was a mistake to let him have a curtain thank you, since Rooney used it to express what was bugging him. This included giving the news of the Lockerbie air disaster, which left them traumatized rather than with the desired warm glow of a wonderful evening.

Miller was acutely aware of the audiences' expectations, since the show had to have sell-outs to compensate for the salaries both stars were pulling, which left her frustrated over Rooney's antics which put the show into jeopardy. She was also furious when one time he used the oxygen machines the star had in the wings to access after a strenuous routine, with the pair going at it with each other with plenty of profane language. The star also did not appreciate Rooney writing Burchmore a new song for the show that she had no intention of approving.

Miller was interviewed for the British television show *GMTV* about the show. She said working with her co-star was like a little bit of M-G-M stardust and the two of them together were like coffee and cream. They understood each other and the show had been enormously successful because of it. Her previous notion that the Brits would find it too bawdy was now revised after having seen *The Benny Hill Show* on television, and the star hoped her show would release the same kind of nostalgia here that had occurred in the United States.

She was referenced in the October 8 episode of the television comedy *The Golden Girls* entitled "Yes, We Have no Havanas." This was written by Mort Nathan and Barry Fanaro and directed by Terry Hughes. In the show Blanche (Rue McClanahan) and Sophia (Estelle Getty) are caught in a love triangle with an elderly Cuban cigar mogul Fidel Santiago (Henry Darrow). At his funeral, Sophia comments, "The man's face has more powder on it than Ann Miller's and she's giving him to me."

Despite the advance box office for *Sugar Babies* the star had the premonition it would close early, though Debbie Zehnder refused to have the hotel porter bring up their suitcases for packing. She didn't want to leave, since Miller had longed to visit the magical city of history and beauty, and did as much sightseeing as possible. The Tower of London was opened early for a private tour and showing of the crown jewels just for her, she went to the state opening of Parliament in the Royal Gallery, and the American Embassy for supper and to watch the televised American election returns. The star and Rooney were received by Prime Minister Margaret Thatcher in her office after they heard her speak in the House of Commons.

Miller thought she was a fabulous lady, who told her to please keep singing and dancing because the world needed more music and laughter. The stars were also presented to Her Majesty Queen Elizabeth the Queen Mother and HRH The Princess Margaret in the lobby of the London Palladium Theatre before *The Royal Variety Performance* of November 21. Miller gave a bouquet of flowers before she and Rooney had to dash back to do *Sugar Babies*. However the couple returned to sing and dance the McHugh medley from the show for the television special that was broadcast on November 26 on the BBC.

On November 25, 1987, *The New York Times* interviewed Paul Stamper, the stagehand at the Savoy, who told of the star's preparation of the stage for each show. He had to stand onstage, hammer and nails at the ready, while she tapped her way over every square inch. If Miller found a loose nail or an uneven floor seam she would drop a Kleenex square for his attention. The star told him she had broken her ankle years ago on an upraised nail to explain her strategy, and they often found two or three things a day that needed fixing.

In early December Miller met Fergie, the Duchess of York, at the *Evening Standard* Newspaper Awards. The December 14 *Daily News* reported Fergie had told her Princess Diana had wanted to take tap dancing lessons and the star volunteered to be the teacher, though it is not known what the reply was.

Miller and Rooney were both nominated for a Lawrence Olivier Award, the British equivalent of the Tony Awards. But the late opening of *Sugar Babies* had indeed had an impact on sales, with the shopping hordes leaving West End theaters half empty. However the cast was still stunned when David Martin announced one day before a matinee the show was closing on December 31, 1987. The star gave a small Christmas party and everyone bought gifts but it didn't help. Miller told her dresser she would return one day and said to keep her hair dryer, coffee grinder, and electric fan on standby. They laughed politely and the star found the British to be the most endearing people she had ever met.

Miller attended the New Year's Eve party thrown by Rhonda Burchmore at her bedsit apartment. Although it was supposed to be a dress casual affair, Miller wore tailored slacks, a black cashmere sweater and a giant emerald necklace and draped over her shoulders a full-length diamond mink coat. She entertained the small group until 4 a.m. as the star drank French champagne, telling stories. These included the botched nose job done at M-G-M, and Fred Astaire, and making *Easter Parade* which led her to perform "Shakin' the Blues Away" again. When Miller was leaving she smiled and said, "I'm pissed [drunk] but elegant."

The star packed her clothes in a hurry, having to vacate her hotel room on a certain date to avoid paying another month's rent, and planned a trip with Debbie to St. Moritz to have some Christmas spirit in the snow. There they checked into the Andre Badrutts' Palace Hotel, overlooking a frozen lake. The two went for a sleigh ride over the lake, up into the mountains and trees, seeing Swiss chalets. They bought cuckoo clocks and chocolate for their friends back home, gave each other watches, and went to the Hanzelmans Café for hot chocolate and pastry and watched the skiers come in. Then they went up the funicular to the restaurant on the side of the mountain to see the skiers going down. After a final dinner in the Hotel's dining room they said a reluctant goodbye to Switzerland.

Back in the United States the two travelled to Cincinnati to pick up Miller's dogs and after a few days, returned to Los Angeles. The next month Ann received another psychic message—they had to leave right away for Sedona. The two houses the star had purchased that had been on the market for three years were going to be sold. They travelled the next day and on arrival were told of the sale of one of the houses. She hoped the other would also sell, to allow her to build a dream home Santa Fe Indian adobe. The star consulted the psychic Ann Klein who channeled an Arab man. He said this was to be her last life, but she had lived many past ones in different areas and was guided by several Masters, especially a Hindu one. The Arab confirmed what Char had said— that her spirit guide was John the Baptist—and the trouble Miller had had with her land would be resolved. She would continue dancing but only when the star wanted to and would be a guiding light for other young dancers. There was also another husband in the future—a tall, white-haired and wealthy man she would meet in London.

Miller appeared on the January 27, 1989, episode of the news and television talk show *Good Morning America*, shot in New York and broadcast on ABC. She was seen in the rehearsal room of her house dancing in a leotard which the star did to keep fit, though she added you also had to get at least eight hours of sleep and eat lots of fruit and vegetables. For Miller, dance was youth itself in body mind and spirit. On February 14 she attended the Nancy Reagan luncheon held at the Beverly Hilton Hotel. On February 23 the star was at the Bob Hope Center Awards, aka the Second Annual America's Hope Awards, held at the Bob Hope Cultural Center in Palm Desert. She performed an unknown number with June Allyson, Cyd Charisse, Robert Stack, and Margaret O'Brien.

Miller was a guest on the CBS television special *America's All-Star Tribute to Elizabeth Taylor* held in Palm Desert, California, and broadcast on March 9. This was the second annual Hope Award honoring Taylor's humanitarian achievement, with the show written by Stephen Pouliot, Ken Welch, and Mitzi Welch, and directed by Marty Pasetta. Miller appears twice, first preceded by a clip of "Shakin' the Blues Away" from *Easter Parade*, as a fellow M-G-M star. She recalls the M-G-M diet, then signs the autograph book and joins June Allyson, Cyd Charisse and Margaret O'Brien to sing "My Friend, Here's to You." The star is also on stage for the M-G-M High Prom Night, in the background as Carol Bayer Sager and Stevie Wonder sing "That's What Friends Are For."

She was in Sedona when Lucille Ball died on April 26. Miller participated in a conversation with Gale Gordon for television about her friend, with the star saying she was heartbroken. On April 30 Miller attended *The Disney-MGM Studios Theme Park Grand Opening* which was televised as an episode of the adventure and biographical series *Disneyland* and broadcast on NBC. The special was written by Lane Sarasohn and directed by Jeff Margolis. That month she also had a lunch with White Bear Fredericks, the elder of the Sedona Hopi tribe, where they discussed his people and spiritualism. In addition the star went to the Hopi reservation to see the sacred, long-haired Kachina dance, something to which the public was rarely invited to.

She was referenced in a play by John Sayles called *New Hope for the Dead*, produced as part of the Renegade Theater Company's annual One-Act Play Festival which ran from May 14 to 21, 1989, in New York. A character named Candace is a would-be actress and tap dancer who prattles on about Miller. It received a mixed reaction from Alvin Klein in *The New York Times*.

The star attended the 19th Annual Nosotros Golden Eagle Awards held at the Beverly Hilton Hotel televised on June 9 by NBC. On June 25 the *New York Post* reported she was to join the Catholic Church's

Carmelite order as a nun, but they had confused her with the New York socialite with the same name. The stage and screen Ann Miller hoped now she would no longer get her namesakes' I. Magnin fur bills.

In August the star went to Santa Fe for the Indian Art Show and stayed at the Rancho Encantado. She met the potters Rodina Huma and Mary Trujillo at the Cochiti Pueblo, and bought some of their pottery.

Miller received a psychic message that she would be invited on another tour and began rehearsing again to stay in shape. The star also wanted new clothes and arranged fittings, now believing there would be no time after the announcement came. The call she received was from Kris Larson from the M-G-M Studio Video Department who were promoting a package of movie musicals and wanted to pay stars handsome salaries to appear across the country. The first stop was in Las Vegas at the national video convention, with Miller invited to stay three nights at the Las Vegas Hilton. She was expected to make a one hour appearance at the M-G-M booth where the star signed autographs and met Ted Turner, the Atlanta TV tycoon.

A week later she was taken to the old M-G-M studios, now called Lorimar Productions, by Larson and M-G-M executive and film historian George Feltenstein. Miller saw how the lion logo that had been on top of the studio had been moved to the top of a new building across the street, and she was ill at ease over lunch held at the Louis B. Mayer's private dining room in the commissary. The star tried to make conversation, all the while sensing the ghosts of Mayer, Clark Gable, Spencer Tracy, and Judy Garland hovering around her. In the new M-G-M building she admired a black satin jacket and watch in the gift shop, which her companions bought for her to commemorate her visit. But as Miller walked back to her car she couldn't help but be sad remembering what had been lost with time. On October 6 the star attended the Jewel Gala held at the Beverly Hilton Hotel.

She attended the America's Dance Honors held on January 18, 1990, at the San Diego Convention Center but broadcast as a music television special on July 5 by ABC. The event saw the National Academy of Dance present the first annual Gypsy Awards, with the show written by Bruce Vilanch and directed by Tony Charmoli. In March Miller was presented with a plaque honoring her career by the University of Southern California drama department. It was reported that every year a scholarship would be given in her name to the best drama student at the university.

On May 4 she attended the third annual Ambassadors Ball for Afghanistan held at the Regent Beverly Wilshire Hotel in Beverly Hills. Miller was a special guest star on the May 19 episode of the television family comedy series *Out of This World*, entitled "Diamonds Are Evie's

Best Friend," which was shot at the Universal Studios in Hollywood. The teleplay was by Laura Levine and the director was Bob Claver. The show had teenager Evie (Maureen Flanagan) "gleep" up a diamond necklace from the collection of a wealthy socialite, Elsie Vanderhoff (Miller), for an Antares Mother's Day gift. The star is billed ninth after the show's title, appearing in three scenes. She wears her natural hair off her forehead and in a neck roll, and a blue patterned long-sleeved floor-length dress by costumers Victoria Dekay and David Baca.

We see her dance briefly with Buzz (Buzz Belmondo) and Miller gets some funny lines. Elise orders two guards to carry Beano (Joe Alaskey) "bodily off the premises" and when they hesitate because of his size, she adds, "Well, just push him out the door." Then she tells Evie and Donna (Donna Pescow) to excuse her as she has to talk to some people that are "much more important than you." The teleplay also is self-referential when Elsie tells Evie she just saw *Sugar Babies*, "the most wonderful play with the most divine dancer who had the most incredible legs." On the same night as the broadcast the star attended the 36th annual Share Boomtown Party held at the Santa Monica Civic Auditorium.

She went on a trip to Gallup, New Mexico, where a Catholic priest took her to the Zuni Reservation and into their Catholic church to watch the Indians make their jewelry. At a charity party in Beverly Hills, Miller met actor Ted Danson, who hailed from Sedona and had land there. He was involved in a group called "Futures for Children" to help the Indian children, which interested her. The two also shared an interest in the ancient history of the Indian tribes, believing that the white man had never treated the American Indian fairly.

The star told of her experience of having a big snake slither past her and out the kitchen door of her Sedona home, which she took to be a warning that problems were coming her way over the land. This perception was right but Miller had been able to resolve the problems. Another time she had found a perfect white Indian stone arrowhead while hiking on her land, learning that the Sinagua Indians had formerly used it as a camping site, and the star believed her mind power brought her closer communication with the ancient ones.

But she could have psychic experiences in other locations, as when Miller was in a department store. She had gone to get a new perfume and the Swedish saleslady told her she could see the star's aura—the energy field which surrounded every living being. Miller did not have this gift but the lady reported her aura had blue, purple, yellow and orange in it, which meant she was a very spiritual person and very psychic.

Her second book, *Tapping Into the Force: Ann Miller's Psychic*

World, written with Dr. Maxine Asher, was published by Hampton Roads Publishing Company on June 1, 1990. She dedicated it to her mother, Clara. In late July the star was photographed in Beverly Hills holding a copy of the book, and reported to be considering a tour of the show *Call Me Madam* in which she would tap and sing Irving Berlin's songs. Miller also promoted the book on the television show talk *Sally Jessy Raphael* on an unknown date, and was joined by a psychic investigator and an astrologist A.J. Abadie who did readings for her. The star discussed Ouija boards, psychic channeling and inner voices, UFOs, being an Egyptian princess, crystals, love, and hypnosis. She told of the latter when, after never having been able to be hypnotized before, it was accomplished by the parapsychologist Dr. Thelma Moss from UCLA at her home on an undisclosed date. During the three hours Miller recalled being the Egyptian princess poisoned by a rival prince who had her suffocated with sand with her pet lion. The suffocation became the star's claustrophobia in her present life and the lion was represented by her stuffed toy lions, ceramic lions and how fans sent her the same. Moss also reported that the reading had Miller's dead child speak, calling herself Mary.

She was in Sedona when her closest friend Hermes Pan died on September 19, but the star was unable to be reached in time to attend his funeral. On September 20 she participated in the Chabad telethon "L'Chaim! To Life!" On October 13 Miller was an honoree of the 35th Annual Thalians Gala held at the Century Plaza Hotel in California with the event televised for NBC.

The star attended a performance of *Madama Butterfly* on July 3, 1991, although the location is unknown. On July 16 she attended the 10th Annual Video Dealers Association Convention at the Sands Hotel in New York. Though the day date is unknown, in 1991 Miller was a guest on the television talk show *Movie Memories with Debbie Reynolds* which was shot in Hollywood and broadcast on American Movies Classics. The show had Reynolds introduce a classic Hollywood film, then return afterwards to talk with legendary movie stars about their careers and experiences during Hollywood's Golden Age.

On June 5, 1992, Ann attended the 22nd Annual Nosotros Golden Eagle Awards held at the Beverly Hilton Hotel. On August 10 she attended the first annual MGM Girls Reunion held at the Tse Yang Restaurant in Beverly Hills, with Esther Williams, June Allyson, and Zsa Zsa Gabor. On August 15 she was at the 10th Annual Golden Boot Awards held at the Century Plaza Hotel in Hollywood. Miller was a guest on the September 7 episode of the syndicated television talk show *Vicki!* with host Vicki Lawrence. On September 12 she participated in the ninth Annual American Cinema Awards held at the Beverly Hilton Hotel and broadcast as a television special on NBC.

On October 1, 1992, the Glenn Plaskin book *Turning Point: Pivotal Moments in the Lives of America's Celebrities* (Carol Publishing Group) had a chapter on the star. On October 30 she kicked off a fundraising drive for Phoenix, Arizona's 63-year-old Orpheum Theatre by placing a personalized brick on the Avenue of the Stars, being chairman of the Stars program. In October Miller also attended a luncheon for Ginger Rogers as part of "Ginger Rogers Day," held at the Beverly Hilton Hotel in honor of her 60 years in show business.

She was in the February 3, 1993, episode of the family television comedy *Home Improvement* entitled "Dances with Tools." This was shot at the Walt Disney Studios in Hollywood and broadcast on ABC. The show was written by Rosalind Moore and directed by Andy Cardiff. Miller is billed in the end credits as a special guest appearance as Mrs. Keeney, an ex–June Taylor dancer and ballroom dancing instructor who attempts to teach television host Tim "The Tool Man" Taylor (Tim Allen) and his wife Jill (Patricia Richardson) the cha-cha. She only has one scene, wearing her natural hair off the forehead and in a neck roll, and a red knee-length, long-sleeved, high-collared dress with a layered skirt and matching scarf by Valerie Laven and Nicole Gorsuch. The star is seen from the back first and we see her dance solo, showing her legs as she twirls, and briefly with Tim, with choreography by Dirk Lumbard. Miller is funny playing a theatrical woman and screams to make the scene button work, where she is spun by Tim out of the room and crashes off-screen into a piano.

The star was interviewed for the television musical comedy documentary *Lucy and Desi: A Home Movie*, which was broadcast on NBC on February 14, 1993. The show had a story by Laurence Luckinbill with special script material by Lonnie Reed, and was directed by Lucie Arnaz. Scenes are also shown from *Too Many Girls*. The show received a mixed reaction from Rick Marin in *Variety* but won the Outstanding Informational Special Emmy Award.

She was the subject of an April 14 episode of *This Is Your Life* broadcast on Thames Television. The show was directed by Brian Klein and Malcolm Morris and shot at the CBS studios in Hollywood. Miller was surprised by studio guests Jimmy Doolittle, Betty Garrett, Jane Withers, Howard Keel, Kathryn Grayson. George Sidney, Dina Merrill, Joe Bowab, Rip Taylor who threw confetti on her, and Ginger Rogers, with Mickey Rooney, Cyd Charisse, Donald O'Connor, Esther Williams, Jane Powell, and Debbie Reynolds on video. The show also had clips of "Prehistoric Man" from *On the Town*, "Too Darn Hot" from *Kiss Me*

Kate and the scene of Miller dancing with Ginger Rogers from *Stage Door*.

Jane Withers said she and Miller shared the same birthday as well as the same hairdo and a husband at different times, and brought her friend a hankie for the night. She added that the star was also a stepmother to her three children. Dina Merrill remembered their time together when Miller went swimming in Waikiki, seeing her smiling little face as the star was waist deep in the water. Then she looked up and said "How do I stop?" Miller added to the story by reporting that later in a Los Angeles pool she sank right to the bottom after jumping in. Recalling her "String Bean" name on *Stage Door*, Rogers commented that the star was still a string bean though Miller replied "not as much as I used to be." O'Connor said that he always loved her for being a great actress and singer and dancer. Reynolds reported she wore fuchsia just for the star.

She appeared in the November 30, 1993, episode of *Biography* entitled "Gene Autry: America's Singing Cowboy." The show was written by Cress Darwin and Alex Gordon and directed by Del Jack. Miller attended the opening night performance of *Sunset Boulevard* on December 9 held at the Shubert Theatre in Los Angeles. On the way out Andrew Lloyd Webber told her she would be great in the show and he would call her, but the show's composer never did. The star thought that she could have sung the hell out of that part and her casting would have been more appropriate than the other ladies who played Norma Desmond. Miller *was* from old Hollywood except she didn't stay at home watching her old cockamamie movies.

On March 28, 1994, the star attended the *2nd Annual Comedy Hall of Fame* taping held at the Beverly Hilton Hotel in Hollywood. This television comedy special was broadcast on August 29.

She appeared in the M-G-M documentary *That's Entertainment! III* (1994), the sequel to *That's Entertainment!* (1974) and *That's Entertainment, Part II* (1976). Written and directed by Bud Friedgen and Michael J. Sheridan, it featured former M-G-M musical stars reviewing the studio's history of musicals. Miller was billed sixth in the alphabetical listings of the special appearances, and was seen doing "I've Gotta Hear that Beat" from *Small Town Girl*, "Shakin' the Blues Away" and "It Only Happens When I Dance with You" from *Easter Parade*, the title number of *On the Town*, and the "Dance of Fury" from *The Kissing Bandit*. Ann also hosted and narrated the segment on Fred Astaire, entering a rehearsal room from a door that has her name and a gold star on it. Miller talks about *Easter Parade*, commenting with pathos, "What I wouldn't give to do it just one more time again."

The film premiered in Los Angeles on April 28 which she attended, and was released on May 6. It was praised by Todd McCarthy in *Variety*, Caryn James in *The New York Times*, and Roger Ebert. The star was also interviewed in the video documentary *That's Entertainment III: Behind the Screen*, directed by David Engel with behind-the-scenes footage of her making the film. We see her hugging Gene Kelly where it appears she is at the M-G-M Studios though her scenes were said to be filmed at a dance studio in a section of Hollywood that was bombed out in riots.

A slate shows Miller was filmed on April 17, 1993, and we see her preparing by doing her makeup in a mirror she holds as her hair is managed, and watching a playback with the directors. The star was wanted for the Astaire segment because she had performed with him and was a friend. Miller comments that to be part of history is a very great honor, and doing the film one of the greatest honors given her. She was very proud at having been at M-G-M which was part of her tapestry of life, with the experience being like going to a party every day, despite all the trouble and pain.

The star was a guest on the May 25 episode of the comedy music television talk show *Late Night with Conan O'Brien* shot in New York and broadcast on NBC. On May 29 she was awarded the 1994 Flo-Bert Lifetime Achievement Award for advancing the art of tap at the Tap Dance Extravaganza '94 held at New York's Fashion Institute of Technology. On July 25 Miller attended the Video Software Dealers Association Convention to celebrate M-G-M's 70th anniversary in Las Vegas and was photographed with Mickey Rooney, Debbie Reynolds, Cyd Charisse and June Allyson. She attended *The 1994 Annual Diversity Awards* held at the Beverly Hilton Hotel on September 20 and broadcast on NBC. The show was directed by Bryan Martin. Miller participated in the documentary *A Century of Cinema* which was written by Bob Thomas and directed by Caroline Thomas. The film's release date in 1994 is unknown.

She appeared on the February 22, 1995, episode of the biographical documentary television series *This Is Your Life* devoted to Howard Keel, and broadcast on Thames Television. The star spoke about her memories of working on *Kiss Me Kate*. She also appeared on the March 15 *This Is Your Life* episode on Debbie Reynolds which took place in Las Vegas where Reynolds was performing. The show was written by Roy Bottomley and directed by Brian Klein. Miller introduced herself in voiceover as her "long-legged tappy-toed friend" and reported that they would have three hour telephone talks from 2 or 3 a.m. dishing and having a ball. Reynolds called the star because she was one of the few people still awake at this time, and said nobody danced liked Ann Miller who had the fastest feet in town.

She was referenced in the Rusty E. Frank book, *TAP! The Greatest Tap Dance Stars and Their Stories 1900–1955* (Da Capo Press, March 22, 1993). The chapter on Dance Directors Who Did Not Dance included an interview with her dated February 9, 1989. Three weeks before Ginger Rogers died on April 25, Miller went to the London Dominion Theatre for a benefit. She sang "Everything's Coming up Roses" to Rogers, who was one of the people being awarded, and the wheelchair bound star was brought to the stage to thank her.

In the summer on an unknown date she was interviewed for the BBC television game and talk show *Pebble Mill at One* in her Beverly Hills home. The star had had the house since 1942 and the living room featured a Roger Robles portrait

Portrait of Miller for *That's Entertainment! III* (1994).

of her. Miller had recently met President Clinton in Washington, and she told stories about lying about her age to get the RKO contract, being a tall dancer, M-G-M, and her legendary Christmas Eve parties. The star wanted to do a stage version of the Patrick Dennis book *Around the World with Auntie Mame.*

She was referenced in the film comedy *Jeffrey* (1995), written by Paul Rudnick based on his play, and directed by Christopher Ashley. When actor/cater-waiter Jeffrey (Steven Weber) compares his friends, dancer Darius (Bryan Batt) and interior decorator Sterling (Patrick

Stewart), to her and Martha Stewart, Darius asks Sterling who Ann Miller is. He replies, "Leave this house." This exchange was apparently not in the original play that was produced at the Off Broadway WPA theater and ran from December 31, 1992, to February 14, 1993.

The September 30 episode of the NBC comedy music television series *Saturday Night Live* had a skit entitled "Leg Up," a talk show spoof and a nifty tribute to the star and Debbie Reynolds. It began with stills of the two stars in their Hollywood heydays, with one of Miller in *Sugar Babies*, before Molly Shannon appears in a red sparkly leotard with a long-coated jacket and bouffant wig with a spit curl. She and the Reynolds character played by Cheri Oteri interview real-life Quentin Tarantino, and propose that he make a *Pulp Fiction II* or *Reservoir Cats* film with them. The skit was revisited on the shows of November 11, December 16 and March 23, 1996.

Shannon reported the star was not amused by the antics, which also had Miller and Frank Sinatra talking dirty about their Vegas escapades, menopause, and trashing stars' aging faces. The original Miller thought it very dirty. She participated in the Turner Classic Movies documentary *Inside the Dream Factory* which was broadcast on November 1. It was written by Maureen Corley and Bob Waldman, and directed by Mark Woods. On the same day the star made an in-store appearance at Towers Records in Hollywood to promote the release of the *That's Entertainment!* DVD box set.

She was in the February 4, 1996, episode of the British television documentary series *Lights, Camera, Action!: A Century of the Cinema* which was entitled "The Sound of Music." The show was written by Tony Bilbow and directed by Frank Simmonds. The episode showed clips from *Kiss Me Kate*. On May 13 Miller attended the California Museum Foundation honoring Jane Goodall.

She was interviewed for an article in *The New York Times* of June 13 about remembering musicals. The star admitted their plots were rotten—boy meets girl, fight and make up—but the movies were like a big candy box with glorious songs and dances and costumes and sets. She had attended a fund-raising event at the Beverly Hills Hotel that day called "Ladies of the American Musical," sponsored by American Movie Classics. They aimed to salvage and restore the classic song-and-dance films that were in disrepair. When Gloria De Haven told of Mickey Rooney being her M-G-M assigned escort, Miller rolled her eyes and said, "Don't talk to me about Mickey Rooney! I was with him for nine years in *Sugar Babies*. Nine years with Mickey Rooney!" Asked if there was any prospect that musicals would be revived, she said to keep your fingers crossed.

The star was interviewed for the episode of *Great Performances* entitled "Musicals Great Musicals: The Arthur Freed Unit at MGM" that was broadcast on December 2, 1996. The show was directed by David Thompson, with Miller again seen doing "Shakin' the Blues Away" in *Easter Parade* and the title number in *On the Town*.

In 1996 on an unknown date she was interviewed at her home by Carole Langer about her career. The star reported she received 50 fan letters a week and, with Debbie Reynolds, had given a luncheon at a Chinese restaurant in Los Angeles for her M-G-M sorority sisters that the press was not invited to. Among those who attended were Ann Rutherford, Esther Williams, Margaret O'Brien, Kathryn Grayson, Janet Leigh, and Cyd Charisse. Miller reported that they started at half-past noon and didn't get out till 5 p.m. because of all the dishing that went on. She had recently gone to a premiere in a print dress with beadings, earrings and ring but felt like an overdone Christmas tree compared to the others, who looked like slobs from lower Slobovia. The star therefore refused to go the party afterward.

She also had an anecdote about Joan Crawford whom Miller knew socially. This very tough and stylish lady was a great actress and one of her screen favorites, but they had tangled over an unnamed beau. Crawford stole him away by buying the man suits but after he dumped her, the man wanted to come back to the heartbroken Miller, and she refused. The ladies met later in life at a nightclub when Miller had a date with Dan Dailey. Crawford called the star over to her table and said she wanted Miller to portray her if Crawford's story was ever told. She felt they were alike, both loving life and dancing, which Miller took as a great compliment and which diffused her anger. Miller said Christina Crawford should never have written her book because after someone was dead it was dirty pool, even if what she claimed happened was true.

She appeared in the March 11, 1997, episode of *Biography* entitled "Sonja Henie: Fire on Ice," broadcast on A&E. The show was written by Guidion Phillips, Jeff Scheftel and Andrew Thomas, and directed by Scheftel. The star also appeared in the March 23 episode of *Biography* entitled "Judy Garland: Beyond the Rainbow." The show was written by Peter Jones and John Fricke based in part on the book *Judy Garland: World's Greatest Entertainer* by Fricke, and directed by Jones.

Miller reported that she had recently gone to see Tina Turner and Michael Bolton in concerts. The star was the subject of the July 3 episode of the television talk show *Private Screenings*, which appears to have been recorded in early June but broadcast on July 3 on Turner Classic Movies. The show had her interviewed by Robert Osbourne, and was written by Maureen Corley and directed by Tony Barbon. A lot of film clips were shown with Miller in both dancing and non-dancing scenes. The star felt she had never had the chance to do a dramatic part which she would be good at as she was more than just the empty-headed show-girl with a heart of gold who went tapping into the sunset. Some of the reported Millerisms, the verbal insanities as famous as Sam Goldwyn's Goldwynisms, were true. Examples included the star saying she didn't do game shows when asked what she was doing for Passover, and being amazed to discover that Christmas always fell on Christ's birthday. Miller said things in innocence and they came out funny.

Despite her wacky reputation the star was a serious person who knew what she wanted and wouldn't settle for less. If Miller had not been a dancer she would have been a dress and jewelry designer. She owed the public everything and people stopped her in public to thank her for all the years of entertainment the star had given, this even occurring when Miller was in an Alaska restaurant. She still danced once or twice a week in her house's rehearsal room, but claimed to have no health routine, and was just lucky to have inherited her mother's good looks. Of the new dancers Miller admired Bebe Neuwirth, whom she had seen in shows in Los Angeles a long time ago and predicted would be a big star.

Her advice to newcomers in show business was to be seen as much as possible since you never knew who might discover you for a better job. The credo that got the star through tough times was "the show must go on" and she would keep going on as long as possible, even rolling in a wheelchair to get to a ballet or stage show or go to a premiere. Her work had been her joy; Miller had met marvelous people and travelled the world over. She had been approached to do *Call Me Madam* to take to Broadway. While the star believed she had one more show left in her, there was a hesitance about this offer because nobody could have topped Ethel Merman in it.

On June 10 on what would have been Judy Garland's 75th birthday Miller hosted an evening at a restaurant in Los Angeles for Julie Sheppard, who impersonated Garland. Ann had never seen a performance like it and after the show was over, the star told the audience that she believed Garland had been reincarnated. On June 23 Miller attended the opening night of *Master Class* at the Doolittle Theatre in Los Angeles.

She appeared on the television news talk show *The Charlie Rose Show* broadcast on July 14 with bandleader Skitch Henderson, Cyd Charisse and Van Johnson to reflect on their experiences in M-G-M musicals and the current state of the genre. The interview was preceded by film clips including the "Dance of Fury" from *The Kissing Bandit*. The star said her favorite musical was *Kiss Me Kate* but bemoaned the modern filmmaker's lack of ability to make musicals, citing the film of the historical biography *Evita* (1996) which failed to capture the brilliance of the stage show. Miller appeared at Carnegie Hall on July 15 and 16 at an evening to celebrate the M-G-M musical. The show was overseen by Michael Feinstein and Roddy McDowall, and *The New York Times* reported that one of the most spectacular sequences had the star seen from one film to the next in a continuous, swiveling whirl of brass and flash. She received a tumultuous reception, reminding the audience of not having made a film since 1954, and leaving her misty-eyed.

On October 21 at *The 1997 Diversity Awards* held at the Beverly Hilton Hotel Miller was presented with the Lifetime Achievement Award by the Multicultural Motion Picture Association. She was recognized for her contribution to diversity in the cinematic arts, with the Lifetime Achievement Award recognizing artists whose years of performances have been outstanding, and applauded by peers and audiences alike. The star was interviewed for the 1997 video documentary *Hollywood Musicals of the 1950's*, which was written and directed by Robert Weaver. She spoke about *Kiss Me Kate*, Judy Garland, and being discovered by Lucille Ball and Benny Rubin. Miller was also seen in clips from *Lovely to Look At*, *Kiss Me Kate*, and *Hit the Deck*.

She was in the March 11, 1998, episode of the television series *Great Performances* entitled "Frank Sinatra: The Very Good Years." The show was written and directed by Ted Newsom. The star reportedly had dinner in the spring, though the date is unknown, with Fred Astaire's widow Robyn, to have Chinese food. She found Robyn to be a sweet girl who loved planes and Miller had no problem with how the widow had allowed a clip of Astaire dancing in the M-GM musical comedy *Royal Wedding* (1951) to be used for a Dust Devil vacuum cleaner commercial. The action had caused a flap among film purists but Robyn rationalized it by needing the money for her air cargo business.

The star was considered for the role of Carlotta Campion in a revival of the Stephen Sondheim and James Goldman musical *Follies* to be done at the Paper Mill Playhouse in New Jersey by director Robert Johanson. She had to audition for Sondheim singing Carlotta's showbiz anthem to survival, "I'm Still Here," which made her nervous as Miller had heard he was very difficult. However she found him kind and the show's designer Michael Anania reported when the star performed there were tears in the composer's eyes. There was a question of her holding the note at the end of the song, but Sondheim said that she made it real. Ann Miller had lived that song so she could end it anyway the star wanted to. She loved the musical since it had a good plot, good songs, and Miller got to play a movie actress.

She was hesitant about the pressure of doing back-to-back shows on Saturdays and Sundays, then decided to stir it up again and get the motor running. This time the star did not ask for a tap number to be added because doing one in a short little costume at 75 was silly. Also the self-described beat-up old mountain lion had hearing and a perfect set of teeth but was otherwise worn out. She wore contacts, a torn knee cartilage from having returned to *Sugar Babies* too soon, and had danced off the flesh from the balls of her feet. Now Miller only wanted to sing and act.

She stayed at a house across the street from the theater with *Follies* to open on April 15 and run till May 31, 1998. April 12 was both Easter Sunday and her birthday and after rehearsal there was a party. *Follies* was praised by Robert L. Daniels in *Variety* who wrote that Miller was the epitome of Carlotta, and she stopped the show with her turn. It received a mixed reaction from Alvin Klein in *The New York Times*, though he said she belted the high notes, ringing and steady, right to the balcony, with "I'm Still Here." Regrettably the existing film footage of her doing the number in the show has poor sound having the star drowned out by the orchestra, but we see her wearing a Gregg Barnes gold and blue patterned long-sleeved floor-length dress with a split.

Cast members Phyllis Newman, Kaye Ballard and Dee Hoyt had anecdotes about Miller. Newman reported they never exchanged an unpleasant word, but the star used childish euphemisms of the word vagina to name her six jet-black stage wigs, like "Twat" and "Pussy." After the show closed Newman gave a cast party at her New York apartment which had a big terrace overlooking Central Park West and a spectacular view of the city. When Miller saw it she commented, "Well, kiddo— you sure dipped your ass in a honey pot!" Ballard said nothing was more thrilling than looking up and seeing the star on top of the stairs for her big number, and she was destroyed when the decision was made not to take the show to Broadway. Dee Hoyt found Miller hilarious. At one matinee the theater had a subscription audience whose reaction was quiet, but after she did "I'm Still Here" the star came offstage and told the cast that the audience had liked her.

She was interviewed by Alex Witchel for The *Times* of May 3. He reported on the impact Miller made when, dressed in a red suit with epaulets of gold braid and a gold watch and gold earrings, appeared in the theater's lobby and divided the box office line. She was like Moses parting the Red Sea and a woman gasped, saying "Isn't that something?" The star felt life at its best was not easy, and full of compromise, and happiness only came in moments. She now had no family after the death of her mother and long ago given up on the father that had shacked up with another dame.

Her companions were her secretary, housekeeper and two dogs and they split their time between Beverly Hills and Sedona. Although *Sugar Babies* had provided a nest egg, Miller was not rich and still needed to work. She had recently been to Palm Springs to get a Golden Palm Star on the Walk of Stars in front of the Desert Plaza mall. The star was a guest on the May 27, 1998, episode of the comedy television talk show *The Rosie O'Donnell Show* which was shot in New York and broadcast on Warner Bros. television. In the *Times* of May 31 Michael Anania spoke of his devotion to her, saying he kept going back to *Follies* to see that saucy lady singing that song, but he couldn't get through it without tears in his eyes.

On June 24 the star attended a screening of the digitally restored Civil War romance *Gone with the Wind* (1939) at the Academy of Motion Picture Arts & Sciences. On July 12 she attended Milton Berle's 90th birthday party held at the Beverly Hilton Hotel.

Miller appeared in the September 14 episode of the documentary television series *E! Mysteries & Scandals* entitled "Busby Berkeley." The writer and director of the show is unknown.

A cast recording of *Follies* was released in November by TVT Soundtrax as part of *Follies: The Complete Recording* with cover art depicting the star in her slit-to-the-thigh blue-sequined sheath. The CD featured her recording of "I'm Still Here" and "Can That Boy Fox-trot." She was again skewered by Gerard Alessandrini in his new show *Forbidden Broadway Cleans Up Its Act!* which ran at the Stardust Theatre from November 27. Kristine Zbornik as Miller sang "I'm Still Weird" to the tune of "I'm Still Here," including the lines "In Sugar Babies they kvetch/ old Mickey Rooney was a letch/ but I'm the one that was feared...." However *The New York Times* reported that the new show's skewering was off-point, even repeating the "I killed Louis B Mayer with my hair" line from the original *Forbidden Broadway*.

An anecdote about the star was among those told by Lee Roy Reams in his autobiographical cabaret show *Gotta Sing, Gotta Dance* which ran at the Firebird Café in New York from December 21 to January 2, 1999.

CHAPTER 10
• • • • • • • • • • • • • • • • •

Mulholland Drive

$\mathcal{M}$iller appeared in the mystery thriller *Mulholland Drive* (2001), initially shot as a television pilot from February 8 to May 1999 at Paramount Hollywood Studios and at locations around California. However after ABC rejected the show, funding was provided for the material to become a feature film with additional shooting in September 2000. It was written and directed by David Lynch and centered on Betty (Naomi Watts), a perky Hollywood hopeful from Deep River, Ontario, who helps a woman amnesiac calling herself Rita (Laura Elena Harding).

Miller is billed fourth after the title in the supporting part of Coco Lanois, the manager of the Hollywood apartment building where Betty stays, and also as the mother of Adam (Justin Thoreaux) in an alternate universe. Coco is a theatrical person, which gives context to the star's theatrical makeup and dyed hair with kiss curls. Her costumes are by Amy Stofsky with a notable long strand of pearls worn over a black suit. While Miller has little to do, her Coco is funny and the best scene is perhaps when she realizes that Betty is lying to her and says, "What you're telling me is a load of horse pucky."

The film premiered at the Cannes Film Festival on May 16, 2001, with a screening on October 6 at the New York Film Festival that the star attended. It eventually opened in the United States on October 19 with the taglines "Beware what you dream for...," "An actress longing to be a star. A woman searching for herself. Both worlds will collide ... on Mulholland Drive," and "A woman in search of stardom. A woman in search of herself—in the city of dreams. A key to a mystery—lies somewhere on Mulholland Drive." It was praised by Stephen Holden in *The New York Times*, Roger Ebert, and Peter Travers in *Rolling Stone*, who called Miller's cameo frisky, but received a mixed reaction from Toddy McCarthy in *Variety*. The film was a box office success and earned Lynch a Best Director Academy Award nomination.

Miller said Lynch wrote the part of Coco with her in mind and it

Stills from *Mulholland Drive* (2001). Miller is seen at top right with Naomi Watts.

was bigger in the original 125 minute pilot. The star found Betty's lesbian scene in the film hot stuff, which would have made Louis B. Mayer turn over in his grave. She described Lynch as a quiet and gentle man, but his things were so way out! He said Miller was a real straight shooter, just the kindest, most professional, anything-goes great gal you would ever want to meet. Lynch had seen all her movies growing up and she was like Jimmy Stewart—just someone who people instantly liked. While being a regular person Miller lived the star's life, very aware of her appearance and loving to dress up. After filming was over they talked on the phone and they became great friends.

The star's voice was used in the documentary *The Lady with the Torch* (1999; working title had "...with the Lamp"), written by Joan Kramer and David Heeley, and directed by Heeley. The film celebrated the 75th anniversary of Columbia Pictures and footage from *You Can't Take It with You, Reveille with Beverly, Hey, Rookie* and *Eve Knew Her Apples* was included. It was released January 8, 1999. On March 3 she attended the American Cinema Editors 49th Annual "Eddie" Awards held at the Beverly Hilton Hotel. On May 27 Miller was at a luncheon at New York's Supper Club by the Theater Development Fund for the 18th Annual Astaire Awards for best dance on Broadway.

Esther Williams reported in *The New York Times* of September 2 that she drove the star to the funeral of James Stewart on July 7 in Beverly Hills, and they got a traffic ticket on the way. On October 4 Miller participated in *Radio City Music Hall's Grand Re-Opening Gala*, televised and broadcast by NBC on December 18. The show was a benefit for the Lustgarten Pancreatic Cancer Research Foundation in honor of Marc A. Lustgarten, a Madison Square Garden executive who had recently died of the disease.

She was the subject of the January 13, 2000, episode of *Biography* entitled "Ann Miller: I'm Still Here." The show was written and directed by Amy Enns-Ford and included comments by June Allyson, Cyd Charisse, Betty Garrett, Art Linkletter, David Lynch, Tony Martin, and Debbie Reynolds. The star was interviewed for the August 23 episode of *Biography* entitled "The Gabors: Fame, Fortune and Romance," broadcast on the A& E Television Network. She commented that when you walked into a restaurant and you saw them they were like table-top beauties, like flowers, and every head in the room turned to look. Miller also commented on Zsa Zsa's marriage to Conrad Hilton.

She was interviewed for the January 14, 2001, episode of *E! True Hollywood Story* entitled "The Last Days of Judy Garland." The star appeared in the February 24 episode of the British music biographical documentary television series *Omnibus* entitled "Fascinatin' Rhythm: The History of Tap," which was broadcast on the BBC. The show was directed by Ian Leese. On the show she spoke about Busby Berkeley. Miller was a guest on the June 27 episode of the news television talk show *Larry King Live*, broadcast on CNN. She spoke about Judy Garland, remembering her great talent and love of the business, who busted her butt on stage even when she was ill toward the end of her life. On August 11 the star attended the 19th Annual Golden Boot Awards held in Beverly Hills. On September 7 she was at the *Michael Jackson: 30th Anniversary Celebration* held at New York's Madison Square Garden and broadcast on CBS on November 19. The show was directed by Bruce Gowers.

Gerard Alessandrini once again satirized Miller in his show *Mr. President*, a reworking of the Irvin Berlin musical which ran on Broadway from October 20, 1962, to June 8, 1963. The new show was directed by John Znidarsic and Alessandrini and ran at the Douglas Fairbanks Theater from August 6 to 12. Amanda Naughton played Kathleen Harris, a bespangled creature who led a ballot-counting song called "Shakin' the Chads Away" to the tune of "Shakin' the Blues Away." On November 5 the star attended Lloyd Klein & David Hayes 2002 Collection Fashion Show held at the Cicada Restaurant in Los Angeles.

By 2002 Ann was reportedly suffering from osteoporosis and lung cancer, which made her lose weight and look alarmingly thin and frail. Miller said she regretted never having children or having found someone with whom to share her last years. No matter what the star had achieved, being unloved made her nothing but a hound dog. She could still tap, but who wanted to pay an old lady to tap sitting down? On February 21 Miller attended the engagement party for Liza Minnelli and David Gest held at the Mondrian in West Hollywood. In May she was interviewed for the documentary *Goodnight, We Love You* about the last live stand-up concert given by 84-year-old comedian Phyllis Diller at the Suncoast Hotel & Casino in Las Vegas. This was written and directed by Greg Barson and the film would premiere at the San Diego Film Festival on October 2, 2006. The star said that the world would never forget Diller because there was only one and she was the best. On June 17, 2002, Miller attended the annual opening of the HBO Bryant Park Film Festival where *On the Town* was screened. On August 10 she was at the 2002 Golden Boot Awards held at the Beverly Hilton Hotel.

The star hosted the video documentary short *Cole Porter in Hollywood: Too Darn Hot* written and directed by Peter Fitzgerald about the making of *Kiss Me Kate* and released on April 22, 2003. She tells anecdotes about the film and we see her in photographs on the set and in the footage of the 1949 M-G-M anniversary lunch. Miller was also the on-camera host for the video documentary music short *Cole Porter in Hollywood: Begin the Beguine* which was released on April 22 as a special feature also by Peter Fitzgerald on the DVD of the M-G-M musical *"Broadway Melody of 1940."* She talks about the film and its musical numbers in a humorous manner, and about the stars Fred Astaire and Eleanor Powell, and her experience of working with him on *Easter Parade.*

Miller was in the music historical documentary *Broadway: The Golden Age, By the Legends Who Were There*, written and directed by Rick McKay. He had spent six years conducting interviews and collecting archival footage to tell the story of Broadway in the 30s, 40s, and 50s. She spoke about doing the *George White Scandals* and provided McKay with some color home movies of herself in it, with her also seen in 1950s footage at El Morocco. Finally the star sang part of the song "Broadway Rhythm" under the film's end credits in outtakes, as an example of how many of the legends sang spontaneously in their interviews. The film premiered at the Palm Beach International Film Festival in April and then opened its theatrical run on June 11, 2004. It was praised by Scott Foundas in *Variety* and Peter Travers in *Rolling Stone*, but received a mixed reaction from Stephen Holden in *The New York Times*. The film was the first part in a trilogy with two follow-ups titled *Broadway: Beyond the Golden Age.*

She was interviewed for the television documentary *The Desilu Story; The Rags to Riches Success of the Desilu Empire* which was broadcast on August 24, 2003, on Bravo. The show was written by Kurt Fethke and directed by Marshall Flaum. Miller was also interviewed for the television biographical documentary on Rita Hayworth entitled *Rita*, broadcast on TCM on September 9. The show was written by Caren Roberts-Frenzel and Elaina Archer and directed by Archer. Miller's interview appears to have been filmed at the Chateau Marmont in Hollywood. She commented on her friend's equally rocky marriages and relationships with men. A lot of people tried to slip on Hayworth's blind side but if it got to the point where the she didn't like it, Hayworth was out the door.

A hilarious story and imitation of Miller was reportedly performed by Carol Channing in her show the *Singular Sensations* series at New York's Off Broadway Village Theater. It ran from November 3 to 9, 2003. The star was interviewed about *Room Service* for the documentary *Inside the Marx Brothers* which was written by Henry Stephens and released on November 11. She was in the British music television documentary *The 100 Greatest Musicals*, broadcast on December on Channel 4. The show was written by Robin Ince and Stewart Williams and directed by Deepak Gattani. The countdown had been voted by the British public through Channel 4's website and readers of The Mail newspaper with each entry represented by film, clips. The Miller films included were *Easter Parade*, *On the Town*, and *Kiss Me Kate*.

The star died on January 22, 2004, at Cedars-Sinai Hospital in Los Angeles at the age of 80. The cause was lung cancer, reported her friend and former publicist Esme Chandlee, and there were no immediate survivors. A funeral service was held on January 28 at the St. Mel Catholic Church in California. Those in attendance included Ann Rutherford, Renee Taylor, Jayne Meadows, Kathryn Grayson, June Haver, Margaret O'Brien, Nicholas Fayard, Connie Stevens, Esther Williams, and Robert Stack. Miller was buried in the Holy Cross Cemetery in Culver City, California, with the remains of her daughter, Mary Milner, who had only lived on November 12, 1946.

It was said that the girl's remains had been found in 1999 by a friend of the star's and had been exhumed so that her coffin could be laid on top of her mother's, with the inscription "Beloved Mother" and "Beloved Baby Daughter." They were buried together next to Miller's mother Clara. *The New York Times* obituary by Richard Severo identified her as the voluptuous dancer with the lacquered raven hair and Nefertiti eye makeup whose tap-dancing athleticism made her a staple of big-screen musicals in the 1940s and 50s. *Variety* noted how Miller became a legit star later in life and she charmed stage, screen and television audiences for almost 70 years.

The *10th Annual Screen Actors Guild Awards* was held at the Shrine Auditorium in Hollywood on the same day the star died and she was included in the Memorial Tribute. The show was directed by Ron de Moraes and televised by TNT. On February 6 Miller was among those honored in `A Tribute to Tap Giants" at New York's Town Hall. The event was part of the World Music and Dance Festival and had Michela Lerman deliver a happy-go-lucky solo to the star. She was also included in the Memorial Tribute at *The 76th Annual Academy Awards* held on February 29, 2004, at the Kodak Theatre in Hollywood and televised by ABC. Footage of her performing "Too Darn Hot" from *Kiss Me Kate* and "Shakin' the Blues Away" from *Easter Parade* was shown to represent Miller in the montage. The show was directed by Louis J. Horvitz and Troy Miller and was nominated for the Outstanding Variety, Music or Comedy Special Emmy Award.

On September 19 and 20, 2004, the Ann Miller estate sale was held at the Bonham and Butterfield Auction House in Los Angeles. She made a posthumous appearance in the video documentary *That's Entertainment! The Masters Behind the Musicals* that was released on October 12. It had uncredited direction by Peter Fitzgerald and had the star commenting on M-G-M, Jack Cummings, Joe Pasternak, Arthur Freed, Hermes Pan, Busby Berkeley, and Stanley Donen. The video showed her in scenes from *The Kissing Bandit, On the Town, Small Town Girl* with a photograph of her with Joe Pasternak, *Kiss Me, Kate,* and *Hit the Deck.*

She appeared to have been interviewed simultaneously for the 2008 video musical documentary *Hollywood Singing and Dancing: The 1970s, Diversity Rocks the Movies.* This was written by Mark McLaughlin with additional writing by Eric Hornberger, directed by McLaughlin, released on May 19, 2009. The show introduced Miller with the Great American Soup commercial and featured snippets of her dancing in *Time Out for Rhythm* and "Shakin' the Blues Away" from *Easter Parade.* She commented that musicals were out of fashion because audiences now loved violence and realism but expressed her admiration for Barbra Streisand.

The star had also been interviewed for the video documentary short *Easter Parade: On the Avenue* which was a Special feature on the Special Edition DVD release of the film on March 15, 2005. Written and directed by an uncredited Peter Fitzgerald, her interview appears to have been done before 2002 since Miller does not look as frail as she would later be. She speaks about Louis B. Mayer, her casting in the film, and "Shakin' the Blues Away." Judy Garland biographer John Fricke also comments on the star's relationship with Mayer and her dancing with

Fred Astaire. Her name was referenced in the August 19 premiere episode of the television animated comedy series *Hopeless Pictures*. The character of Traci (voiced by Jennifer Coolidge) is a six-figure salaried executive of Hopeless Pictures who says she doesn't read but is pretty sure that Arthur Miller is Ann Miller's husband. The series was broadcast on IFC.

An anecdote about an encounter with a mouthy Miller at a Hollywood Bowl event was in Alan Cumming's cabaret show which ran at New York's Feinstein's at Loews Regency from April 28, 2010, for five nights. Cummings had performed with her at the Bowl in 1997, where she sang "I'm Still Here," and apparently the star said something which included the word "pussy."

Her work with Jack Cole on *Eadie Was a Lady* was referenced in the revue produced at New York's Off Broadway Queens Theater in the Park entitled "Heat Wave: The Jack Cole Project." It was conceived and directed by Chet Walker and ran from May 9 to 20, 2012.

A surreal photograph of Miller hilariously placed amid a garden of violins appeared in "Dancing the Dream," an exuberantly diverse exhibition at the National Portrait Gallery in Washington that surveyed dance in America over the last 100 years. The show ran from March 6 to July 13, 2014.

A chapter entitled "Too Darn Hot" was devoted to her in the Brian Siebert book *What the Eye Hears: A History of Tap Dancing*, published by Farrar, Straus and Giroux on November 17, 2015. She was also referenced in Megan Pugh's book, *America Dancing: From the Cakewalk to the Moonwalk*, published by Yale University Press on the same date. Pugh claims that the star was present when Fred Astaire took a lesson from the black tapper John Sublett aka John W. Bubbles. Bubbles reported that Astaire couldn't catch the dancing as quickly as Miller, so he taught her so she could teach Fred to save time.

Rick McKay's musical historical documentary *Broadway: Beyond the Golden Age* was screened at the 27th annual Palm Springs International Film Festival on January 8, 2016. This continued the story of American theater from the legendary Broadway season of 1959, the revolutionary 70s, and up to the opening night of David Merrick and Gower Champion's 42nd Street in 1980. Once again, McKay used personal interviews with legends, with Miller reportedly talking about why certain talents made it on Broadway but a very few could also work in films. The release of the film and the third in the trilogy, *Broadway: The Next Generation*, would be hampered by the death of McKay on January 29, 2018.

Miller was referenced in the David Fantle and Tom Johnson book,

Hollywood Heyday: 75 Candid Interviews with Golden Age Legends published by McFarland on April 9, 2018. The star was covered in a chapter entitled Tops in Taps and the writers reported they had met her in the spring of 1998. She claimed that Michael Flatley, the lead dancer of the Riverdance troupe of Celtic highsteppers had stolen two of her steps, and Miller had bought the video to revisit the steps that got Flatley big applause. *The New York Times* of July 4 reported that the male tap dancer Caleb Teicher performed a solo that sampled female tappers, including the star, in #SpeakingInDance, a weekly visual exploration of dance on Instagram.

She was referenced in the Jeanine Basinger book, *The Movie Musical!* released on November 5, 2019, by Knopf. Basinger writes that Miller was a great tapper and a glamorous star, a description that she would have no doubt been pleased by.

Appendix:
Appearances in Theatre,
Film, Television,
Shorts and Videos

Theatre

The final element of each entry is the part played,
including Herself and Unknown.

Scandals aka George White's Scandals (August 28 to November 5, 1939). Alvin Theatre, New York. Herself.

Scandals National Tour including December 11 for two weeks, 1939 Forrest Theatre Philadelphia; December 25 to date unknown Erlanger Theatre, Chicago; dates unknown, Detroit; March 24, 1940, for two weeks Biltmore Theatre, Los Angeles; April 15 to date unknown Curran Theatre, San Francisco.

Can-Can (Dates unknown, 1968). Theatre unknown, Huston. Unknown.

Glad Tidings (Dates unknown in October 1968). Pheasant Run Theatre, Chicago. Maude Abbott.

Mame (March 1969 to unknown date). Parker Playhouse, Fort Lauderdale. Mame Dennis.

Mame (May 26, 1969, to January 3, 1970). Winter Garden Theatre, New York. Mame Dennis.

Mame (Week of September 1, 1970). Packard Music Hall in Warren and the Memorial Hall in Dayton, Ohio. Mame Dennis.

Hello, Dolly! (Dates unknown in summer, 1971). Packard Music Hall Theatre in Warren, the Veterans Memorial Theatre in Columbus and Memorial Hall in Dayton, Ohio. Dolly Gallagher Levy.

Can-Can (dates unknown; summer, 1972). Packard Music Hall Theatre in Warren, the Veterans Memorial Theatre in Columbus and Memorial Hall in Dayton, Ohio. Unknown.

Blithe Spirit (September 18 to 30, 1973). Little the Square in Sullivan, Illinois. Elvira.

Anything Goes (March 27 to May 12, 1974). Paper Mill Playhouse in Millburn, New Jersey; (June 1974) Westchester Playhouse in Yonkers, New York. Reno Sweeney.

197

Anything Goes (August 1975). Summer Star Theater, Miami. Reno Sweeney.

Panama Hattie (June 9 to 27, 1976) Paper Mill Playhouse in Milburn, New Jersey. Unknown.

Panama Hattie (August 3 to 8, 1976). Syracuse Symphony Famous Artists Playhouse in New York; August 9 to 21, 1976 Westchester Playhouse in Yonkers, New York. Unknown.

The 24th Annual Milliken Breakfast Show (June 2 to 15, 1977). Waldorf-Astoria Hotel's Grand Ballroom, New York. Herself.

Anything Goes (August 22 to 27, 1977). Sikithville Theatre, New Jersey; September 6 to 11 and 13 to 28, 1977 American Shakespeare Theater in Stratford, Connecticut. Reno Sweeney.

The 25th Annual Milliken Breakfast Show (June 8 to 21, 1978). Waldorf-Astoria Hotel's Grand Ballroom, New York. Herself.

Cactus Flower (Dates unknown, 1978). National tour, including Dallas, Texas, and Scottsdale, Arizona. Stephanie.

Sugar Babies (October 8, 1979, to August 28, 1982). Mark Hellinger Theatre, New York. Herself.

Sugar Babies National Tour including: June–July 1983 Met Center, Boston; August 9 to September 3, 1983, Shubert Theater, Philadelphia; July 3 to 11, 1984 San Jose Center for the Performing Arts; January 8 to 13 and January 29 to February 3, 1985, Shubert Performing Arts Center, New Haven; March 19 to 24, 1985 Riverside Theatre in Milwaukee, Wisconsin; June 1985 Music Fair Theater in Valley Forge, Pennsylvania; on February 25, 1986, Fort Lauderdale, Florida; February 26 to April 5 Sunrise Musical Theatre in Sunrise, Florida; March 25 to April 1986 Fort Lauderdale.

Sugar Babies (September to December 31, 1987). Savoy Theatre, London. Herself.

Follies (April 15 to May 31, 1998). Paper Mill Playhouse, New Jersey. Carlotta Campion.

Film

The final element of each entry is the part played, including Herself.

Anne of Green Gables (1934). Uncredited schoolgirl.

Ferenc Molnar's "The Good Fairy" (1935). Uncredited schoolgirl in orphanage.

The Devil on Horseback (1935). Uncredited chorus dancer.

New Faces of 1937 (1937). Herself.

The Life of the Party (1937). Betty.

Stage Door (1937). Annie.

Having Wonderful Time (1938). Uncredited camp guest.

Radio City Revels (1938). Billie.

Frank Capra's You Can't Take You (1938). Essie Carmichael.

Room Service (1938). Hilda.

Tarnished Angel (1938). Violet McMaster.

Too Many Girls (1940). Pepe.

Hit Parade of 1941 aka *Romance and Rhythm* (1940). Annabelle Potter.

"Melody Ranch" (1940). Julie Shelton.

Time Out for Rhythm (1941). Kitty Brown.

Go West, Young Lady (1941). Lola.

Meet the Stars #8: Stars Past and Present (1941). Herself.

Screen Snapshots Series 21, No. 1 (1941). Herself.

True to the Army (1942). Vicki Marlow.

Hedda Hopper's Hollywood No. 2 (1941). Herself (uncredited).

Priorities on Parade (1942). Donna D'Arcy.

Reveille with Beverly (1943). Beverly Ross.

What's Buzzin', Cousin? (1943). Ann Crawford.

Hey Rookie (1944). Winnie Clark.

Jam Session (1944). Terry Baxter.

Sailor's Holiday (1944). Herself (uncredited).

Carolina Blues (1944). Julie Carver.

Eve Knew Her Apples (1945). Eve Porter.

Eadie Was a Lady (1945). Edithea "Eadie" Alden.

The Thrill of Brazil (1946). Linda Lorens.

Irving Berlin's Easter Parade (1948). Nadine Hale.

The Kissing Bandit (1948). Fiesta Specialty Dancer.

On the Town (1949). Claire Huddesen.

Watch the Birdie (1950). Miss Lucky Vista.

"Two Tickets to Broadway" (1951). Joyce Campbell.

Texas Carnival (1951). Sunshine Jackson.

(1952). "Bubbles" Cassidy.

Small Town Girl (1953). Lisa Bellmount.

Kiss Me Kate (1953). Lois Lane/"Bianca."

My Heart (1954). Guest Star in "Artists and Models."

Hit the Deck (1955). Ginger.

The Opposite Sex (1956). Gloria.

The Great American Pastime (1956). Doris Patterson.

Won Ton Ton: The Dog Who Saved Hollywood (1976). President's Girl 2.

That's Entertainment! III (1994). Herself.

The Lady with the Torch (January 8, 1999). Herself—Voice.

Mulholland Drive (2001). Coco Lanois.

Broadway: The Golden Age, By the Legends Who Were There (2003). Herself.

Goodnight, We Love You (2006). Herself.

Broadway: Beyond the Golden Age (2016). Herself.

Television

All appearances are as herself except the few
marked otherwise.

Toast of the Town (November 1, 1953).

Lux Video Theatre: "Three Just Men" (December 10, 1953). Intermission guest.

Toast of the Town: ""MGM's 30th Anniversary Tribute" (February 14, 1954).

What's My Line? (October 7, 1956). Mystery guest.

The Bob Hope Show (October 6, 1957).

The Big Record (October 16, 1957).

The Dinah Shore Chevy Show (December 29, 1957).

The Perry Como Show (November 8, 1958).

The Arthur Murray Party (November 17, 1958).

The Juke Box Jury (August 1, 1959).

Toast of the Town aka The Ed Sullivan Show (Jun e 19, 1960).

The Hollywood Palace (December 12, 1964).

That Regis Philbin Show (February 4, 1965).

That Regis Philbin Show (March 4, 1965).

The Hollywood Palace (May 22, 1965).

Late Night with Johnny Carson (October 6, 1965).

The Bell Telephone Hour: "Music of the Movies" (March 13, 1966).

The Hollywood Palace (April 2, 1966).

Girl Talk (January 19, 1967).

The Hollywood Palace (March 11, 1967).

House Party (May 4, 1967).

The John Gary Show (Date unknown, 1967).

The Mike Douglas Show (January 22 to 25, 1968). Co-Host.

The Woody Woodbury Show (January 28 or June 4, 1968).

The Hollywood Squares (March 4 to 8, 1968).

The Pat Boone Show (March 8, 1968).

The Hollywood Squares (July 1 to 5, 1968).

The Joey Bishop Show (August 20, 1968).

George Jessel's Here Come the Stars: "Mickey Rooney" (September 15, 1968).

The Jonathan Winters Show (October 2, 1968).

Talking Pictures (Date unknown, 1968).

Laugh-In (March 3, 1969).

Laugh-In (March 17, 1969).

What's My Line? (Date unknown, 1969).

Allen Ludden's Gallery (July 9, 1969).

Philbin's People (April 24, 1970).

The Rosey Grier Show (May 23, 1970).

It's Your Bet (June 1, 1970).

The Hollywood Squares (June 7, 1971).

The Virginia Graham Show (June 29, 1971).

The Mike Douglas Show (September 14, 1971).

Sea (November 15, 1971). Mona Kent.

The Bob Braun Show (June 29, 1972).

Love, American Style (November 17, 1972). Unknown.

Today (December 5, 1972).

The Merv Griffin Show (December 8, 1972).

The Mike Douglas Show (January 1, 1973).

Joanne Carson's VIPs (January 17, 1973).

Dinah's Place (January 26, 1973).

The Merv Griffin Show (September 4, 1973).

The Merv Griffin Show (March 12, 1974).

Grammy Salutes Oscar (March 30, 1974).

The 46th Annual Academy Awards (April 2, 1974).

The Merv Griffin Show (July 23, 1974).

The Merv Griffin Show (November 20, 1974).

This Day Tonight (Date unknown; December 1974).

At Long Last Cole (April 10, 1975).

The Mike Douglas Show (February 20, 1976).

The Mike Douglas Show (October 10, 1976).

The Mike Douglas Show (October 10, 1977).

The Merv Griffin Show (Date unknown, 1977).

The Joe Franklin Show (Date unknown, 1977).

Macy's Thanksgiving Day Parade (November 22, 1979).

The Kennedy Center Honors: A Celebration of the Performing Arts (December 29, 1979).

This Is Your Life: "Stewart Granger." (March 5, 1980).

The 52nd Annual Academy Awards (April 14, 1980).

The 34th Annual Tony Awards (June 8, 1980).

The Merv Griffin Show (October 21, 1980).

Eyewitness News: "Nothing's higher than being on top" (May 5, 1981).

The 35th Annual Tony Awards (June 7, 1981).

Macy's Thanksgiving Day Parade (November 26, 1981).

Hour Magazine (January 12, 1982).

The Love Boat "The Musical/My Ex-Mom/The Show Must Go On/ The Pest/My Aunt, the Worrier" (February 27, 1982). Connie Carruthers.

Night of 100 Stars (March 6, 1982).

The 36th Annual Tony Awards (June 6, 1982).

This Is Your Life: "Mickey Rooney" (February 4, 1984).

The 26th Annual Grammy Awards (February 28, 1984).

Hour Magazine (March 13, 1984).

The Tonight Show Starring Johnny Carson (April 13, 1984).

The Merv Griffin Show (May 27, 1984).

All-Star Party for "Dutch" Reagan (December 8, 1985).

The 58th Annual Academy Awards (March 24, 1986).

Late Night with David Letterman (November 18, 1986).

Happy 100th Birthday, Hollywood (May 18, 1987).

The 18th Annual Nosotros Golden Eagle Awards (May 13, 1987).

The Royal Variety Performance (November 26, 1987).

Good Morning America (January 27, 1989).

America's All-Star Tribute to Elizabeth Taylor (March 9, 1989).

The Disney-MGM Studios Theme Park Grand Opening (April 30, 1989).

The 19th Annual Nosotros Golden Eagle Awards (June 9, 1989).

Out of This World: "Diamonds Are

Evie's Best Friend" (May 19, 1990). Elsie Vanderhoff.

America's Dance Honors (July 5, 1990).

L'Chaim! To Life! (September 30, 1990).

The 35th Annual Thalians Gala (October 13, 1990).

Sally Jessy Raphael (Date unknown, 1990).

Movie Memories with Debbie Reynolds (Date unknown, 1991).

Vicki! (September 7, 1992).

The 9th Annual American Cinema Awards (September 12, 1992).

Home Improvement: "Dances with Tools" (February 3, 1993). Mrs. Keeney.

Lucy and Desi: A Home Movie (February 14, 1993).

This Is Your Life: "Ann Miller" (April 14, 1993).

Biography: "Gene Autry: America's Singing Cowboy" (November 30, 1993).

The 2nd Annual Comedy Hall of Fame (August 29, 1984).

Late Night with Conan O'Brien (May 25, 1994).

The 1994 Annual Diversity Awards (September 20, 1994).

A Century of Cinema (Date unknown, 1994).

This Is Your Life: "Howard Keel" (February 22, 1995).

This Is Your Life: "Debbie Reynolds" (March 15, 1995).

Pebble Mill at One (Date unknown, 1995).

Inside the Dream Factory (November 1, 1995).

Lights, Camera, Action!: A Century of the Cinema: "The Sound of Music" (February 4, 1996).

Great Performances: "Musicals Great Musicals: The Arthur Freed Unit at MGM" (December 2, 1996).

Biography: "Sonja Henie: Fire on Ice" (March 11, 1997).

Biography: "Judy Garland: Beyond the Rainbow" (March 23, 1997).

Private Screenings: "Ann Miller" (July 3, 1997).

The Charlie Rose Show (July 14, 1997).

Great Performances: "Frank Sinatra: The Very Good Years" (March 11, 1998).

The Rosie O'Donnell Show (May 27, 1998).

E! Mysteries & Scandals: Busby Berkeley (September 14, 1998).

Radio City Music Hall's Grand Re-Opening Gala (October 4, 1999).

Biography: "Ann Miller: I'm Still Here" (January 13, 2000).

Biography: "The Gabors: Fame, Fortune and Romance" (August 23, 2000).

E! True Hollywood Story: "Last Days of Judy Garland" (January 14, 2001).

Omnibus: "Fascinatin' Rhythm: The History of Tap" (February 24, 2001).

Larry King Live (June 27, 2001).

Michael Jackson: 30th Anniversary Celebration (November 19, 2001).

The Desilu Story; the Rags to Riches Success of the Desilu Empire (August 24, 2003).

Rita (September 9, 2003).

The 100 Greatest Musicals (Date unknown; December 2003).

Shorts and Videos

Miller appeared as herself in all of the listings.

Mighty Manhattan, New York's Wonder City (1949).

Screen Snapshots: Salute to Hollywood (1958).

Taste of the Big Apple (1982).

That's Entertainment III: Behind the Screen (1994).

Hollywood Musicals of the 1950's (1997).

Cole Hollywood: Too Darn Hot (2003).

Inside the Marx Brothers (2003).

Cole Hollywood: Too Darn Hot (2003).

That's Entertainment!: The Masters Behind the Musicals (2004).

Easter Parade: On the Avenue (2005).

Hollywood Singing and Dancing: The 1970s, Diversity Rocks the Movies (2009).

Bibliography

Alexander, Ron. "The Evening Hours." *The New York Times*, December 2, 1982. Retrieved July 11, 2019 from http://www.nytimes.com.

_____. "The Quandary of Christmas Tipping." *The New York Times*, December 17, 1981. Retrieved July 8, 2019 from http://www.nytimes.com.

Anderson, Jack. "Tapping into the Past." *The New York Times*, February 13, 2004. Retrieved July 29, 2019 from http://www.nytimes.com.

Arcen, Gene. *Brooklyn's Scarlett: Susan Hayward: Fire in the Wind*. Albany, GA: BearManor Media, 2010.

Arnold, Jeremy. "Articles: Deep in My Heart (1954)." *Turner Classic Movies*. Retrieved May 10, 2019 from http://www.tcm.com.

_____. "Articles: The Good Fairy (1935)." *Turner Classic Movies*. Retrieved January 13, 2019 from http://www.tcm.com.

_____. "Articles: Watch the Birdie (1951)." *Turner Classic Movies*. Retrieved April 19, 2019 from http://www.tcm.com.

Astaire, Fred. *Steps in Time: An Autobiography*. New York: Harper, 1959.

Astaire McKenzie, Ava, and John Fricke. *Easter Parade* DVD Audio Commentary. Warners DVD, 2005.

Atkinson, Brooks. "The Play: George White Throws Out the First 'Scandals' of the Season at the Alvin." *The New York Times*, August 29, 1939. Retrieved February 28, 2019 from http://www.nytimes.com.

Autry, Gene, with Mickey Herskowitz. *Back in the Saddle Again*. Garden City, NY: Doubleday, 1978.

Ball, Lucille. *Love, Lucy*. New York: Putnam Adult, 1996.

Barnes, Clive. "Ann Miller Brings Zest to a Still Lively 'Mame.'" *The New York Times*, June 20, 1969. Retrieved June 4, 2019 from http://www.nytimes.com.

Basinger, Jeanine. *Gene Kelly*. New York: Pyramid, 1976.

_____. *The Movie Musical!* New York: Knopf, 2019.

Baxter, John. *Hollywood in the Thirties*. London: Tantivy Press, A.S. Barnes, 1968.

Bellison, Lillian. "Future Events..." *The New York Times*, September 28, 1980. Retrieved July 6, 2019 from http://www.nytimes.com.

Berger, Joseph. "Harry Rigby Dead." *The New York Times*, January 18, 1985. Retrieved July 12, 2019 from http://www.nytimes.com.

Bird, David, and Robert McG. Thomas. "Notes on People; Traditions." *The New York Times*, December 18, 1981. Retrieved July 9, 2019 from http://www.nytimes.com.

Blau, Eleanor. "Where the Hoofas Meet the Divas." *The New York Times*, October 27, 1981. Retrieved July 8, 2019 from http://www.nytimes.com.

Botto, Louis. "Stage and Screen Icon Ann Miller on Sugar Babies, Co-Star Feuds, and Those Wigs." *Playbill*, April 12, 2019. Retrieved June 2, 2019 from http://www.playbill.com.

Boyd, Gerald M. "Hollywood Stars Honor President." *The New York Times*, December 2, 1985. Retrieved July 14, 2019 from http://www.nytimes.com.

Brady, Kathleen. *Lucille: The Life of Lucille Ball*. New York: Hyperion, 1994.

Brantley, Ben. "Theater Review." *The New York Times*, May 8, 1998. Retrieved July 21, 2019 from http://www.nytimes.com.

＿＿＿. "Theater Review." *The New York Times*, August 6, 2001. Retrieved July 24, 2019 from http://www.nytimes.com.

Brown, Peter H. "Blithe Spirit Keeps Star Image." *Star News*, December 8, 1973. Retrieved June 25, 2019 from http://www.news.google.com.

Brown, Peter Harry, and Pat H. Broeske. *Howard Hughes: The Untold Story*. New York: Dutton, 1996.

Buckley, Tom. "For Mickey Rooney, Happiness Is Broadway." *The New York Times*, October 10, 1979. Retrieved July 1, 2019 from http://www.nytimes.com.

＿＿＿. "Joey Bishop, At 63, Savors Debut." *The New York Times*, February 10, 1981. Retrieved July 6, 2019 from http://www.nytimes.com.

Burchmore, Rhonda, with Frank Howson. *Legs 11: My Life in Front of the Lights and Backstage*. Sydney: New Holland Publishers, 2010.

Calta, Louis. "...2 Musicals Slate Openings." *The New York Times*, November 30, 1971. Retrieved June 8, 2019 from http://www.nytimes.com.

Canby, Vincent. "Theater." *The New York Times*, May 24, 1998. Retrieved July 21, 2019 from http://www.nytimes.com.

Capra, Frank. *Frank Capra: Interviews*. Jackson: University Press of Mississippi, 2004.

Carey, Gary. *All the Stars in Heaven: Louis B. Mayer's MGM*. New York: Dutton, 1981.

Chartier, Roy. "You Can't Take It with You." *Variety*, September 7, 1938. Retrieved January 22, 2019 from http://www.variety.com.

Clarity, James F. "Notes on People." *The New York Times*, August 16, 1972. Retrieved June 8, 2019 from http://www.nytimes.com.

＿＿＿. "Notes on People." *The New York Times*, August 18, 1972. Retrieved June 8, 2019 from http://www.nytimes.com.

＿＿＿. "Notes on People." *The New York Times*, September 7, 1972. Retrieved June 8, 2019 from http://www.nytimes.com.

Coleman, Emily R. *The Complete Judy Garland: The Ultimate Guide to Her Career in Films, Records, Concerts, Radio, and Television, 1935–1969*. New York: Harper & Row, 1990.

Collins, Glenn. "So Many Key, So Few Pockets, Such Ire." *The New York Times*, April 16, 1981. Retrieved July 7, 2019 from http://www.nytimes.com.

Colt, George Howe. "To Spice Up a Long Run, Add a Dash of Mickey Rooney." *The New York Times*, April 12, 1981. Retrieved July 7, 2019 from http://www.nytimes.com.

Connor, Jim. *Ann Miller Tops in Taps: An Authorized Pictorial History*. New York: Franklin Watts, 1981.

Corry, John. "Broadway." *The New York Times*, July 15, 1977. Retrieved June 25, 2019 from http://www.nytimes.com.

＿＿＿. "Broadway...." *The New York Times*, June 12, 1981. Retrieved July 8, 2019 from http://www.nytimes.com.

Crowther, Bosley. "Frank Sinatra, Kathryn Grayson Head Cast of Lavish 'Kissing Bandit' at the Capitol." *The New York Times*, November 19, 1948. Retrieved April 9, 2019 from http://www.nytimes.com.

＿＿＿. "...'Hit Parade of 1941' at Loew's Criterion." *The New York Times*, December 5, 1940. Retrieved March 5, 2019 from http://www.nytimes.com.

_____. "'On the Town,' Yuletide Picture at Radio City, Is Musical to Please the Family." *The New York Times*, December 9, 1949. Retrieved April 13, 2019 from http://www.nytimes.com.

_____. "The Screen in Review; 'Kiss Me Kate,' an Inviting Film Adaptation of Stage Hit..." *The New York Times*, November 6, 1953. Retrieved May 5, 2019 from http://www.nytimes.com.

_____. "The Screen in Review; 'Too Many Girls' Makes Appearance at Loew's Criterion." *The New York Times*, November 21, 1940. Retrieved March 1, 2019 from http://www.nytimes.com.

_____. "The Screen in Review; Red Skelton in 'Watch the Birdie,' New Comedy..." *The New York Times*, December 12, 1950. Retrieved April 19, 2019 from http://www.nytimes.com.

_____. "The Screen in Review; Romberg Film, Mostly Music, at Radio City." *The New York Times*, December 10, 1954. Retrieved May 10, 2019 from http://www.nytimes.com.

_____. "The Screen in Review...." *The New York Times*, December 26, 1940. Retrieved March 8, 2019 from http://www.nytimes.com.

_____. "The Screen in Review...." *The New York Times*, November 22, 1951. Retrieved April 21, 2019 from http://www.nytimes.com.

_____. "The Screen in Review." *The New York Times*, September 6, 1946. Retrieved April 2, 2019 from http://www.nytimes.com.

_____. "The Screen; 'Texas Carnival' Opens at State..." *The New York Times*, October 13, 1951. Retrieved April 23, 2019 from http://www.nytimes.com.

_____. "The Screen; Very Blue." *The New York Times*, December 8, 1944. Retrieved March 22, 2019 from http://www.nytimes.com.

_____. "The Screen: ... 'The Opposite Sex.'" *The New York Times*, November 16, 1956. Retrieved May 19, 2019 from http://www.nytimes.com.

_____. "The Screen." *The New York Times*, July 10, 1941. Retrieved March 11, 2019 from http://www.nytimes.com.

Cummings, Judith. "...Ann Miller Moved by Popularity of the Ann Miller Look." *The New York Times*, February 4, 1980. Retrieved July 5, 2019 from http://www.nytimes.com.

Curtis, Charlotte. "Theater Life, Second Love." *The New York Times*, June 19, 1984. Retrieved July 12, 2019 from http://www.nytimes.com.

Daley, Suzanne. "A Tearful Goodbye for 'Sugar Babies.'" *The New York Times*, August 30, 1982. Retrieved July 10, 2019 from http://www.nytimes.com.

Daniels, Robert L. "Follies." *Variety*, May 11, 1998. Retrieved July 21, 2019 from http://www.variety.com.

Davis, Ronald L. *Hollywood Beauty: Linda Darnell and the American Dream*. Norman: University of Oklahoma Press, 1991.

_____. *Van Johnson: MGM's Golden Boy*. Jackson: University Press of Mississippi, 2001.

Dick, Bernard F. *That Was Entertainment: The Golden Age of the MGM Musical*. Jackson: University Press of Mississippi, 2018.

Dunning, Jennifer. "'Dancing Ladies' of Screen at the Regency; 'Ruby Pointed the Way.'" *The New York Times*, January 25, 1980. Retrieved July 5, 2019 from http://www.nytimes.com.

_____. "Rip Taylor Barges in for Rooney." *The New York Times*, June 29, 1981. Retrieved July 8, 2019 from http://www.nytimes.com.

Dupont, Joan. "David Lynch in Competition for 4th Time." *The New York Times*, May 19, 2001. Retrieved July 24, 2019 from http://www.nytimes.com.

Eames, John Douglas. *The MGM Story*. London: Octopus Books, 1975.

_____ *The Paramount Story*. London: Octopus Books, 1985.

Ebert, Roger. "Mulholland Drive." October 12, 2001. Retrieved July 24, 2019 from http://www.rogerebert.com.

_____. "That's Entertainment! III." July 22, 1994. Retrieved May 4, 2019 from http://www.rogerebert.com.

Eder, Richard. "Miss Kahn Lifts 'Won Ton Ton." *The New York Times*, May 27, 1976. Retrieved June 27, 2019 from http://www.nytimes.com.

Elliot, Mark. "That's Entertainment! 50 Years Of MGM." *ABC Late Night*. Jack Haley, Jr. Productions, 1974.

Erickson, Glenn. "Articles: Small Town Girl (1953)." *Turner Classic Movies*. Retrieved April 28, 2019 from http://www.tcm.com.

Eyman, Scott. *Lion of Hollywood: The Life and Legend of Louis B. Mayer*. New York: Simon & Schuster, 2008.

Fantle, David, and Tom Johnson. *Hollywood Heyday: 75 Candid Interviews with Golden Age Legends*. Jefferson, NC: McFarland, 2018.

Faris, Jocelyn. *Ginger Rogers: A Bio-bibliography*. Westport, CT: Greenwood Publishing, 1994.

Feaster, Felicia. "Articles: Kiss Me Kate (1953)." *Turner Classic Movies*. Retrieved May 5, 2019 from http://www.tcm.com.

_____. "Articles: Stage Door (1937)." *Turner Classic Movies*. Retrieved January 16, 2019 from http://www.tcm.com.

_____. "Articles: That's Entertainment! III (1994)." *Turner Classic Movies*. Retrieve May 4, 2019 from http://www.tcm.com.

Ferretti, Fred. "The Evening Hours." *The New York Times*, May 15, 1981. Retrieved July 7, 2019 from http://www.nytimes.com.

Fitzgerald, Peter. *What a Glorious Feeling: The Making of 'Singin' in the Rain.'* Turner Entertainment/Warner Home Video/ FitzFilm, 2002.

Ford, Peter. *Glenn Ford: A Life*. Madison: University of Wisconsin Press, 2011.

Fordin, Hugh. *M-G-M's Greatest Musicals: The Arthur Freed Unit*. New York: Da Capo Press, 1996.

Foundas, Scott. "Broadway: The Golden Age." *Variety*, June 29, 2003. Retrieved July 28, 2019 from http://www.variety.com.

Franceschina, John. *Hermes Pan: The Man Who Danced with Fred Astaire*. New York: Oxford University Press, 2012.

Frank, Leah D. "Theater Review...." *The New York Times*, October 7, 1984. Retrieved July 12, 2019 from http://www.nytimes.com.

_____. "Theater Review." *The New York Times*, June 9, 1985. Retrieved July 12, 2019 from http://www.nytimes.com.

_____. "Theater Review." *The New York Times*, July 7, 1985. Retrieved July 12, 2019 from http://www.nytimes.com.

Frank, Rusty E. *TAP! The Greatest Tap Dance Stars and Their Stories 1900–1955*. Boston: Da Capo Press, 1995.

Frankel, Haskel. "Yokum Hokum." *The New York Times*, August 7, 1977. Retrieved June 25, 2019 from http://www.nytimes.com.

Freedland, Michael. *Fred Astaire*. New York: Grosset & Dunlap, 1977.

Freedland, Michael B. *Judy Garland: The Other Side of the Rainbow*. London: JR Books, 2010.

Freedman, Samuel G. "When an Actor Is Taken Captive by a Single Role." *The New York Times*, December 23, 1984. Retrieved July 12, 2019 from http://www.nytimes.com.

Fricke, John. *Judy: A Legendary Film Career*. Philadelphia: Running Press, 2010.

Fristoe, Roger. "Articles: Jam Session (1944)." *Turner Classic Movies*. Retrieved March 26, 2019 from http://www.tcm.com.

_____. "Articles: Lovely to Look At (1952)." *Turner Classic Movies*. Retrieved April 25, 2019 from http://www.tcm.com.

Gamarekian, Barbara. "Kennedy Center Honors Five for Life Achievements in Arts." *The New York Times*, December 2, 1979. Retrieved July 5, 2019 from http://www.nytimes.com.

Garrett, Betty. *Betty Garrett and Other Songs: A Life on Stage and Screen*. Lanham, MD: Madison Books, 1999.

Gates, Anita "Human Sharks Feeding in an Animated Hollywood Aquarium." *The New York Times*, August 19, 2005. Retrieved July 30, 2019 from http://www.nytimes.com.

Gehring, Wes. *Red Skelton: The Mask Behind the Mask*. Indianapolis: Indiana Historical Society, 2008.

Gold, Gerald. "About Records...." *The New York Times*, June 6, 1982. Retrieved July 9, 2019 from http://www.nytimes.com.

Gottfried, Martin. *All His Jazz: The Life and Death of Bob Fosse*. New York: Bantam, 1990.

Granger, Farley, and Robert Calhoun. *Include Me Out: My Life from Goldwyn to Broadway*. New York: St. Martin's Press, 2007.

Green, David. "BWW Interview: The Show Goes On!" *Broadway World*, June 4, 2018. Retrieved August 4, 2019 from http://www.broadwayworld.com.

Gussow, Mel. "Theater: Barbara Perry as All of the 'Passionate Ladies.'" *The New York Times*, May 7, 1981. Retrieved July 7, 2019 from http://www.nytimes.com.

Haley, Jack, Jr. *That's Entertainment!* M-G-M, 1974.

Harland Smith, Richard. "Articles: Radio City Revels (1938)." *Turner Classic Movies*. Retrieved January 20, 2019 from http://www.tcm.com.

Harmetz, Aljean. "Mickey Rooney, Master of Putting on a Show, Dies at 93." *The New York Times*, April 7, 2014. Retrieved August 2, 2019 from http://www.nytimes.com.

Henson, Jim. *The Great Muppet Caper*. Muppet Studios/Jim Henson Pictures/ITC Entertainment, 1981.

Herman, Robin, and Laurie Johnston. "New York Day by Day." *The New York Times*, January 5, 1983. Retrieved July 11, 2019 from http://www.nytimes.com.

Hess, Earl J., and Pratibha A. Dabholkar. *Singin' in the Rain: The Making of an American Masterpiece*. Lawrence: University Press of Kansas, 2009.

Higham, Charles. *Merchant of Dreams: Louis B. Mayer, M.G.M. and the Secret Hollywood*. New York: Donald I. Fine, 1993.

_____, and Joel Greenberg. *Hollywood in the Forties*. New York: A. S. Barnes. 1968.

Higham, James. "Ann Miller." *Nourishing Obscurity*, December 17, 2016. Retrieved April 9, 2019 from http://www.nourishingobscurity.com.

Hirschhorn, Clive. *The Columbia Story*. London: Pyramid Books, 1989.

_____. *The Universal Story*. London: Octopus Books, 1983.

Hodgson, Moira. "The Evening Hours." *The New York Times*, April 2, 1982. Retrieved July 9, 2019 from http://www.nytimes.com.

_____. "An Old-Fashioned Movie Star Scores on Broadway." *The New York Times*, October 28, 1979. Retrieved July 1, 2019 from http://www.nytimes.com.

Holden, Stephen. "Cabaret Review." *The New York Times*, December 21, 1998. Retrieved July 22, 2019 from http://www.nytimes.com.

_____. "Film Festival Review." *The New York Times*, October 6, 2001. Retrieved July 24, 2019 from http://www.nytimes.com.

_____. "Film Review; Legends and Lore Dished Up with After-Theater Panache." *The New York Times*, June 11, 2004. Retrieved July 25, 2019 from http://www.nytimes.com.

_____. "Four Brash Musicals...." *The New York Times*, August 1, 1986. Retrieved July 13, 2019 from http://www.nytimes.com.

_____. "A Mischievous Charmer, Showing Vulnerability." *The New York Times*, April 28, 2010. Retrieved August 1, 2019 from http://www.nytimes.com.

_____. "Stars of Old Movie Musicals Bask in Their Own Light." *The New York Times*, July 17, 1997. Retrieved July 19, 2019 from http://www.nytimes.com.

Hoty, Dee. Interview. *Behind the Curtain*, January 15, 2019. Retrieved August 5, 2019 from http://www.behindthecurtainpodcast.blog.

Hudson, Edward. "2 Theaters in Trouble." *The New York Times*, June 12, 1977. Retrieved June 25, 2019 from http://www.nytimes.com.

James, Caryn. "Critic's Notebook...." *The New York Times*, November 13, 1995. Retrieved July 18, 2019 from http://www.nytimes.com.

_____. "Review/Film; Waste Not, Want Not: MGM's Outtakes Are a Movie." *The New York Times*, May 6, 1994. Retrieved May 4, 2019 from http://www.nytimes.com.

Jefferson, Margo. "Theater Review." *The New York Times*, November 8, 2003. Retrieved July 28, 2019 from http://www.nytimes.com.

Jewell, Richard B, and Vernon Harvin. *The RKO Story*. London: Octopus Books, 1982.

Johnson, David. "'I'm like a cat with nine lives.' Ann Miller Begins Her Fourth Career." *After Dark* 11, no. 6 (1969): 52–55.

Juneau, James. *Judy Garland*. New York: Pyramid Publications, 1975.

Kael, Pauline. *5001 Nights at the Movies*. New York: Holt, Rinehart and Winston, 1984.

Kantor, Michael. *Broadway: The American Musical*. Ghost Light Films/Thirteen/WNET New York/NHK/BBC/Carlton International, 2004.

Keel, Howard, with Joyce Spizer. *Only Make Believe: My Life in Show Business*. Fort Lee, N.J.: Barricade, 2005.

Kehr, Dave. "At the Movies." *The New York Times*, October 12, 2001. Retrieved July 24, 2019 from http://www.nytimes.com.

Kelly, Erin St John. "Playing in the Neighborhood." *The New York Times*, May 29, 1994. Retrieved July 18, 2019 from http://www.nytimes.com.

Kelly, Gene. *That's Entertainment, Part II*. M-G-M, 1976.

Kerr, Walter. "Stage: 'Sugar Babies,' Burlesque Is Back." *The New York Times*, October 9, 1979. Retrieved July 1, 2019 from http://www.nytimes.com.

Kisselgoff, Anna. "Dance View." *The New York Times*, February 10, 1985. Retrieved July 12, 2019 from http://www.nytimes.com.

Klein, Alvin. "In Person." *The New York Times*, May 31, 1998. Retrieved July 21, 2019 from http://www.nytimes.com.

_____. "'New' Shubert Theater Weathers Its First Year." *The New York Times*, December 30, 1984. Retrieved July 12, 2019 from http://www.nytimes.com

_____. "Theater Reviews." *The New York Times*, May 3, 1998. Retrieved July 20, 2019 from http://www.nytimes.com.

_____. "Theater; What to Expect in Coming Season." *The New York Times*, September 23, 1984. Retrieved July 12, 2019 from http://www.nytimes.com.

_____. "Theater...." *The New York Times*, March 1, 1987. Retrieved July 13, 2019 from http://www.nytimes.com.

_____. "Theater...." *The New York Times*, April 12, 1998. Retrieved July 20, 2019 from http://www.nytimes.com.

_____. "Theater...." *The New York Times*, May 14, 1989. Retrieved July 15, 2019 from http://www.nytimes.com.

Klemesrud, Judy. "The Evening Hours." *The New York Times*, August 27, 1982. Retrieved July 10, 2019 from http://www.nytimes.com.

_____. "Weaving Stars and Stripes Together." *The New York Times*, June 8, 1977. Retrieved June 24, 2019 from http://www.nytimes.com.

Kobal, John. *People Will Talk. Personal Conversations with the Legends of Hollywood.* London: Aurum Press, 1991.

Kourlas, Gia. "Sounding Out 'Great Heights' in Heels." *The New York Times*, July 4, 2018. Retrieved August 4, 2019 from http://www.nytimes.com.

Krebs, Alvin, and Robert McG. Thomas, Jr. "Moe and Joe, Frick and Frack, and Friends." *The New York Times*, May 20, 1981. Retrieved July 7, 2019 from http://www.nytimes.com.

_____, _____. "Notes on People...." *The New York Times*, February 19, 1981. Retrieved July 6, 2019 from http://www.nytimes.com.

_____, _____. "Non-Dream Fulfilled." *The New York Times*, March 10, 1982. Retrieved July 9, 2019 from http://www.nytimes.com.

_____, _____. "'Sugar Babies' Turns 2." *The New York Times*, October 14, 1981. Retrieved July 8, 2019 from http://www.nytimes.com. Kresh, Paul. "From 1917 to 1984...." *The New York Times*, August 12, 1984. Retrieved July 12, 2019 from http://www.nytimes.com.

Landazuri, Margarita. "Articles: New Faces of 1937 (1937)." *Turner Classic Movies.* Retrieved January 13, 2019 from http://www.tcm.com.

_____. "Articles: Texas Carnival (1951)." *Turner Classic Movies.* Retrieved April 23, 2019 from http://www.tcm.com.

_____. "Articles: The Opposite Sex (1956)." *Turner Classic Movies.* Retrieved May 19, 2019 from http://www.tcm.com.

_____. "Articles: Two Tickets to Broadway (1951)." *Turner Classic Movies.* Retrieved April 21, 2019 from http://www.tcm.com.

Lawson, Carol. "...Debut for Mickey Rooney." *The New York Times*, June 13, 1979. Retrieved June 28, 2019 from http://www.nytimes.com.

Leaming, Barbara. *If This Was Happiness: A Biography of Rita Hayworth.* New York: Viking, 1989.

Leigh, Janet. *There Really Was a Hollywood.* New York: Berkley Pub. Group, 1985.

Leigh, Spencer. *Frank Sinatra: An Extraordinary Life.* Carmarthen, United Kingdom: McNidder and Grace, 2015.

Lertzman, Richard A., and William J. Birnes. *The Life and Times of Mickey Rooney.* New York: Gallery Books, 2015.

LoBianco, Lorraine. "Articles: Anne of Green Gables (1934)." *Turner Classic Movies.* Retrieved January 8, 2019 from http://www.tcm.com.

Loney, Glenn. *Unsung Genius: The Passion of Dancer-Choreographer Jack Cole.* New York: Franklin Watts, 1984.

Macaulay, Alastair. "A Nation's Soul, Tapping and Twirling." *The New York Times*, March 6, 2014. Retrieved August 2, 2019 from http://www.nytimes.com.

Marin, Rick. "Lucy and Desi: A Home Movie." *Variety*, February 11, 1993. Retrieved July 17, 2019 from http://www.nytimes.com.

Marks, Peter. "Critic's Notebook." *The New York Times*, November 27, 1998. Retrieved July 21, 2019 from http://www.nytimes.com.

Martin, Frank. *MGM When the Lion Roars Part Three: The Lion in Winter.* Turner Pictures/Joni Levin/Point Blank Productions, 1992.

Martin, Len D. *The Republic Pictures Checklist: Features, Serials, Cartoons, Short Subjects and Training Films of Republic Pictures Corporation, 1935–1959.* Jefferson, NC: McFarland, 2015.

Maslin, Janet. "Critic's Notebook...." *The New York Times*, September 19, 1980. Retrieved July 6, 2019 from http://www.nytimes.com.

_____. "Night Of RKO Memories." *The New York Times*, July 9, 1982. Retrieved July 10, 2019 from http://www.nytimes.com.

McCarthy, Peggy. "Theater Museum Planned." *The New York Times*, November 11, 1984. Retrieved July 12, 2019 from http://www.nytimes.com.

McCarthy, Todd. "Mulholland Drive." *Variety*, May 16, 2001. Retrieved July 24, 2019 from http://www.variety.com.

_____. "That's Entertainment! III." *Variety*, April 25, 1994. Retrieved May 4, 2019 from http://www.variety.com.

McGilligan, Patrick. *Ginger Rogers: Pyramid Illustrated History of the Movies*. New York: Pyramid Publications, 1975.

McKay, Holly. "Molly Shannon Says Ann Miller Hated Famous 'SNL' Impersonation." *Fox News*, September 12, 2011. Retrieved July 18, 2019 from http://www.foxnews.com.

McKay, Rick. Interview for Broadway: The Golden Age. *Behind the Curtain*. Retrieved July 30, 2019 from http://www.behindthecurtainpodcast.blog.

McWhorter, John. "'What the Eye Hears' and 'America Dancing.'" *The New York Times*, December 4, 2015. Retrieved August 3, 2019 from http://www.nytimes.com.

Miller, Ann, with Maxine Asher. *Tapping into the Force: Ann Miller's Psychic World*. Norfolk, VA: Hampton Roads Publishing, 1990.

Miller, Ann, with Norma Lee Browning. *Miller's High Life*. Garden City, NY: Doubleday, 1972.

Miller, Frank. "Articles: Easter Parade (1948)." *Turner Classic Movies*. Retrieved April 5, 2019 from http://www.tcm.com.

_____. "Articles: Hit the Deck (1955)." *Turner Classic Movies*. Retrieved May 13, 2019 from http://www.tcm.com.

Miller, John H. "Articles: The Great American Pastime (1956)." *Turner Classic Movies*. Retrieved May 17, 2019 from http://www.tcm.com.

Montgomery, Paul L. "President, Visiting New York...." *The New York Times*, March 15, 1981. Retrieved July 6, 2019 from http://www.nytimes.com.

Morella, Joe, and Edward Z. Epstein. *Forever Lucy: The Life of Lucille Ball*. New York: Berkley Books, 1990.

Nemy, Enid. "Broadway." *The New York Times*, February 7, 1986. Retrieved July 12, 2019 from http://www.nytimes.com.

_____. "Broadway." *The New York Times*, September 28, 1984. Retrieved July 12, 2019 from http://www.nytimes.com.

_____. "Chronicle." *The New York Times*, February 22, 1994. Retrieved July 18, 2019 from http://www.nytimes.com.

_____. "A Good Time at the Ziegfeld Ball Extravaganza." *The New York Times*, November 5, 1979. Retrieved July 4, 2019 from http://www.nytimes.com.

_____. "On Stage." *The New York Times*, January 1, 1988. Retrieved July 13, 2019 from http://www.nytimes.com.

_____. "On Stage." *The New York Times*, November 25, 1988. Retrieved July 14, 2019 from http://www.nytimes.com.

Neuhaus, Mel. "Articles: The Kissing Bandit (1948)." *Turner Classic Movies*. Retrieved April 9, 2019 from http://www.tcm.com.

Newman, Phyllis. "How Do You Get from Peter Pan to Alan Cummings by Way of Ann Miller?" June 29, 2010. Retrieved August 1, 2019 from http://www.phyllisnewman.com.

Nixon, Rob. "Articles: Room Service (1938)." *Turner Classic Movies*. Retrieved February 20, 2019 from http://www.tcm.com.

_____. "Articles: Stage Door (1937). " *Turner Classic Movies*. Retrieved January 16, 2019 from http://www.tcm.com.

Nugent. Frank S. "Review | 'You Can't Take It with You.'" *The New York Times*, September 2, 1938. Retrieved January 22, 2019 from http://www.nytimes.com.

_____. "The Screen....." *The New York Times*, March 21, 1938. Retrieved January 18, 2019 from http://www.nytimes.com.

_____. "The Screen: 'Room Service,' Which Was Daffy Enough Even Without the Marxes, Skips Lightly into the Rivoli." *The New York Times*, September 22, 1938. Retrieved February 1, 2019 from http://www.nytimes.com.

_____. "The Screen: 'Stage Door,' Hollywood Edition, Opens at the Music Hall." *The New York Times*, October 8, 1937. Retrieved January 14, 2019 from http://www. nytimes.com.

_____. "The Screen: 'The Life of the Party' and Other Cut-Ups at the Rivoli." *The New York Times*, October 4, 1937. Retrieved January 13, 2019 from http://www. nytimes.com.

_____ "The Screen: A Suspicious Glance at 'New Faces of 1937.'" *The New York Times*, July 2, 1937. Retrieved January 13, 2019 from http://www.nytimes.com.

_____. "The Screen: Changed a Bit, 'Having Wonderful Times' Reaches the Music Hall." *The New York Times*, July 8, 1938. Retrieved January 21, 2019 from http:// www.nytimes.com.

_____. "The Screen: ... 'Tarnished Angel' at Rialto." *The New York Times*, November 15, 1938. Retrieved February 28, 2019 from http://www.nytimes.com.

O'Brien, Daniel. *The Frank Sinatra Film Guide*. London: Pavilion Books, 2014.

O'Connor, John J. "The Academy Awards Ceremony." *The New York Times*. March 26, 1986. Retrieved July 12, 2019 from http://www.nytimes.com.

_____. "Television Review...." *The New York Times*, October 2, 1995. Retrieved July 18, 2019 from http://www.nytimes.com.

_____. "TV Weekend; Bash Aboard 'Love Boat.'" *The New York Times*, February 26, 1982. Retrieved July 9, 2019 from http://www.nytimes.com.

_____. "TV: Some Network Specials Do Not Always Turn Out to Be So." *The New York Times*, November 17, 1971. Retrieved June 5, 2019 from http://www.nytimes. com.

Osborne, Robert. Private Screenings interview with Stanley Donen. *Turner Classic Movies*, 2006.

Otler, John. *Jean Arthur: The Actress Nobody Knew*. New York: First Limelight, 1997.

Parrish, James Robert, and Michael R. Pitts. *Hollywood Songsters: Singers Who Act and Actors Who Sing. A Biographical Dictionary. Volume 2: Garland to O'Connor*. Oxfordshire: Routledge, 2003.

Parrish, James Robert, and Ronald L. Bowers. *The MGM Stock Company: The Golden Era*. London: Ian Allen, 1973.

Passafiume, Andrea. "Articles: Go West, Young Lady (1941)." *Turner Classic Movies*. Retrieved March 12, 2019 from http://www.tcm.com.

_____. "Articles: Having Wonderful Time (1938)." *Turner Classic Movies*. Retrieved January 21, 2019 from http://www.tcm.com.

_____. "Articles: The Thrill of Brazil (1946)." *Turner Classic Movies*. Retrieved April 2, 2019 from http://www.tcm.com.

_____. "Articles: You Can't Take It with You (1938)." *Turner Classic Movies*. Retrieved February 19, 2019 from http://www.tcm.com.

Phillips, Brent. *Charles Walters: The Director Who Made Hollywood Dance*. Lexington: University Press of Kentucky, 2014.

Plaskin, Glenn. *Turning Point: Pivotal Moments in the Lives of Celebrities*. New York: Carol Publishing, 1992.

Porter, Darwin. *Howard Hughes: Hell's Angel*. New York: Blood Moon Productions, 2005.

_____. *Katharine the Great: A Lifetime of Secrets Revealed*. New York: Blood Moon Productions, 2004.

Powell, Jane. *The Girl Next Door...And How She Grew*. San Francisco: Untreed Reads, 2014.

Propst, Andy. *They Made Us Happy: Betty Comden and Adolph Green's Musicals and Movies*. New York: Oxford University Press, 2019.

Pryor, Thomas M. "...Ann Miller in 'Lili.'" *The New York Times*, December 28, 1951. Retrieved February 15, 2019 from http://www.nytimes.com.

Puig, Claudia. "First Off...." *Los Angeles Times*, May 30, 1989. Retrieved July 15, 2019 from http://www.latimes.com.

Purdum, Todd S. "At Home With: Esther Williams." *The New York Times*, September 2, 1999. Retrieved July 22, 2019 from http://www.nytimes.com.

Quin, Eleanor. "Articles: Carolina Blues (1944)." *Turner Classic Movies*. Retrieved March 22, 2019 from http://www.tcm.com.

_____. "Articles: Too Many Girls (1940)." *Turner Classic Movies*. Retrieved March 1, 2019 from http://www.tcm.com.

_____. "'Easter Parade,' With Berlin's Hit Tunes, Astaire's Nimble Feet, at Loew's State." *The New York Times*, July 1, 1948. Retrieved April 5, 2019 from http://www.nytimes.com.

Quinlend, Anna. "About New York...." *The New York Times*, August 15, 1981. Retrieved July 8, 2019 from http://www.nytimes.com.

Reynolds, Debbie, with David Patrick Columbia. *Debbie: My Life*. New York: Morrow, 1988.

_____, with Dorian Hannaway. *Unsinkable: A Memoir*. New York: William Morrow, 2013.

Rogers, Ginger. *Ginger: My Story*. New York: HarperCollins, 1991.

Rule, Sheila. "On a Dazzling Day...." *The New York Times*, November 27, 1981. Retrieved July 8, 2019 from http://www.nytimes.com.

Schechter, Scott. *Judy Garland: The Day-by-Day Chronicle of a Legend*. New York: Cooper Square Press, 2002.

Schiro, Anne-Marie. "The Evening Hours." *The New York Times*, June 18, 1982. Retrieved July 10, 2019 from http://www.nytimes.com.

Schultz, Margie. *Eleanor Powell: A Bio-Bibliography*. Westport, CT: Greenwood, 1994.

Sen, Mayukn. "In 1970, Heinz Made a Woman Tap Dance on an 8-Foot Can of Soup." *Flood52.com*, October 7, 2016. Retrieved May 28, 2019 from http://www.food52.com.

Sennwald, Andre. "Anne Shirley and "Anne of Green Gables," at the Roxy." *The New York Times*, December 22, 1934. Retrieved January 8, 2019 from http://www.nytimes.com.

_____. "The Screen; The Radio City Music Hall Presents a Screen Version of Molnar's Fantastic Comedy, 'The Good Fairy.'" *The New York Times*, February 1, 1935. Retrieved January 13, 2019 from http://www.nytimes.com.

Severo, Richard. "Ann Miller, Tap-Dancer Starring in Musicals, Dies." *The New York Times*, January 23, 2004. Retrieved July 27, 2019 from http://www.nytimes.com.

Shales, Tom. "ABC's Shipshape Musical 'Love Boat' Special." *The Washington Post*, February 27, 1982. Retrieved July 8, 2019 from http://www.washingtonpost.com.

Shepard, Richard F. "Broadway...." *The New York Times*, June 6, 1980. Retrieved July 5, 2019 from http://www.nytimes.com.

Shipman, David. *The Great Movie Stars: The International Years*. New York: Hill and Wang, 1980.

_____. *Judy Garland: The Secret Life of an American Legend*. New York: Hyperion, 1993.

Siebert, Brian. "Theater Review: Following in the Footsteps of Gwen Verdon and

Ann Miller." *The New York Times*, May 9, 2012. Retrieved August 2, 2019 from http://www.nytimes.com.

Sirkin, Elliott. "Breakfast of Superstars." *New York Magazine*, June 18, 1979. Retrieved June 29, 2019 from http://www.books.google.com.au.

Snyder, Camilla. "Marriott Is Guest (of Honor) for Once." *The New York Times*, September 8, 1973. Retrieved June 9, 2019 from http://www.nytimes.com.

Sondak, Eileen. "Dance...." *Los Angeles Times*, January 22, 1990. Retrieved July 16, 2019 from http://www.latimes.com.

Soren, David. *Vera-Ellen: The Magic and the Mystery*. Baltimore: Luminary Press, 2003.

Spivak, Jeffrey. *Buzz: The Life and Art of Busby Berkeley*. Lexington: University Press of Kentucky, 2011.

Stafford, Jeff. "Articles: Reveille with Beverly (1943)." *Turner Classic Movies*. Retrieved March 18, 2019 from http://www.tcm.com.

Starr, Steve. "Actress Ann Miller—A Bitter, Sweet Life." *The Entertainment Magazine*. Retrieved July 29, 2019 from http://www.emol.org.

Steffen, James. "Articles: On the Town (1949)." *Turner Classic Movies*. Retrieved April 13, 2019 from http://www.tcm.com.

Stern, Caryl. "Can Burlesque Succeed on Broadway—After 50 Years?" *The New York Times*, October 7, 1979. Retrieved June 28, 2019 from http://www.nytimes.com.

Stern, Lee Edward. *The Movie Musical. Pyramid Illustrated History of The Movies*. New York, Pyramid, 1974.

Strauss, Theodore. "At the Abbey." *The New York Times*, April 24, 1943. Retrieved March 18, 2019 from http://www.nytimes.com.

_____. "At the Central." *The New York Times*, November 24, 1941. Retrieved March 12, 2019 from http://www.nytimes.com.

_____. "At the Central." *The New York Times*, June 15, 1942. Retrieved March 13, 2019 from http://www.nytimes.com.

_____. "The Screen; 'Priorities on Parade'" *The New York Times*, July 23, 1942. Retrieved March 15, 2019 from http://www.nytimes.com.

Summerhays, Jane. Interview. *Behind the Curtain*, April 22, 2018. Retrieved August 5, 2019 from http://www.behindthecurtainpodcast.blog.

Taraborrelli, J. Randy. *The Hiltons: The True Story of an American Dynasty*. New York: Grand Central Publishing, 2014.

Tatara, Paul. "Articles: You Can't Take It with You." *Turner Classic Movies*. Retrieved February 19, 2019 from http://www.tcm.com.

Terrace, Vincent. *Television Specials: 5,336 Entertainment Programs, 1936–2012*. Jefferson, NC: McFarland, 2013.

Thames, Stephanie. "Articles: Eve Knew Her Apples (1945)." *Turner Classic Movies*. Retrieved March 29, 2019 from http://www.tcm.com.

_____. "Articles: The Life of the Party (1937)." *Turner Classic Movies*. Retrieved January 13, 2019 from http://www.tcm.com.

Thomas, Tony. *That's Dancing!* New York: Abrams, 1984.

Thompson, Howard. "M-G-M Technicolor Musical Opens Here." *The New York Times*, May 7, 1953. Retrieved April 28, 2019 from http://www.nytimes.com.

Travers, Peter. "Broadway: The Golden Age." *Rolling Stone*, June 2, 2004. Retrieved July 28, 2019 from http://www.rollingstone.com.

_____. "Mulholland Drive." *Rolling Stone*, November 8, 2001. Retrieved July 24, 2019 from http://www.rollingstone.com.

Tucker, David C. *Eve Arden: A Chronicle of All Film, Television, Radio and Stage Performances*. Jefferson, NC: McFarland, 2012.

Van Gelder, Lawrence. "Footlights." *The New York Times*, May 6, 1999. Retrieved July 22, 2019 from http://www.nytimes.com.

Weiler, A.H. "At Loew's State." *The New York Times*, July 23, 1943. Retrieved March 20, 2019 from http://www.nytimes.com.

_____. "'Lovely to Look At,' Based on Musical Comedy, 'Roberta,' Arrives at Music Hall." *The New York Times*, May 30, 1962. Retrieved April 25, 2019 from http://www.nytimes.com.

_____. "Screen: 'Hit the Deck'; Reveille for a Retired Navy Musical." *The New York Times*, March 4, 1955. Retrieved May 13, 2019 from http://www.nytimes.com.

Weinraub, Bernard. "Movie Musicals: Remembering." *The New York Times*, June 13, 1996. Retrieved July 19, 2019 from http://www.nytimes.com.

Weisman, Steven R. "For Reagan's Second Night on a Town..." *The New York Times*, March 16, 1981. Retrieved July 6, 2019 from http://www.nytimes.com.

Whitney, Craig R. "Britain Imports Mason Just for Fun." *The New York Times*, November 23, 1988. Retrieved July 14, 2019 from http://www.nytimes.com.

Williams, Esther, and Digby Diehl. *The Million Dollar Mermaid: An Autobiography*. New York: Simon & Schuster, 1999.

Wilson, John S. "Revue; Satire of Theater." *The New York Times*, February 16, 1982. Retrieved July 9, 2019 from http://www.nytimes.com.

_____. "Upper West Side Is Home to Offbeat Music." *The New York Times*, March 12, 1982. Retrieved July 9, 2019 from http://www.nytimes.com.

Winner, Michael. *Michael Winner: Winner Takes All: A Life of Sorts*. London: Portico Books, 2005.

Witchel, Alex. "Theater...." *The New York Times*, May 3, 1998. Retrieved July 20, 2019 from http://www.nytimes.com.

Index

Numbers in **_bold italics_** indicate pages with illustrations